Contents

This book is dedicated to Alastair, Francesca and Trish.

EVENTS AND THE ENVIRONMENT

Robert Case

 Routledge
Taylor & Francis Group

LONDON AND NEW YORK

First published 2013
by Routledge
2 Park Square, Milton Park, Abingdon, Oxon OX14 4RN

Simultaneously published in the USA and Canada
by Routledge
711 Third Avenue, New York, NY 10017

Routledge is an imprint of the Taylor & Francis Group, an informa business

© 2013 Robert Case

The right of Robert Case to be identified as author of this work has been asserted by
him in accordance with sections 77 and 78 of the Copyright, Designs and Patents Act
1988.

British Library Cataloguing in Publication Data
A catalogue record for this book is available from the British Library

Library of Congress Cataloging in Publication Data
Case, Robert.
  Events and the environment / Robert Case.
    p. cm.
    Includes bibliographical references and index.
  1. Special events–Management. 2. Special events–Environmental aspects. I. Title.
  GT3405.C37 2012
  394.2–dc23   2012016305

ISBN: 978–0–415–60595–3 (hbk)
ISBN: 978–0–415–60596–0 (pbk)
ISBN: 978–0–203–08432–8 (ebk)

Typeset in Garamond
by Swales & Willis Ltd, Exeter, Devon

Permission to reproduce extracts from British Standards is granted by the British Standards Institution (BSI).
No other use of this material is permitted. British Standards can be obtained in PDF or hard copy formats
from the BSI online shop: http://shop.bsigroup.com or by contacting BSI Customer Services for hard copies
only: Tel: +44 (0)20 8996 9001, Email: cservices@bsigroup.com.

MIX
Paper from
responsible sources
FSC
www.fsc.org **FSC® C004839**

Printed and bound in Great Britain by
CPI Group (UK) Ltd, Croydon, CR0 4YY

List of figures

List of tables

Acknowledgements

I should like to acknowledge the help of many people in the preparation of this book and the evolution of ideas contained within it. First to the staff at the British Antarctic Survey (BAS) with whom I worked on the *Antarctic Schools Pack* and who gave me insight into the environmental problems of Antarctica, and who made specific suggestions for images used in the book. Second, to staff at Hampshire County Council from whom I gained information about how the authority was tackling climate change. Third, to staff at Europe Direct (European Law Monitor) with whom I collaborated in the delivery of the Climate Change Conference at Winchester University. Fourth, to Jane Fairclough, who was a patient listener and supporter whilst I ran the Event Management Course at the University of Winchester. Fifth, and it will be a surprise to him, Steve Williams, who first got me involved in the delivery of small-scale, musical events. Sixth, to Sue Warn and others who have given permission to use materials cited in the book – my apologies to any I may have inadvertently overlooked. Finally, to the organizers of the 1969 Isle of Wight Pop Festival, who provided my first, and never to be forgotten, experience of this type of event.

1 Introduction

Aims

The aims of this introduction are to:

- outline the purpose of the book;
- define the terms 'event' and 'environment';
- outline the relationship between events and the environment as it has changed over time;
- identify some significant aspects of the relationship between events and the environment:
  - positive and negative impacts;
  - the relationship between environmental and other impacts;
  - the changing nature and scale of environmental impacts;
  - models of the environment;
  - the interactive, two-way relationship between events and the environment;
  - feedback from the environment; and
- outline the structure and content of the book.

Introduction

Events are designed to have impacts and impacts are intrinsic to their nature. As events take place in the physical environment, whether that is a built or natural one, it is not surprising that they have impacts on that environment. Historically, the discussion of event impacts has tended to focus on cultural, social and economic outcomes and until recently the environmental impacts have been relatively neglected. However, changes in society are forcing a reappraisal of the impacts. Environmental degradation, climate change and resource shortages are threatening global lifestyles and that includes delivery of and participation in events. Resource constraints dictate that we reconsider the environmental inputs into the event industry. The relationship between events and the environment is two-way. The environment affects where and how events are delivered – the nature of the physical landscape will influence the siting and design of venues, the weather the timing and location of events and resource availability, the quality of venues and the event accessories such as food and drink. This book explores in detail the nature of the relationship between events and the environment.

The purpose of this book

The purpose of this book is to bring together in one volume discussion of all aspects of the relationship between events and the environment. Recent publications such as *Sustainable Event Management* and *Event Management and Sustainability* have looked at aspects of the relationship. As their titles indicate they have focused on sustainability issues. Their discussion of event impacts is limited, although much is implied in their approach to sustainable management techniques. Similarly, discussion of the environment as a resource is covered in part but not as a topic in its own right. This book attempts to be all-embracing, though not exhaustive, in its coverage of the interface between events and the environment and introduce topics that hitherto have appeared only in books on geography or environmental science. It tries to avoid excessive duplication with the volumes cited.

The volume is a textbook. It reports on research but includes limited original field research. It attempts to review many of the developments in the subject area that have emerged in the past 50 years, many of them outside the events literature. It is targeted at undergraduate students of event management who increasingly have to study the environment as part of their courses and who will have to manage the relationship with the environment in their future careers. Many find such study tiresome and outside their comfort zone as they have no background in subjects such as geography. This book should ease their progress by providing coverage of the topic and pointers to other sources in one volume. It may also be of use to those studying event management at advanced and postgraduate levels and those already in the industry who seek an overview of the relationship between events and the environment.

What are events and what is the environment?

It is essential to define some key terms, what is meant by an 'event' and what is meant by the 'environment'. This is far from straightforward. In his seminal work, *Events Studies*, Donald Getz describes an event as 'an occurrence at a given place and time; a special set of circumstances; a noteworthy occurrence' (Getz 2007: 18). He goes on to note that events,

> by definition, have a beginning and an end. They are temporal phenomena, and with planned events the event programme or schedule is generally planned in detail and well-publicised in advance. Planned events are also usually confined to particular places although the space involved might be a specific facility, a very large open space, or many locations. (ibid.)

Getz also notes that events are unique. Even when events may appear similar the unfolding of the events and the experiences of participants may be different.

More recently Page and Connell have noted in their introduction to *The Routledge Handbook of Events* that:

> the term 'event' covers a broad spectrum . . . [including] . . . significant international events requiring huge capital investment which attract an enormous

number of people and global media attention (known as *mega-events*) and *hallmark events* used to literally 'hallmark' or define and distinguish the destination such as the Rio Carnival or Munich Oktoberfest, characterised by a high level of media exposure, positive imagery and perceived value in gaining competitive destination advantage. (Page and Connell 2011: 12)

Both *Events Studies* and *The Routledge Handbook of Events* go on to produce typologies of events which include categories such as cultural celebrations, arts and entertainment, sports competitions and private events. For the purpose of defining events in the context of this book, Getz's definition of planned events will be used. These are events

> created to achieve specific outcomes, including those related to the economy, culture, society and environment. Event planning involves the design and implementation of themes, settings, consumables, services and programs that suggest, facilitate or constrain experiences for participants, guests, spectators and other stakeholders. Every event experience is personal and unique, arising from the interactions of setting, program and people. (Getz 2007: 21)

This definition is attractive when discussing events and the environment as the term environment is not only used directly within it but is also implied in mention of settings and stakeholders. The relationships to other aspects of events such as economy, culture and society is also consistent with the remit of this book.

The *New Oxford Dictionary of English* defines the environment as either 'the surroundings or conditions in which a person, animal or plant lives or operates (or) the natural world as a whole or in a particular geographical area, especially as affected by human activity' (Pearsall and Hanks 2001: 617). These definitions may appear straightforward but people use the term environment in many different ways. As Belshaw notes, the word has many meanings, some of them competing with each other. He discusses a number of meanings and concludes:

> that we think in the main of there being one environment, rather than many, and that we think of this environment as it exists in outdoor places (so excluding the home and the office), whether inhabited by human beings or not (and so including both cities and the few wild places that are left on earth), but inhabited nonetheless (and so excluding, at least until we get there, the distant reaches of outer space). (Belshaw 2001: 2)

This 'definition' is helpful as it restricts the term environment to the earth, excludes internal environments, i.e. those inside buildings, but not the environment created by buildings themselves, and encompasses all external environments whether they are inhabited by human beings or not. Thus this book will focus on the relationship between events and the external natural and built environment on this planet.

The changing relationship of events and the environment over time

Ever since the first planned 'event', whenever that was, a relationship has existed between events and the environment in which they take place. This is inevitable – events take place in the environment, effectively using it as one of their resources, and they cannot avoid having impacts on it. Some events have long been intrinsically environmental. The Greek and Roman civilisations designated some event outcomes as environmental. The Greeks, for example, developed rituals intended to guarantee good harvests and held harvest festivals that followed them. Examples included the Little Panathenaia:

> a night festival of dancing and singing, a procession, a contest for 'circular choruses' and war dances (or) the great festivals of Demeter, Athena, and Dionysis [which] had as their foundation a very much older conception of deity: the possibility that life was renewed in the spring. (Webster 1969: 85)

As Chapter 3 of this book shows, the creation of venues – critical aspects of events – involves significant modification of the environment – indeed the nature of the environment is a major determinant of venue locations. Early development of such venues can still be seen today in the theatre at Epidaurus or the amphitheatre in Pompeii. Some venues were designed to create different types of environment, such as the Coliseum in Rome, which could be used dry or flooded to allow water-based spectacles. Some events were designed to produce environmental impacts. In Athens, for example, the festival of Adonis involved 'tiny gardens that sprang up and withered quickly on the tops of houses' (Levi 1980: 165).

In addition to these intended and known impacts there were impacts that had accidental and often unfortunate consequences. Some of these were tolerated, some were not apprehended, perhaps because they could not be observed or measured. The original Olympics (Olympia) were an example of an event with striking impacts:

> oxen . . . were axed before a crowd, and the precincts steeped with their blood. Ash, bones, and bovine offal piled up over centuries into a huge pyramid: it must have reeked to high heaven. Could we have endured this for the sake of Olympia's pride: the great, original Olympic Games? Again, it is doubtful. (Spivey 2004: xviii)

Additionally the 'festival was noisy . . . [and] . . . hideously congested, and for hundreds of years deprived of adequate accommodation, water supply, and sanitation; not to mention marred by the standard plagues of heat, flies, and hucksters' (ibid.).

Waste, therefore, was clearly an environmental impact of the former category, those that were tolerated. Carbon dioxide and resource depletion were examples of the latter type, those that were not apprehended. A lesson can be learnt from this, namely that it is useful to distinguish between intended and unintended or accidental impacts. Both can be damaging but for many centuries the latter were unconsidered, tolerated or not understood. It is only relatively recently that the event industry has begun to anticipate, as far as it is able, the full impacts of its actions. This is partly the result of a change in the zeitgeist symbolised by a growing awareness of environmental fragility, the emergence of a plethora of green initiatives, the development of a range of environmental standards and reporting systems, and increasing amounts of legislation.

Despite that, some parts of the event industry still appear to care little about the environmental consequences of its activities, intended or otherwise. This can be seen not only in the behaviour of the industry but also in the education system. Undergraduates on event courses have expressed frustration at having to study the environmental dimension of events and even some lecturers, who should know better, have asserted that the environment is irrelevant to the study of event management. Optional courses with environmental themes can fail to recruit sufficient students to be viable. A relatively recent example of such lack of concern could be seen at Confex 2009. This featured a seminar, with prominent speakers, on Green Events, which attracted fewer than 30 attendees in an event that attracted tens of thousands.

Recent initiatives, such as BS8901 and ISO14001 (discussed later), and the emphasis put on sustainability by the 2012 Olympics in London, are beginning to have an effect, although much lip service is paid to green issues for image reasons. However, much remains for the industry to do to improve its environmental performance. Fortunately, the environmental dimension of events is coming under increasing academic scrutiny, although much of this remains tourism oriented rather than focused on the plethora of events, local and national, that do not involve overnight stays by attendees. It is hoped that this book will augment two recently published volumes on events and sustainability in promoting the attention paid to environmental issues.

Positive and negative environmental impacts

Environmental discussion has often tended to dwell on negative impacts on the environment. There are good reasons for this. For a long time the environment was ignored by all but a small fraction of the population until the consequences of resource issues such as oil shortages and the manifestation of serious environmental damage such as the reduction in the ozone layer and global warming became political and media issues. However, as indicated above, not all environmental impacts created by events are negative. The prime purpose of some events is to have a beneficial environmental impact, indeed some are designed to promote a green agenda. Others strive to improve the environment as a by-product which may be permanent or temporary. Positive effects are intended and manifested at a range of scales, from mega-events such as the Olympics, where the intended environmental legacy now forms part of the bid, to community events that focus on cleaning up litter in local open spaces. In between are events such as the garden festivals that were held in Liverpool (1984) and South Wales (1992). Such events have grown considerably in recent years. Both positive and negative impacts are discussed later in the book in Chapters 4 and 5.

The relationship between environmental and other impacts

As noted earlier, environmental impacts do not exist in isolation from other types of impact. They are often intrinsically linked to each other. Additionally, environmental impacts themselves may, for example, have effects on economy, society and polity. Environmental damage can be expensive to clear up, it may upset local residents and it may embarrass politicians. Vandalism by attendees at events can cause direct damage to the built or natural environment which may have to be repaired by the local council at a cost to taxpayers. Meanwhile, the desecration can offend the local, permanent community and they in turn can vent their frustration and irritation on their elected representatives who are prompted to enact new legislation or change policies. Similarly, positive impacts, such as clearing up litter, can increase enjoyment of open spaces, not least by making them safer, with consequent social benefits. Thus, although identification of environmental impacts is a useful analytical device, it needs always to be aware of the connections with other impacts in a wider context. Such interaction is also recognised in business concepts, such as the triple bottom line, that assess entrepreneurial outcomes in economic, social and environmental terms.

The changing scale and nature of environmental impacts

As has been established, the environmental impacts of events have a long history. However, those impacts have changed in scale and nature. Mega-events, such as the Olympics, take place on an unprecedented scale not only in the host city but globally through coverage by the mass media. The supply chains for such events are complex and their use of resources extensive. Their ecological footprints are very substantial, in particular their carbon footprints. The wastes they create are diverse, complicated and difficult to process both physically and legally, in an era of increasing environmental legislation. However, the impacts and their consequences are better understood and metrics have been established by which they can be quantified, an issue extensively discussed in Chapter 10.

Some idea of the scale of impacts that can result from mega-events is given by a study for the London Organising Committee of the Olympic and Paralympic Games (LOCOG), which produced an estimate of the carbon footprint to be generated by the 2012 Olympics. It concludes that 'the London 2012 reference footprint is estimated to be 3.4 million tonnes of carbon dioxide equivalents (3.4MtCO$_2$e)' (LOCOG 2010a: 27). This is a substantial carbon footprint and is discussed further in Chapter 5.

Events, systems and models of the environment

It is useful to consider how events might relate to models of the environment. Models are useful tools, their selective, structural and suggestive nature making them useful tools against which to test reality. They became very popular in the 1960s. A system can be described as 'a set of objects together with the relationships between the objects and their attributes' (Haggett 1965: 17). Blunden (1977: 110) used such a systems approach to visualise human use of the environment. The present author adapted this in his chapter in *The Routledge Handbook of Events* to illustrate the role of events in processing environmental inputs to create a series of outputs that can either be recycled or 'dumped' to the environment, though in the latter case they may be recycled over geological time (see Figure 1.1).

Another systems approach to the environment was developed by James Lovelock, who instigated the concept of Gaia. This conceptualised the earth as a system which had for centuries been in a state of dynamic equilibrium. Dynamic equilibrium is a feature of systems theory. Simply put, it suggests that when changes in one part of a system occur other parts adjust to dampen down the effects of change. In this way a degree of stability is maintained. Recently, Lovelock has taken an alarmist line with respect to global warming, arguing that the planetary system has passed a threshold and can longer maintain a balance – the dynamic equilibrium has been lost (Lovelock 2006).

The event industry is a significant contributor to this transformation of the planet, as is discussed in Chapters 4 and 5.

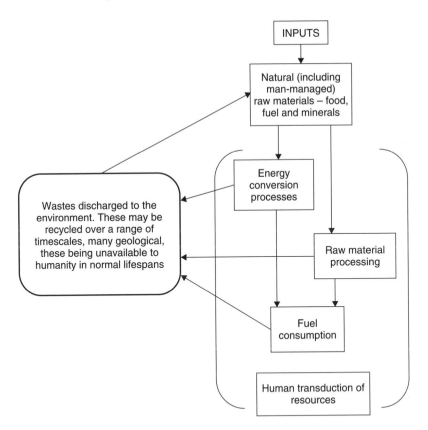

Figure 1.1 A systems approach to the environmental context of the event industry

Source: Case 2011 (adapted from Blunden 1977)

Event industry interactions with the environment

The interactions of the event industry with the environment fall into two types. These form the basis of some of the different parts of this book. The first concerns the use of environmental resources in delivering the event and is discussed extensively in Chapter 2 and to a lesser extent in Chapter 3. The second concerns environmental outputs which can be analysed at two levels, the macro and the micro. The latter can be further broken down into short and long term. Some authorities, such as the IOC (International Olympic Committee), also distinguish between direct and indirect impacts, the former being the result of the actions of event deliverers themselves, and the latter the result of the actions of external organisations such as governments, who improve transport infrastructure for mega-events and tourist activities which the IOC deem to be outside the Games themselves (a debatable proposition). These outputs are discussed in Chapters 4 and 5. An overview of the relationship between events and the environment can be seen in Figure 1.2.

The event industry uses a very wide range of inputs in its supply chain – food, materials and energy. Many of these are limited or stock resources which have a limited lifespan, such as oil. Some of these resources can be substituted, but some are more difficult to replace. Even if substitution is possible, the alternatives may be more expensive. This is an issue of which there seems to be limited awareness in the event industry except at the mega-event level, although recent standards such as the *Event Organizers Sector Supplement (EOSS)* recognise this.

The event industry also uses the environment in a very direct way. Events take place on land, water and in the air. Temporary and permanent venues are constructed in the

Figure 1.2 Relationships between events and the environment

built and natural environment. These can result in temporary or permanent loss of such phenomena as biodiversity and visual amenity. Choice of locations needs careful consideration but selection involves social, economic and political factors as well as environmental ones. This is discussed further in Chapter 3. Some events require specific types of environment and others are greatly affected by changing environmental conditions. Those planning sailing events need to consider winds, tides and currents. Skiing events need reflection on probabilities of snowfall. Athletics records can only be broken if certain wind velocities are not exceeded. Again, these issues are discussed in Chapter 2.

Feedback from the environment on its misuse

Ironically, some of the environmental impacts to which the event industry contributes are beginning to have an impact on the event industry itself. One example is climate change. Global warming appears to be melting glaciers in parts of Europe and changing patterns of weather may affect snow-based events in the Alpine regions of Europe. An increase in extreme weather events, such as hurricanes and tornadoes, is likely to cause more disruption to planned events. Sea-level rise may damage traditional sailing venues, and possibly, in the longer term, the potential venues for mega-events – many of the world's great cities including Tokyo, New York and London are close to sea level. At a local scale soil erosion caused by events may damage environments to such an extent that they can no longer sustain the environment needed for events such as cross-country running. Flooding may damage venues. One-off disasters such as fires caused by lightning and exacerbated by high winds can damage venues beyond repair.

Structure of the book

Of the ten chapters which follow, the first two focus on the event industry's use of the environment as a resource. This is a relatively neglected area in the events literature. Chapter 2 is a broad-ranging chapter that looks at the environment as an input to the event industry. It looks at phenomena such as the atmosphere, land and sea and shows how these can influence and, at times, determine the nature of events. It demonstrates that many events need particular environmental conditions: obvious examples would be skiing, which requires snow, and sailing, which requires both water and wind. Other events are seriously affected by environmental conditions. Cricket, for example, is affected by cloud cover and humidity which influence the swing of the ball. Catastrophic meteorological events such as hurricanes can cause cancellation of events and inflict great damage on event venues. The chapter provides a case study of the Vancouver Winter Olympic Games, which had problems with adequate snow at some of their venues.

Chapter 3 looks at the environmental context of venue location. It investigates in particular the key location factors that determine the site venues. It develops a typology of venues and explores the complex interaction of environmental issues with political and social factors. It provides case studies that look at the relocation of Southampton

Football Club and Hampshire County Cricket Club as well as looking at the decision-making that led to the 2012 Olympics being sited in the East End of London.

The next three chapters look at the environmental impacts of events in some detail. Chapter 4 looks at impacts at a micro or local scale. It examines a range of issues such as trampling and erosion, localised air and noise pollution and problems of liquid and solid wastes. It provides case studies of Dartmoor, the Beijing Olympics, the Knebworth concerts, the Reading Festival and the Avon Descent in Australia. Chapter 5 moves from the micro to the macro scale and investigates how the event industry contributes to global environmental problems such as acid rain, the depletion of the ozone layer and greenhouse emissions, and their impact on climate change. These global issues do not result from the activities of the event industry alone, so some of them are discussed in general terms to illustrate the scale of the problems that confronts society. Responses to these problems are also discussed and the case studies provided relate to Hampshire County Council, the carbon footprint of the 2012 Olympics and the Sydney Olympics.

Chapter 6 looks at a specific set of impacts related to urban regeneration. The creation of a positive urban legacy has been a motive for bidding for many large-scale events. Events such as the Olympics have in the past generated benefits such as new sports facilities, new housing facilities, improved transport systems, developments in cultural infrastructure and environmental improvement. However, the success of events in producing these benefits has been variable and the chapter compares case studies of the Athens and Barcelona Olympics to illustrate this.

Chapter 7 charts the history of environmental legislation and standards and how these affect what businesses can and cannot do environmentally at local, national and international levels. Standards that have evolved within the industry are also discussed. Case studies are provided of BS 8901, Antarctica and Cape Breton.

The next two chapters look at the issue of sustainability. Chapter 8 considers the nature of the concept and how this has developed both within and outside the event industry. It shows that sustainable development is a contested concept and that defining sustainability is problematic. It is noted that the Brundtland definition is often accepted uncritically and has become a de facto benchmark within the sustainability debate. The chapter looks at movements within the event industry and provides a case study of the green meetings initiative. Chapter 9 focuses on the practical aspects of sustainable management. It tries to minimise overlap with Meegan Jones's book (Jones 2010) and examines some of the practical guidance available to event organisers in the form of lists, tips and flyers, mini-guides and books. The case studies include the World Summit on Sustainable Development in Johannesburg and the Ninth International Conference on Southern Hemisphere Meteorology and Oceanography in Melbourne.

Chapter 10 focuses more closely on standards and reporting by looking at how events can be monitored. It looks at the history of environmental performance monitoring and discusses a wide range of monitoring approaches and initiatives. Case studies are provided of Defra's Environmental Key Performance Indicators, the *Event Organizers Sector Supplement* and the DIT-ACHIEV Model.

Chapter 11 concludes the book by examining some future issues that confront the event industry in its relationship to the environment. It looks at the impact of environmental scepticism, economic recession, the education system, the political process, the provision of incentives for sustainable behaviour and the intrinsic nature of events themselves. It concludes by commenting positively on the progress that has been made within the event industry on becoming more sustainable and more responsible in its attitude to the environment. However, it also notes that there is no room for complacency and that much remains to be done if some of the major environmental threats are to be avoided.

Each chapter states its aims at the outset and concludes by referring back to these. Many case studies are provided at a range of scales from the local to the international. The case studies come from many different parts of the world – Africa, Europe, Asia, Australasia and North America. Many tasks are suggested aimed at applying and consolidating the knowledge and skills acquired through reading the material outlined. Each chapter is fully referenced and provides recommendations for further reading.

Conclusion

The aims of this chapter were to:

- outline the purpose of the book;
- define the terms 'event' and 'environment';
- outline the relationship between events and the environment as it has changed over time;
- identify some significant aspects of the relationship between events and the environment:
  - o positive and negative impacts;
  - o the relationship between environmental and other impacts;
  - o the changing nature and scale of environmental impacts;
  - o models of the environment;
  - o the interactive, two way relationship between events and the environment;
  - o feedback from the environment; and
- outline the structure and content of the book.

This chapter has noted that the book is a textbook aimed at bringing together all aspects of the relationship between events and the environment in a way that has not been attempted before. It has discussed the terms 'event' and 'environment' and produced working definitions of both. It has provided a brief history of the complex relationship between events and environment and has identified a number of significant themes. Finally, it has described the way the book is structured and outlined the content to be expected in each chapter.

2 Environmental resources for the event industry

Aims

The aims of this chapter are to:

- identify the nature and scope of the environment as an input into the event industry;
- examine the environmental influences on venues in both the natural and built environments;
- explore the ways in which the environment impacts on the running of events; and
- unravel the environmental context of the event supply chain.

Introduction

Much of the discussion about events and the environment has tended to focus on event outputs and how these impact on the environment. Equally important, however, is the environmental input into the event industry. This takes several forms:

- the natural environment as a venue for events to take place;
- the built environment, notably towns and cities, and their potential as event venues;
- environmental constraints on events such as the weather; and
- the environment as a supplier of products in events – the supply chain and its limitations.

These elements are interconnected, as are their relationships to output impacts. Thus the natural environment provides venues for events and resources for use in them, and puts constraints on the nature and scope of events. Similarly, the use of environmental resources creates impacts. However, it is useful to analyse these elements separately to highlight their nature. The remainder of this chapter will discuss the inputs focusing on the constraints and supply chain. The next chapter will focus on the issue of venue location and later chapters will discuss environmental impacts and the environmental legacies of events.

The natural environment as a venue for events

Defining the term environment is problematic, as was noted in Chapter 1. The natural environment is equally difficult to define. For the purposes of this book the natural environment will be defined as that part of the earth's outdoor environment that exists independently of man. It thus includes the atmosphere, hydrosphere (oceans, rivers and lakes) and the biosphere (living matter) excluding man. These spheres are characterised by systems and processes that exist and operate whether man is present or not. This does not mean that man's influence is absent. Many would regard the moorlands of Dartmoor or Exmoor as natural, even wild, yet they are highly managed and look the way they do partly because of human decision-making. The natural environment provides a venue for a substantial range of events. These vary from small, impromptu or informal events such as a sponsored clean-up of rubbish in a local beauty spot to large-scale, premeditated or formal events such as the Ten Tors walk on Dartmoor.

Such events use the environment in many ways. Some may use it as an attractive place in which to undertake an activity that does not intrinsically need that type of location. A sponsored walk, for example, may take place in a national park – however, such a walk could be equally effective in raising funds if it were to involve a transect of Toronto or Paris. Others may use the natural environment as an extreme challenge – examples of this include sponsored treks across parts of the Arctic or Antarctica. Many sporting events make use of the natural environment as it meets specific requirements, such as the oceans for sailing (e.g. the Sydney to Hobart race), skiing (e.g. Kitzbühel) or fell running (e.g. in the Lake District of north-west England). In these cases the environment, or how to manage it, often gave rise to the sport in the first place.

The infrastructure associated with such events varies. This is discussed in more detail in the following chapter but briefly it can be said that the infrastructure may range from the temporary and minimal (e.g. for the fell running already mentioned) to the permanent and extensive (e.g. the sites of many Winter Olympics). The impacts of such events are discussed later. Overall, within the context of this chapter, it is sufficient to note the massive potential of the natural environment to host a wide range of events.

TASK

Working on your own or in small groups, identify 20 events that make use of the natural environment. State how each uses the environment e.g. as an extreme challenge, or as a resource that meets given requirements. For example, Henley Regatta takes place on the River Thames as it requires a stretch of water of a particular length and width. Try to classify the events into groups which share similar characteristics.

Try to think of a new event that exploits the potential of the natural environment. What type of infrastructure would it need? Would this be temporary or permanent? Could it only take place in the natural environment?

The built environment as a venue for events

The built environment can be defined as that constructed by human activity on a substantial scale. Occasional buildings can be found in predominantly natural environments, even in the extreme wilderness of Antarctica, but what is being discussed here is the environment created by the accretion of buildings that occurs in towns, cities and agglomerations such as the megalopolises that can be found in central Honshu and the north-eastern United States seaboard. These areas are virtually devoid of natural environment although they may encompass green spaces such as parks or golf courses. Where these occur they are entirely man-managed. Such environments are distinct from natural environments in many ways. They are centres of densely packed population with extensive industrial and service facilities and sophisticated communication networks. While they are unable to offer many of the characteristics of natural environments, they offer another layer of event opportunities. Again, they offer events that can be local, impromptu or informal, e.g. a picnic in the park, or large-scale, premeditated and formal, such as the Notting Hill Carnival in London or Mardi Gras in Rio de Janeiro.

Again, some events may use such environments because, for example, they are local rather than have intrinsic value, but others are located here because of the nature of the urban environment – street parties are an obvious example. Many exploit the market of a large population or capital status. Wembley and Stade de France are examples of venues built to exploit both. The infrastructure associated with urban environments can be temporary and minimal but much is permanent and large scale. Two prominent stadia have already been mentioned but many different types of venue could also be mentioned – the Philharmonic Hall in Berlin, Sydney Opera House and Flushing Meadow in New York are well-known examples. The siting of such venues is discussed in the next chapter and the impacts later in the book.

TASK

Working in small groups, identify 20 city based venues. In each case note its function and reason for being in an urban environment. Reflect on whether they can be classified into different groups.

Think of a new event that exploits the potential of the built environment. What type of infrastructure would it need? Would this be temporary or permanent? Could it only take place in an urban environment?

Environmental constraints on events

Anyone who has organised a garden fete, sailed in a regatta, or attended a cricket match knows about the importance of the weather. Although perhaps the most important constraint imposed by the environment on events, weather is not the only one. A discussion of the other constraints will precede an extensive discussion of the weather.

Non-weather environmental constraints

Extreme events such as earthquakes and volcanic eruptions can disrupt events or reduce the probability of events being held in areas subject to frequent manifestations of such phenomena. Less spectacular natural hazards such as avalanches and rock slides can also affect events and decisions on where to locate events. These are linked to weather – prolonged snowfall or rain – but are also independent of current weather as they are affected by topography, rock type and human intervention. Tides and currents affect sailing and rowing events. Some events cannot take place at low tide, others at high tide. An example of the former is the annual boat race between the Universities of Cambridge and Oxford on the River Thames in London. The Thames is tidal over the course between Putney and Mortlake and the race can only take place when the tide is sufficiently high. This means the timing of the event varies from year to year. This is usually only a matter of a few hours but sometimes it can lead to it being on a different day – Sunday rather than Saturday.

Case study: cricket on shingle banks in the Solent

At the other end of the scale is a very unusual event that was held in the Solent, a stretch of water off the southern English coast. This area has shallows comprising shingle banks that are only exposed at times of extreme low tide. Each year a cricket match was held on the shingle to mark this event. The size and nature of the shingle is also affected by the circulation of material in Christchurch Bay, which is somewhat complex. The prevailing longshore drift carries material from west to east but there is also thought to be some movement offshore which returns some of the material westwards. This movement is ultimately the result of prevailing winds and their strength and fetch (the distance over which the wind blows). The winds here are mainly south-westerly. The fetch is very long – several thousand kilometres – so waves can be very large and longshore drift very powerful. However, it can be easily upset by human intervention. Intervention in this area has involved dredging and the installation of groynes to preserve beaches. Defensive measures to protect cliffs can also affect the rates of erosion and thus the supply of new material to the cliff base. The banks are still substantial and human intervention is now coordinated by the Environment Agency. In the past local authorities had carried out their own coastal measures which often had adverse effects on the coast down-drift. This had happened in the bay in the past, when Bournemouth Council had built a major groyne at Hengistbury Head and reduced the flow of material into Christchurch Bay from the west. Although this is a very unusual event it does show how complicated environmental factors can be in determining when and how an event can take place.

A fuller discussion of the problems of this section of coast can be found in Case 1997.

Topography imposes its own constraints. Some sporting events need relatively flat pitches. Football and cricket are obvious examples. While human intervention largely determines the exact surface, natural topography provides the broad context and natural events can modify surfaces through flooding (such as at Worcester Cricket

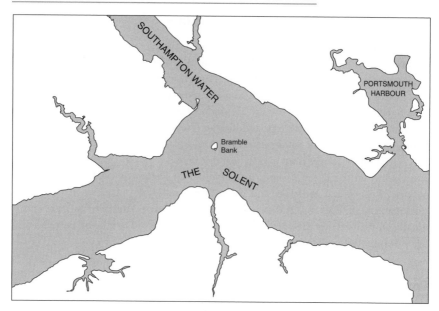

Figure 2.1 Bramble Bank in the Solent

Ground in 2010) or wind erosion. Although some variation is permitted, this can have a significant impact on the event. The famous slope at Lord's Cricket Ground can affect seam and spin. Players who can exploit the slope may take more wickets than those who cannot. Such a topic provides the basis of much punditry in the media. At a micro level unevenness can affect cricket and many other sports. Small bumps may lead to the ball rising or turning sharply and unexpectedly. Such phenomena have led to endless 'gardening' of the pitch by batsmen trying to eliminate such uncertainty. The option to roll the pitch between innings shows how seriously cricket teams take the micro-condition of the environment in their quest to win matches. There are serious consequences for venue owners who fail to provide satisfactory pitches – they can be fined or eliminated from consideration for future events such as test matches.

Cricket is not the only sport to need flat or perfect surfaces. Bowls and curling are others. The need for perfect surfaces in bowls has led to bowling greens being used as metaphors for perfect lawns. In curling the players prime the surface to affect movement.

In golf, topography plays a critical part in the challenge of a course. Slopes, vegetation, water hazards and sand are used by designers to make course interesting. Although the detail of these is human-built, the broader context is natural. Obvious examples of this are the links courses built in fragile sand dune environments. These are famed for the particular type of golf they offer and also substantially alter the ecology of the landscapes they occupy. Indeed it may be suggested that the greater the role the environment has in determining the nature and location of venues, the more likely those venues are to have, in turn, a major impact on the environment in which they are situated. Although this is a generalisation with many exceptions and opportunities for damage limitation, it is a useful thought for planners to consider when contemplating the use of particular environments for event use.

Some events require more extreme topography. Fell running is an obvious example. Without the fells (hills/mountains) there is no event. Such events in England require the Lake District or Peak District – they cannot be held in the fenlands of East Anglia or Somerset Levels. Similarly an event such as the Ten Tors expedition needs an environment with tors – Dartmoor, where it is held, is a perfect landscape for such an event. Skiing is another sport that requires mountains for most of its events. While cross-country skiing can take place in relatively flat environments, the most spectacular events such as the downhill or giant slalom require steep slopes (and snow – discussed later). Not all mountains are suitable – vertical slopes are unsuitable except for very short sections. Topography is not the only reason for location – history, tradition, media rights and population distribution are also factors. However, nearly all the famous venues for skiing are in high mountain ranges such as the Rockies in North America and the Alps in Europe. These areas include famous venues such as Aspen and Kitzbühel.

TASKS

(i)   Investigate the Ten Tors expedition online. Identify the type of landscape in which it takes place. Consider geology and landforms (the tors). Review other landscapes in which a similar event could take place – there is no need to confine yourself to the UK.

(ii) Consider the environments where skiing takes place. There are similar landscapes in many parts of the world. Identify some of these. Suggest reasons why they have fewer (or no) skiing events. Suggest and provide a rationale for future developments.

(iii) Identify examples of sports events where human ingenuity (and the necessary money) has been used to overcome deficiencies in the physical environment. Start by looking at sport in the deserts of the Middle East.

(iv) Suggest other types of event that depend considerably on the physical environment. What are they and what are their needs? Identify some event locations and show how they meet the needs. An annotated sketch-map might be a useful way of doing this.

Meteorology

The environmental constraint that most of us are aware of is meteorology. Few reading this text will have avoided an event that has not been ruined by the weather. This may have been a cricket match stopped by bad light, a tennis tournament interrupted by rain, a regatta curtailed by high winds, a religious event hit by excessive temperatures or a skiing event postponed or relocated through too much, or too little, snow.

In terms of event planning the weather operates at two levels. The first is the climatic or macro level. This relates to the overall pattern of weather that occurs in regions over long periods of time. It is often, inaccurately, referred to as average weather. Thus skiing events are not generally planned for hot desert regions where snow is rare and short-lived and cricket tends not to thrive in the Arctic where it is too cold for the necessary types of grass to grow naturally. The second is the weather or micro scale. This relates to day-to-day variability that occurs within the overall pattern. Both levels are critical to the success of events. The former can be predicted to an extent, although extreme events can occur in any climate and global warming is exacerbating these. Some climates are more constant than others. The latter is much more difficult to predict although long-term forecasting has greatly improved over the past 50 years. Once again, however, global climate change appears to be creating more extreme weather events, making it problematic to predict their likelihood months in advance.

Climate

The world's climates can be classified into a number of general types. The classification produced by the UK Meteorological Office is shown in Figure 2.2. It is based on maximum and minimum temperatures and the temperature range as well as the total and seasonal distribution of precipitation.

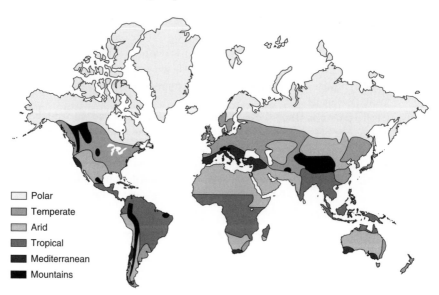

Figure 2.2 World climate types

Source: Internet Geography (2012); image courtesy of the UK Meteorological Office

The types are:

- Tropical

  This climate occurs close to the equator where the sun is always high in the sky. Temperatures are therefore high throughout the year. High temperatures generate a great deal of convection, which in turn leads to rainfall. The climate tends to be monotonous – most days start sunny but cloud builds during the morning leading to rainfall. This allows the clouds to disperse and leave clear evenings. On the equator every day has 12 hours' sunlight and 12 hours' night – sunrises and sunsets are very quick. Humidity tends to be high which can affect athletic performance. Snow never occurs except at very high altitude. Away from the equator the climate becomes seasonal with distinct wet and dry seasons; the wet seasons becoming shorter the further away one goes from the equator. The 2014 World Cup will be held in Brazil, a country with zones of this climate, as illustrated by the data for Manaus given below.

Manaus	Jan	Feb	March	April	May	June	July	Aug	Sept	Oct	Nov	Dec
Temp. (°C)	26.0	26.0	25.9	26.0	26.2	26.3	26.5	27.2	27.5	27.5	27.1	26.6
Tropical rainfall (mm)	263.9	262.0	297.9	282.7	203.7	103.1	66.9	45.6	63.0	111.1	161.0	219.8

- Arid

  This climate is generally hot during the day at all times, though at nights and at altitude it can be surprisingly cold. The technical criterion for true desert is less than 250mm per year of precipitation. Some areas such as Insalah receive hardly any rain. When rain occurs in these regions it is often intense, though short-lived, and can cause flash flooding. This can be a severe hazard for events held in these regions, such as the East African Safari.

Insalah	Jan	Feb	March	April	May	June	July	Aug	Sept	Oct	Nov	Dec
Temp. (°C)	12.6	14.8	19.8	24.2	29.7	34.1	37.0	35.8	33.0	26.4	19.8	14.3
Rainfall (mm)	Virtually no rain											

- Mediterranean

  This is often regarded as an ideal climate. It has hot dry summers and warm wet winters. It is a climate particularly suited to tourism where it is ideal for sunbathing. It can border on drought-like and fires can be a problem. It is perceived as ideal for many events, particularly as its summer weather is relatively predictable. Events that have been held in such zones include the Athens and Rome Olympics and the FIFA World Cup in Spain.

- Temperate
  This climate is dominated by westerly air flow and is transitional. Variation is its key – it is very difficult to predict long-term in all but the most general of terms. Away from the coast it tends to be more consistent with cold, relatively dry winters (though with snowfall) and warm wet summers characterised by convectional rain that can often be thundery. Many major events are held in this zone as it generally avoids extremes. The FIFA World Cup in France and the British Open Golf tournament are examples.
- Polar
  This is a cold climate – intensely cold in winter and cool in summer. Precipitation can be low – many areas have less than 250mm per year – and much falls as snow. Many areas have permafrost and ice is a general problem though global warming appears to be modifying this. It is not a popular area for events, but expeditions (often for charity) and husky racing are examples of events held there.
- Mountains
  This type of climate cuts across the regional boundaries of the climates listed above because altitude has a profound effect on climate (temperature, winds and precipitation). Mountainous areas tend to be cold in winter so are useful for snow sports, such as the Albertville Winter Olympics.

Davos	Jan	Feb	March	April	May	June	July	Aug	Sept	Oct	Nov	Dec
Temp. (°C)	–7	–5	–3	2	5	10	12	11	8	3	–1	–6
Rainfall (mm)	46	56	56	56	59	102	125	128	95	69	56	64

TASKS

Consider these climatic types. Giving specific examples, identify some of the types of event ideally suited to such climates. Identify also any types of event that would be impossible or problematic to hold in such climates. Suggest some of the management problems that might occur in holding events in the various climates – referral to the climatic data will help you.

How the weather disrupts events

Weather can disrupt events in many ways. These include:

- Rain
  For many events rain is an irritant that may make conditions more dangerous, but does not stop the event continuing. Football and rugby are obvious examples. Attendance may be affected which will have financial implications. Injuries may

be more likely. Firework and other outdoor festivals may be dampened – Glastonbury is an example of a music festival that is often disrupted by rain. Health and safety risk assessments will have to take account of the impact of rain. Some events are stopped by rain, however: cricket and tennis are obvious examples. Refund policies for cricket are discussed below.

- Hail
  The problems of hail are similar to rain but there are greater implications with regard to injury and damage to venues. These need to be assessed in risk assessments.
- Snow and ice
  Snow may disrupt events if it is heavy. People may not get to the events because of adverse road conditions or disruption to public transport. This may have financial implications. Snow accumulation may cause cancellation of many events such as football matches. In other cases the absence of snow may threaten an event. Skiing is an obvious example, as discussed in the case study below.
- Wind
  High winds can disrupt many events. Playing conditions may be made difficult in many sports. In some sports cancellation may be necessary. Sailing is an obvious example. Where events have continued in very high winds boats have been lost and crew killed, such as in the Sydney to Hobart and Fastnet races. Hurricanes, typhoons and tornadoes may not only lead to cancellation, they may lead to destruction of temporary and permanent event infrastructure.
- Lightning
  Lightning is one of the most dangerous of meteorological phenomena. It is mercifully often short-lived but it can lead to delay in outdoor events, notably in golf, where players holding steel clubs are in particular danger.

TASK

Use the internet to research examples of events that have been disrupted by the weather elements listed above. For each describe the nature of the disruption and the consequences for the organisers. Could the organisers have taken any measures to prevent or mitigate the disruption?

Managing meteorological uncertainty

Uncertainty can be tackled in a number of ways. Care can be taken in selecting the timing and location of the events to maximise the chance of suitable weather prevailing. This can include reference to meteorological data. Contingency measures can be prepared to overcome adverse weather. Assurances can be given to ticket purchasers of refunds if the event does not take place. Insurance can be taken out to help guard against consequential losses if events are cancelled. A number of brief case studies will illustrate some of the issues involved.

Case study: the Vancouver 2010 Winter Olympics

Vancouver is situated in British Colombia in the west of Canada. The regional climate is temperate – west coast cool temperate to be precise – but much of the area is mountainous which makes many areas much colder, particularly in winter. The snow data are shown in Table 2.1. The weather statistics displayed here represent the mean value of each meteorological parameter for each month of the year, over a 30-year sampling period (1961–90).

As the Games were about to begin there were headlines around the world indicating that there might not be enough snow for some of the events to take place.

> Providing snow in the midst of a Canadian winter ought to be relatively uncomplicated. But the efforts of the Vancouver Games organising committee to ensure sufficient snow cover for the opening day on Friday could just about qualify as an Olympic event in its own right.
>
> They have tried airlifting snow by helicopter at five-minute intervals; hauling snow by the lorryload from three hours away; shooting ice and water out of a snow cannon; spreading layers of snow with a Zamboni ice-smoothing truck; and studding the slopes with tubes packed full of dry ice, to keep the snow from melting, and replenishing them every 12 hours.
>
> 'The amount of work that has been done against these conditions is really hard to believe,' Jack Furlong, the head of the committee, said this week.
>
> After an unusually mild winter, organisers first grew alarmed at a lack of snow cover last month, closing the Cypress Mountain resort – where the freestyle skiing and snowboarding competitions are to be held – to preserve the scant covering of white stuff. (Goldenberg 2010)

And yet the problem was known in advance and forecasters had prepared for such an eventuality.

Table 2.1 Snow data for Vancouver International Airport, British Columbia, Canada (latitude 49.11N; longitude 123.10W; altitude: 3m)

Precipitation	J	F	M	A	M	J	J	A	S	O	N	D
Snow (cm)	21	9	4	1	0	0	0	0	0	0	3	19
Snow Depth(cm)	1	1	0	0	0	0	0	0	0	0	0	4

Source: Weathernetwork (2011)

As Doyle has commented:

> A much cooler than normal November and December of 2009 transformed into a significantly warmer January of 2010 under the influence of an increasingly powerful el-Niño and an archetypical blocking and split flow pattern that developed over the west coast of North America during the month . . . and contingency plans were developed by the organizing committee for extremely mild conditions. The amount of artificial snow produced during the November–December period may well have prevented the complete cancellation of events at least at one venue, Cypress Mountain. (Doyle 2010)

The Games did go ahead, but the problems they encountered raise a number of issues. First, should the Games have been awarded to Vancouver in that year when the el-Niño is a known cyclical event? Are such environmentally sensitive issues given adequate scrutiny in the bidding process? Do the evaluation criteria give appropriate weight to such considerations? Are the costs of overcoming such difficulties included in the financial projections for the viability of the event? Second, the case shows the need for contingency planning. This saved the day in this instance, albeit at a financial and publicity cost. It illustrates well the need for event planners to take full account of environmental uncertainty and put in place measures to ensure that the event can take place.

Case study: the Indian Premier League tournament in South Africa

In 2009 the Indian Premier League (IPL), which runs the lucrative Twenty20 cricket competition with a host of world-class cricketers being bid for, was forced to relocate away from India. The United Kingdom and South Africa were both thought to be in the running. Both countries had long histories of running cricket tournaments. They had the grounds and enthusiastic supporters. However, as the BBC reported at the time, South Africa won the day: 'Security concerns in India forced organisers to seek an alternative host, with England a possible destination. But IPL boss Lalit Modi opted for South Africa following talks with Cricket South Africa (CSA), ultimately because of the favourable weather conditions' (BBC News 2009).

In this case weather was clearly a critical criterion and the decision took full account of the meteorological probabilities in each location.

Refunds for UK Cricket Internationals

Refund conditions for test matches in 2012 were as follows.

> If play is restricted or does not take place at the ground on the day for which this ticket is valid, you may claim a refund of only the match ticket value subject to there being:

(a)   no play because the match has been completed – a full refund;

(b)   10 overs or less because of adverse weather conditions or completion of the match – a full refund;

(c)   10.1 overs to 24.5 overs because of adverse weather conditions or completion of the match – a 50% refund.

In no other circumstances can money be refunded. (ECB 2012)

The rules for one-day internationals are different:

If play is restricted or does not take place at the ground on the day for which this ticket is valid, you may claim a refund of the match ticket value subject to there being:

(a)   10 overs or less because of adverse weather conditions and no result is obtained – a full refund;

(b)   10.1 overs to 24.5 overs because of adverse weather conditions and no result is obtained – a 50% refund.

In no other circumstances can money be refunded. (Ibid.)

For Twenty20 the rules are also different:

If play is restricted or does not take place at the ground on the day for which this ticket is valid, you may claim a refund of the match ticket value subject to there being:

(a)   9.5 overs or less of the only or last match of the day because of adverse weather conditions and no result is obtained – a full refund.

In no other circumstances can money be refunded. (Ibid.)

Such conditions have to be carefully considered by the organisers – the absence of refunds could greatly reduce ticket purchases while excessive refunds could undermine the event's viability. It is a difficult balancing act. It also puts pressure on the management of a game. If it starts raining in the tenth over of a Twenty20 umpires must be aware of the implications of coming off too soon even if it is a downpour.

Managing your own event

You can take your own precautions when planning an event. In the UK, and elsewhere, data exist that show the probability of rain, sunshine and wind on any given day. These have been accumulated over a long period of time and access to such data may involve payment. Such data only provide probabilities – in temperate climates such as the UK and western Canada the probability of rain may be only 1 in 5 but it may still rain on your event. However, it is better to have good odds rather than poor ones. An example of such data is given below for Seattle in the United States.

TASK

Look at the data for Seattle in Figure 2.3. Which would be the best month in which to hold an event which avoids rain?

Events within limited time periods can have long-term forecasts provided for them – again this usually involves a charge. Such forecasts may enable postponement or the implementation of contingency measures such as using the village hall for a fete rather than the village green.

Insurance

It is possible to obtain insurance against the effects of the weather on events. Insurers will draw on the types of database already referred to. Premiums will vary not only with the statistical probabilities of meteorological disruption but also on the nature of the event, the contingency measures designed to mitigate adverse consequences and the potential financial losses that may result. With the progression of global warming, however, and an apparent tendency to more extreme weather, insurance may become more difficult to obtain in the future unless the locations and timings of events have been planned with great care.

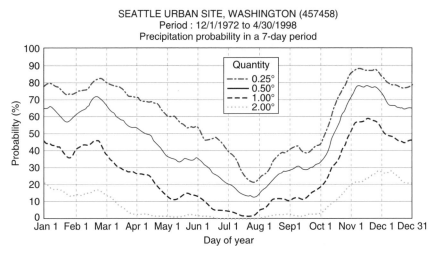

Figure 2.3 Rainfall probability data for Seattle, Washington State, USA

Source: ECO-3 (2012).

The supply chain

Events, like any other facet of human activity, make use of resources. Food can come from a range of sources, such as picking an apple from a tree or consuming an industrially produced chilled chilli con carne; drink can come from a mountain stream or from a soft drinks factory. In all cases resources are used, but there are significant differences in the products and their impacts on the environment. The apple depends on rain, soil and sunlight, which all occur naturally. If eaten in situ it involves virtually no transport. Waste is limited to human faeces and organic decay of materials in the tree. Once cropped for a year the tree will crop again the following year, unless it dies to be replaced by another (assuming human activity has not consumed all the fruit and therefore seeds for future trees). Water from a stream is available as long as the natural climatic cycles continue and human activity does not divert it or cause it to dry up.

By contrast chilled food products are the result of multiple ingredients. Energy is used in transporting them to a factory, processing them and delivering the product to retail outlets. Material is used to package them. Wastes are created from the processing, packaging and the use of energy, and some of these are toxic, such as many of the gases emitted during transportation. Soft drinks are similar. Both products make use of resources that are depleting – some can be renewed, some even sustainably, but others are in finite supply such as oil and gas. When exhausted these resources will be unavailable to future generations.

Owing to their diverse nature, events make use of a vast range of resources. As Meegan Jones puts it, 'A mountain of "stuff" is needed to run most events, much with a once only use' (Jones 2010). These resources involve supplying the needs of the event itself, such as the products needed to run a Formula 1 race; providing hospitality, such as the food and drink needed for attendees, participants and organisers; and providing transport facilities to access the events, such as fuel for the cars used to travel to the event. To audit fully these resources and the life cycles associated with them is difficult for a small event; for a large event it is an immense task, though some mega-events such as the 2012 Olympics are attempting it at least. The scale of the problem is vast and costs may be involved. This can be a deterrent to action unless legislative or moral forces compel it.

A complete audit of the resources used in an event would involve:

* identification of every product used in an event;
* an analysis of all the resources and processes used in the production of those products to identify their depletion implications, carbon footprints and other environmental impacts; and
* the utilisation and disposal implications of the products, including transportation from the event site.

The depletion of some resources is already a serious problem (see Table 2.2).

As can be seen from the table, some minerals critical to industry, such as tin, lead and zinc, have lifespans of less than 50 years, even without any growth in the rate of use since the late 1990s. Although these figures may be modified by a number of factors – discovery of new reserves, use of lower grade ores (usually involves increased energy

Table 2.2 Life expectancies of world reserves: selected mineral commodities

Mineral commodity[a]	1999 reserves[b]	1997–99 average annual primary production[b]	Life expectancy in years, at three growth rates in primary production[c]			Average annual growth in production 1975–99 (5)
Coal	987×10^9	4561.3×10^6	216	84	49	1.1
Crude oil	1035×10^9	23.7×10^9	44	31	23	0.8
Natural gas	5145×10^{12}	80.5×10^{12}	64	41	29	2.9
Aluminium	25×10^9	123.7×10^6	202	81	48	2.9
Cooper	340×10^6	12.1×10^6	28	22	18	3.4
Iron	74×10^{12}	559.5×10^6	132	65	41	0.5
Lead	64×10^6	3070.0×10^3	21	17	14	−0.5
Nickel	46×10^6	1133.3×10^3	41	30	22	1.6
Silver	280×10^3	16.1×10^3	17	15	13	3.0
Tin	8×10^6	207.7×10^3	37	28	21	−0.5
Zinc	190×10^6	7753.3×10^3	25	20	16	1.9

Source: IIED (2002)

a   For metals other than aluminium, reserves are measured in terms of metal content. For aluminium, reserves are measured in term of bauxite ore.

b   Reserves are measured in metric tonnes except for crude oil (in barrels), and natural gas (in cubic feet).

c   Life expectancy figures were calculated before reserve and average production data were rounded. As a result, the life expectancies shown in columns 4, 5 and 6 may deviate slightly from the life expectancies derived from the reserve data shown in column 2 and the annual primary production data shown in column 3.

costs), improved extraction technology, increased cost and the emergence of substitutes – they still indicate severe shortages in the short to medium term.

The processing of such products has other environmental impacts. The energy used in manufacture and delivery of products can be very considerable. According to Robison, 'In 1992, copper mining consumed a total of 46.2 trillion Btu [of energy]' (Robison 2002: 5–12).

Thus energy costs and their associated pollution can be immense in industrial production. The polluting effects can be serious, as the following extracts from a UN Review demonstrate:

Another issue that may have an impact on the future use of copper is its toxicity. Although it is an essential element at low concentrations for all living organisms including humans, large doses can be harmful. The impact on human health increases with both level and length of exposure. Water containing high levels of copper may cause vomiting, diarrhoea, stomach cramps, and nausea, and very high intakes of copper or long-term exposure to high levels of copper in food and water can cause liver and kidney damage that may be fatal. At high concentrations, copper and its compounds are also toxic to aquatic life. Its acute toxic effects may include death of animals and plants. Chronic toxic effects may include shortened lifespan, lower fertility, and changes in appearance or behaviour of animals and lower growth rates in plants. . . . Another major environmental impact associated with copper production is SO_2 emissions that occur in the process of copper smelting; the weight of SO_2 released more than twice that of the metallic copper produced due to the high sulphur content in the ores. . . . Mining copper ore also disturbs the natural environment. Large open-pit operations, which are becoming more common and necessary for companies to stay competitive, alter the local environment permanently. (Dzioubinski and Chipman 1999: 8)

Finally, there are the considerations relating to use and disposal of materials. In the case of copper many of the products of which it is part will be reused in future events. Some may be damaged, however. Copper itself is a valuable mineral and worth recycling. However, its separation from other components may be difficult or costly. Any transportation will involve further energy consumption and potential pollution.

This is an example of just one mineral in a supply chain and a common one at that, as copper can be found in much of the electrical equipment deployed in events, including mobile phones.

A PESTE approach to environmental audit

Beer has suggested a PESTE approach to analysing the food chains used in events (Raj and Musgrave 2009: 160). Such an approach focuses on political, economic, social, technological and environmental aspects of the supply chain. This includes assessing factors such as fair trade and genetic modification of food as well as narrower environmental considerations such as food miles and global warming. Some of these wider issues, many of which raise ethical concerns, have environmental impacts of their own. Genetic modification could greatly ease food supply and thus pressure on farmland but it might lead to interbreeding between genetically modified plants and traditional species, which could have unforeseen, and potentially dangerous, ecological impacts. Some of the PESTE dimensions are beyond the scope of this chapter but readers might reflect on them in the task described below.

TASK

In a group, choose a small local event. Using a brainstorming approach try to identify every product that will be used in the event. For each, try to identify its provenance (where it comes from and how far it has to travel), component materials, its resource limitations (is it scarce or plentiful?), its recyclability, and the environmental impacts its production has had on the environment before its use in the event.

The task of environmental audit is clearly immense and this can be daunting or intimidating for organisers of small events. However, being aware of the issues and implementing measures that can be achieved are worth considering. Adopting a sustainable approach is discussed in Chapter 7. Those wishing to refer to other sources might look at chapter 6 of Meegan Jones's book (Jones 2010).

Conclusion

The aims of this chapter were to:

- identify the nature and scope of the environment as an input into the event industry;
- examine the environmental influences on venues in both the natural and built environments;
- explore the ways in which the environment impacts on the running of events; and
- unravel the environmental context of the event supply chain.

In identifying the nature and scope of environmental inputs the chapter has shown that these are extensive and both direct and indirect. In examining the environmental influences on venues in both the natural and built environments it has shown how important the environment is in selecting the location of venues, designing them and running the events that take place in them. Examples have been given of the ways in which the environment impacts on the running of events, notably in the importance of weather. Finally, it has outlined the environmental context of the event supply chain and shown this to be both substantial and complicated. Overall it has sought to demonstrate an area of environmental importance in running events that has often been neglected, as the event literature has focused on the impacts of events on the environment rather than vice-versa.

Further reading

There is no single book in the events literature that addresses all the issues raised in this chapter. Referral to general geographical textbooks will yield useful background material.

3 Venues and the environment

Aims

The aims of this chapter are to:

- identify the different types of event venue;
- analyse their relationship to the environment;
- explain some of the key location factors in determining sites for venues, including those of a political and ethical nature;
- evaluate, through the provision of case studies, the venue decision-making process; and
- highlight some environmentally friendly practices in construction.

Introduction

Events take place in a wide range of locations. Some of these are relatively natural environments such as moorlands for the Three Peaks Run or the sea for the Clipper Yacht Race. These locations may have temporary facilities such as mobile toilets or catering but the location can be returned to its natural state relatively quickly. Others may make use of parkland or other tightly managed open environments. The use of these can be controversial, such as the use of Greenwich Park for equestrian events in the 2012 London Olympics. Some take place in multi-purpose locations such as schools or churches. Many, however, take place in purpose-built venues designed to house particular events, such as theatres, or to house a range of events, such as the National Exhibition Centre in Birmingham or the O2 Arena in London. These types of arena have a long history. Stonehenge, dating back 3500 years, could be seen as an early venue for (quasi) religious events. The theatre at Epidaurus dates to c.350 BC and the Coliseum in Rome dates to AD 79–82. These venues all have interactions with the environment – the environment influences their location, their design and their function. In turn they have impacts on the local, regional and global environment. These interactions form the basis of this chapter.

A typology of venues

As indicated above, there is a range of venue types varying from the almost natural to the completely artificial and purpose built. Each exhibits a range of characteristics and to some extent these can be categorised, as is shown in Table 3.1. This attempts to differentiate venues according to a number of criteria:

- the naturalness of the environment, which ranges from the almost natural (the world's oceans) to the completely artificial urban environment (the Stade de France);
- the frequency of use of the venue, ranging from the occasional (Global Challenge) to the permanent;
- the degree and length of intervention in the environment involved in using the venue, ranging from the minimal (Global Challenge) to the total (Stade de France); and
- the types of impact – these are variable but range from the minimal and short-term (Global Challenge) to the considerable and frequent (Stade de France).

The naturalness of the environment is not always what it appears to be. British moorlands, such as Dartmoor, may appear natural to the casual observer. However, their characteristics are the result of a long history of management dating back to the Bronze Age. Dartmoor was once extensively forested but is much less so today. It has been mined and reservoirs created in it. Agricultural practice, grazing for example, helps maintain its landscape. Some would argue that in developed countries like the UK there are no natural landscapes. Even in countries like the US and Australia wilderness landscapes are managed at an aggregate level through their designations as national parks. Chaffey has sought to categorise landscape character by reference to the degree of human intervention, as can be seen in Figure 3.1.

Chaffey envisages landscapes as having degrees of wilderness. Nonetheless, for the purposes of this chapter, areas such as Dartmoor will be treated as wilderness or near-natural environments, as they represent the closest to the natural that many highly developed countries with a long history of environmental change and management can achieve. Wilderness is usually much cherished and often highly protected. Organising events in such locations offers many challenges if the quality of the environment is to be maintained, not least because what can seem as a minimal impact such as trampling can have long-term effects – in extreme climatic environments it may take a long time for grass to grow back. Such environments may be better without events at all, or, if the public demands them, they should be infrequent.

As management of the landscape increases a range of venue types emerges. Farmland is highly managed but provides a relatively natural setting for the likes of festivals such as Glastonbury. Parkland is highly managed for recreational purposes which can include temporary events such as the 2012 Olympic Equestrian Events in Greenwich Park. Some natural environments have permanent venues in them, such as the theatre at Epidaurus, while some event venues actually create their own managed semi-natural landscapes, such as golf courses or garden festivals.

Table 3.1 A typology of venues

Environment	Temporary venues in wilderness or near natural environments	Temporary venues in moderately managed natural settings	Temporary venues in highly managed landscapes	Permanent venues in moderately managed natural settings	Permanent venues that create highly managed natural settings	Temporary venues in man-made environments	Permanent venues in man-made environments
Example location	Oceans	Rural Somerset	Greenwich Park, London	Epidaurus, Greece	St Andrews, Scotland	Notting Hill, London	Stade de France, Paris
Example event	Global challenge	Glastonbury Festival	Equestrian events at 2012 Olympics	Plays	Golf tournaments	Street carnival	World Cup football final
Event intervention	Minimal and short-term	High but short-term	High but short-term	Moderate but frequent	Permanent moderate inputs with short-term highs for special events	High but short-term	High and permanent

	Start/finish points Checkpoints	Fencing, parking, gating Staging, camping, toilets	Fencing, parking, gating Seating, toilets	Permanent structures Media infrastructure	Permanent facilities Seating, catering, toilets, communications for big events	Road closures Temporary seating	New arena New car parking facilities
	Health and safety facilities	Health and safety facilities	Competition structures and facilities	Access infrastructure	Media infrastructure	Advertising banners	New transport infrastructure, e.g. access roads, underground stations
Examples of event impacts	Litter Discharges to sea	Litter Trampling, compaction Congestion Noise Light	Litter Trampling, compaction Congestion Noise Light	Litter Congestion Noise Light	Litter Congestion Noise	Litter Vandalism Congestion Noise Light	Litter Congestion Noise Light
	Resource use e.g. food, packaging etc.	Resource use e.g. food, packaging etc.	Resource use e.g. food, packaging etc.	Resource use e.g. food, packaging etc.	Resource use e.g. food, packaging etc.	Resource use e.g. food, packaging etc.	Resource use e.g. food, packaging etc.

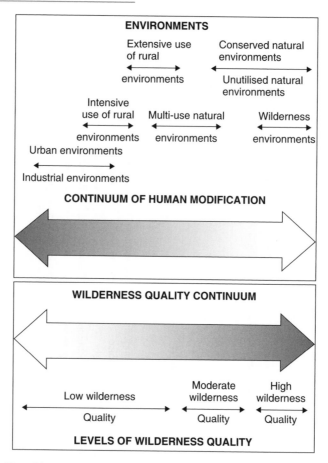

Figure 3.1 The wilderness continuum

Source: Chaffey 1996

At the far end of the environmental scale is the man-made, artificial environment. This is mainly urban. It hosts both temporary and permanent event venues, some purpose-built, some not.

Such an exercise is artificial in many ways though it does provide an analytical tool for reviewing venues.

TASK

Review (or if you are working in a group, discuss) Table 3.1 and its characteristics. What are its strengths and weaknesses? Consider its logic, criteria for differentiation and the adequacy of its categories (e.g. are all the categories mutually exclusive?). Where would you place racecourses, boating lakes and cricket grounds?

Venue location factors

The factors involved in locating venues will depend on the types of venue sought. As can be seen from the preceding discussion there are many venue types. Temporary venues may differ in their location requirements from permanent ones: thus the needs of pop festival venues such as Glastonbury will differ from concert halls such as the Sydney Opera House. Types of venue will vary in their needs: thus racecourses such as Longchamps or exhibition centres such as Earls Court will differ from theatres such as Epidaurus or football stadia such as the Neucamp. Issues such as site size, type of environment (natural or urban), association with traditions and culture or famous people (e.g. Bayreuth) and need for special facilities (e.g. snow for skiing) may therefore vary widely and may be idiosyncratic or unique.

However, a number of location factors are desirable or essential for most types of venue. These include:

- good public transport access;
- access to good roads such as motorways;
- a large population within a reasonable distance;
- available car parking;
- a suitably sized site, including space for ancillary activities;
- a site that is easy to build on;
- sites that will gain planning permission;
- environments compatible with the activities of the venue;
- the need to provide redevelopment in a run-down area;
- sites that minimise the effects of environmental impacts such as noise, litter, light and vandalism; and
- land that is affordable.

The nature of these factors varies widely geographically and environmentally.

Public transport is likely to be at its best in large cities and the centres of towns. Motorway access and car parking are likely to be better on the outskirts of towns. Large populations are found in urban areas and these are often concentrated in particular parts of a country such as south-east England in the UK, the Tokaido megalopolis in Japan or the Paris region in France. Large sites are probably easiest to find in suburban or rural areas though these may be the most difficult places in which to gain planning permission for construction. Greenfield sites are likely to be easier to build on than brownfield (e.g. derelict industrial sites) though they may also face planning restrictions. Compatibility factors will vary: for example, racecourses needing a green environment. Some venue projects have to consider their role in redevelopment. This may be providing a stimulus in a run-down area such as St Mary's in Southampton (see case study below). In the case of events that have to be bid for, such as the Olympics, organisers may have to demonstrate the environmental legacy that will result from a successful bid (see case study of the 2012 Olympics, below).

The minimisation of adverse environmental impacts is problematic for some activities such as football, which is rarely welcome near residential areas because of the noise and light pollution that it generates and the vandalism that is often associated with it, which can create damage to the existing environment. Cost varies enormously. Urban areas are generally more expensive and if the site is brownfield and requires decontamination this may exacerbate costs. On the other hand planning permission and local government support are more likely.

Clearly, venue location is a complex issue and to some extent each location is unique in its requirements. To illustrate this some examples will be discussed: first, the location of Southampton Football Club and Hampshire County Cricket Club, which provide contrasting examples in the same city, Southampton; and second, the London 2012 Olympic Stadium and other facilities, including the controversial decision to site the equestrian events in Greenwich Park.

Case study: Southampton Football Club and Hampshire County Cricket Club

In recent years Southampton has seen both Southampton Football Club (Saints) and Hampshire County Cricket Club move to new stadia. Both clubs applied for greenfield sites on the edge of the city. Southampton FC's plans were turned down though Hampshire's were ultimately approved. In the end Southampton FC moved to a brownfield site in the inner city.

Background

Southampton lies at the head of Southampton Water in southern Hampshire. Its origins as a port date back to Roman times but the modern growth of the city began in the 19th century and it is now a city of some 214,000 people. The late 19th century was a period of increasing leisure time. This led to a growth of leisure facilities, among which were Hampshire County Cricket Club at the County Ground and Southampton Football Club at the Dell. Both were originally on the edge of the city but saw housing develop around them (see Figure 3.2). By the late 20th century both grounds were cramped and a nuisance to neighbours, and occupied valuable suburban real estate. Road access was poor. Both had plans for development turned down so both sought new stadia.

The search for new venues

Southampton Football Club identified a site at Stoneham in the strategic gap between Southampton and Eastleigh. Much of the land was owned by Hampshire County Council. The club proposed a community stadium with associated retail developments, extensive car parking and links to Southampton Parkway station. Although the original idea had the support of Hampshire County Council, Southampton City Council and Eastleigh Borough Council, early planning submissions were turned down. The developers went to appeal and central government overturned the local decisions. Outline planning permission was given by the Secretary of State in 1994.

Following this outline permission, detailed proposals were drawn up in consultation with the various local authorities. In 1997 a formal planning application was made to Eastleigh Borough Council. The proposal was a complex one and included a 25,000 seat

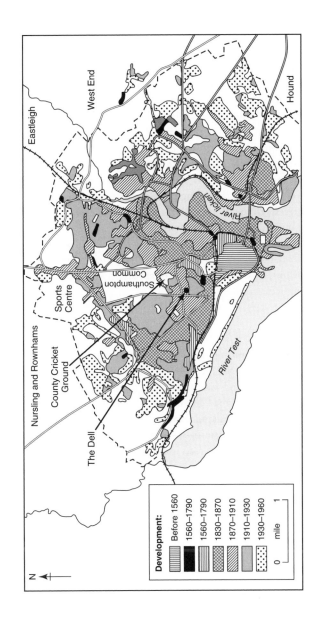

Figure 3.2 Location of the old football and cricket club grounds in Southampton

Source: Case 2007

Development:
Before 1560
1560–1790
1560–1790
1830–1870
1870–1910
1910–1930
1930–1960

0   mile   1

N

Nursling and Rownhams

County Cricket Ground

Sports Centre

The Dell

Southampton Common

Eastleigh

West End

River Itchen

River Test

Hound

stadium for Southampton Football Club, along with community sport facilities, leisure outlets and a retail complex. It offered links to Southampton Parkway station which could maximise use of public transport and proximity to the M3 and M27, which along with road improvements and car parking for 5000 vehicles would avoid congestion in the city centre. Additionally it would release land for property development at the Dell in a city with a high demand for new housing.

The planning authorities did not see the proposal as environmentally friendly and turned it down. They argued that retail developments and a new multiplex in the area were inappropriate and that there would be an unsatisfactory visual impact in the area, which constituted the principal approach to Southampton. They suggested that links to the station were inadequate and envisaged adverse effects on traffic flow on the M27 and on local residents, as a result of cars accessing the parking areas. Overall the county council felt the proposal was incompatible with the area's status as a strategic gap between Southampton and Eastleigh, while Eastleigh Borough Council feared, among other things, that 'its town centre and other local centres might be undermined by major shopping or cinema developments in the wrong place out-of-town' (Case 2007).

Without the commercial interests the developers felt the project would not be viable. As a result, the application to build the stadium was withdrawn.

There were rumours in the area that the project was not welcomed in what was essentially a middle-class area when the bulk of the fans were likely to be of working-class or lower-middle-class origin, a possible example of apparently environmental objections masking other prejudices.

A brownfield site alternative

Southampton City Council quickly came up with an alternative at St Mary's, a brownfield site located in the inner city of Southampton (see Figure 3.3). It had been a former gasworks and was contaminated, and was in a built-up industrial/warehousing area close to the docks with relatively poor road communication. It was in one of the most deprived inner-city areas in southern England. However, it did lie adjacent to the main rail link to London, the Midlands and south-east England, and Southampton Football Club agreed to contribute to the cost of road improvements. Overall it could help regenerate a run-down area (see Chapter 6).

This project was granted planning permission and initial funding of £17 million was secured through loans. The site clearance began in the autumn of 1999 and a new stadium was completed by the summer of 2001. The 32,500 capacity stadium, costing finally £32 million, saw its first match on 11 August 2001.

The new stadium has had many advantages:

- Saints now have a state-of-the-art stadium with more than double the capacity of the Dell;
- the roads in the area have been improved;
- the passage of fans (and earlier the labour force to build the stadium) through the area has brought in additional income, particularly to cafes, pubs and fast-food outlets;
- the Dell site was released to enable the building of 256 new homes.

However, some describe the stadium as soulless. Inevitably the transport difficulties envisaged by many have become a reality. Although the roads have been improved and the club has rented parking spaces from firms and institutions in the area, the area becomes very congested on match days. Big matches have created traffic jams both in and out of the city. Scandalously, in an era of supposed integrated transport infrastructure, no use has been made of the railway that runs along the edge of the site. Cynics have suggested that the establishment of a new station was opposed by commercial interests in the city centre who envisaged that they would benefit from fans having to walk from the station (an unpleasant, exhaust-fume dominated, 20 minute walk alongside busy roads) to the ground. South West Trains, the principal rail operator, have said that the lines already run at capacity. The result is that relatively few fans travel by train, not encouraged by the fact that trains after matches are not at all well timed, especially in the evenings. Not surprisingly a number of councillors, supported by the police, are campaigning for a new station to be built that will enable fans to have direct access to the stadium.

Cricket has green credentials

Hampshire County Cricket Club's proposals had a number of similarities to those of Southampton Football Club's at Stoneham. The new stadium lay on the outskirts of Southampton and in a strategic gap, this time to the north-east of the city. It was close to the M27 and was also part of a larger development proposal. There were some significant differences, however. The main stadium had a capacity of only 10,000 and involved little retail activity. Despite the provision of other leisure facilities

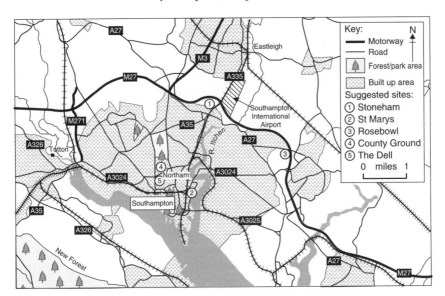

Figure 3.3 The sites of the new Southampton stadia

Source: Case 2007

(hotel/health spa, golf club, indoor bowls and a tennis club) this threatened less disturbance to adjacent residential areas and less pressure on the transport system than a football stadium. However, the initial planning permission was still turned down, largely on the grounds of the stadium being an unsuitable development in a strategic gap. Re-submission of revised proposals, however, gained outline planning permission in 1991.

Despite its middle-class image, cricket is less well financed than football. Funding was a major problem for the club. This created delays and the new Rosebowl stadium itself was not secured until a lottery grant of £7 million was awarded in 1997. It was not completed until 2001. Meanwhile the old county cricket ground was sold for residential development.

The new West End Leisure Park (which includes the Rosebowl) has many advantages. The cricket club has a new state-of-the art stadium holding 10,000 people which has now hosted international test and one-day matches. There are excellent new recreational facilities in an area of rapidly growing population and rapidly growing incomes and the road facilities have been improved in the immediate area. Environmentally there are downsides. Another major development has evolved in a strategic gap in an area where urban coalescence is difficult to prevent; there is additional traffic in the area and an element of disruption and visual intrusion. Access by public transport is still a problem when there are large gates. The cricket club no longer plays at Portsmouth and Bournemouth and only occasionally at Basingstoke – fans from these areas now have to travel to Southampton to see their club.

Conclusion – Southampton stadia

Environmentally, much can be learnt from these two developments. The pressure to move sports stadia from congested 19th-century sites is likely to continue, fuelled by commercial potential for property development and the need for large capacity stadia, particularly since the requirement for all-seater facilities. These factors are compounded by the difficulties of policing congested inner-city grounds and their poor road access. However, new stadia will not inevitably be sited on greenfield sites, despite their advantages of motorway access and ease of policing. The government's emphasis on the use of brownfield sites and on urban renewal may lead to more inner-city stadia such as St Mary's. Planning decisions are not based just on rational environmental appraisal. They reflect values, perceptions and conflicting interest groups. They are about politics. Those wishing to influence those decisions are likely to benefit as much from the study of politics and media manipulation as environmental considerations.

The two decisions were not, on environmental grounds, consistent. Both related to strategic gap locations and ancillary commercial development, yet one was rejected and the other accepted. Critically, however, there were differences in the scale of the proposals, 32,000 fans compared to 10,000, and the nature of them – ancillary retail activity rather than leisure activity. Perceptions relating to the nature of the two sports and their fans may well have influenced the outcomes.

Despite the government's emphasis on public transport, disappointingly this was not an issue that was ultimately given much priority. Access to the Rosebowl is largely by road, and this has led to congestion at some major matches. The same is true for St Mary's. The Stoneham site would have facilitated rail access but was turned down. Despite St Mary's location adjacent to the railway, no station has been built. It would appear that commercial considerations have prevailed over environmental and strategic transport ones.

Finally, the Rosebowl may mark the beginning of the centralisation of county cricket and the loss of matches played locally, such as those at Basingstoke. Whether people will be prepared to travel by car so much in the future with rising fuel prices and increasing congestion remains to be seen.

Case study: the 2012 Olympics in London's East End

The location factors that were involved in the siting of the main Olympic facilities in the East End of London were very complex indeed and operated at several levels.

- At one level was the British Olympics Association (BOA)'s decision to bid for London rather than another British city.
- A second level involved the International Olympic Committee (IOC)'s criteria for awarding the Games.
- A third level involved the long history of redevelopment in east London.
- Other levels included the needs of local government and the availability of specific sites.

The BOA's decision to bid for London followed the failure of Manchester and Birmingham to win the 1992, 1996 and 2000 Olympic Games. Despite the many merits of the cities as venues the BOA was convinced that 'only a London based bid was likely to be taken seriously by the IOC' (Poynter and MacRury 2009: 184). This is an interesting location factor as it represents a quasi-political factor that may be based partly on perception as well as technical assessment and other factors. No doubt environmental factors play a role in the assessment and the perception. Decisions are made by groups of individuals who have their own 'images' of particular cities established through personal experience, education, tastes and visits as well as presentations and media coverage. Evaluating these images, including the environmental dimensions of them, is a risky business but it is not one that can be ignored in the bidding process. It may be an intangible location factor but it is also a powerful one.

Following a feasibility study, further evaluations and complex negotiations with multiple stakeholders a bid was submitted which was finally considered in 2005. The feasibility study had looked at locations in both the west and east of London. The then Mayor of London (Ken Livingstone) insisted that it be in the east where it could enhance 'an existing urban regeneration agenda' (Poynter and MacRury 2009: 184). Having determined the general location within London the bid had to consider the explicit, as well as implicit criteria, for location that would be assessed by the IOC. There are many IOC criteria for assessing bids and these have evolved over the years. Until the 1990s environmental concerns had not been at the forefront of IOC considerations (see Case 2011). Following controversial Winter Games at Albertville the focus began to change.

The 2000 Sydney Games were designated the 'green games'. Sustainability and environmental concerns had become incorporated into the Olympic Charter by the time of London's bid. The IOC mission statement in 2005 stated that the Olympics should provide:

sustainable environmental legacies, such as

- rehabilitated and revitalized sites,
- increased environmental awareness,
- improved environmental policies and practices,
- further encouragement and facilitation of strong environmental actions, technology and product development in a city, country and beyond, through the educational value of good example. (IOC, cited in Digby 2008)

Particularly important was the legacy factor. In this respect the London bid promised:

- To make the UK a world-class sports nation: elite success, mass participation and school sport.
- To transform the heart of East London.
- To inspire a new generation of young people to take part in local volunteering, cultural and physical activity.
- To make the Olympic Park a blueprint for sustainable living.
- To demonstrate that the UK is a creative, inclusive and welcoming place to live in, to visit and for business.
- To develop the opportunities and choices for disabled people. (LOCOG 2007)

London was thought to be running third in the bidding process and it came as a surprise to many when it won. Legacy was seen as a key reason. As Jack Straw noted, 'London's bid was built on a special Olympic vision. The vision of an Olympic Games that would not only be a celebration of sport *but a force for regeneration*' (author's italics; cited in Poynter and MacRury 2009: 185). More specifically, Toyne notes that 'other important factors in deciding London's selection were the desire to use the Games as a catalyst to stimulate the regeneration of a 500-acre site in East London' (Toyne 2009: 234). Thus, while the bid clearly met the IOC's environmental and other criteria, it also promised to utilise land in a run-down and deprived area of east London.

The Lea Valley lies four miles north of Tower Bridge. Many plans had been put forward for its redevelopment. A-level geography students of a certain age may recall evaluating the area in an introductory exercise to the Schools Council Geography Project in the 1980s. Digby, commenting on the Lea Valley, noted in 2008 that:

- A considerable amount of land is contaminated, either with chemicals from wartime munitions dumps, or from bombsite clearance after the Second World War, or from industrial waste, which has been covered over. Mercury, cyanide and lead contamination are common.

- Environmental quality is low. East London is the only area of London where surface pylons transmitted electricity overhead; in all other areas of London, cables took it underground. In 2007 their removal began as a part of the new infrastructure for an energy grid in east London.
- Waste dumping and fly tipping has been ignored or tolerated.
- Industrial decline has led to a proliferation of derelict sites. (Digby 2008)

It is part of a larger area of the East End of London that had declined in the post-war era as industrial activity fell away and the docks moved downstream to avoid the unionised workforce and to take advantage of newer deep-water facilities that would allow for containerisation and larger boats. This left a large area of unused docklands with pockets of surviving industrial estates and residential housing. Much of the area had been transformed by 2000 by the London Docklands Corporation which created, among other things, the Canary Wharf complex. Much of the redevelopment had been very successful in generating new wealth but it had not been without controversy as commerce and middle-class housing supplanted the remnants of industry and working-class communities. The Lea Valley area had not benefited from this regeneration, so it was a natural location for the Olympic facilities from the Mayor of London's and local authorities' point of view.

Like St Mary's in Southampton (see above) much of the land was brownfield and soil decontamination was a necessary part of the development process. Also, as noted above, there was still industrial activity in the area. As Digby noted in 2008:

> At the heart of the new Olympic Park is an area of industrial estates forming one of east London's major industrial areas, Marshgate Lane. Nearly 300 out of a total of 400 companies for whom relocation has been necessary to create the park are located in this area. On July 1st 2007, the site was transferred into the ownership of the ODA [Olympic Delivery Authority], by which time all companies had been relocated. Most companies were service and utility-based e.g. waste recycling, bus depots and office supplies, though a substantial number were manufacturing, including food processing. (Digby 2008)

Not only industry had to move; so did public housing. Although it is intended that the Olympic Village will provide 3000 homes, people have been displaced and their relocation has seen some residents poorer as they were sometimes moved to more expensive accommodation.

The area has now been transformed, with an Olympic Park that houses the main Olympic Stadium, the Aquatic Centre, a multi-sports complex with indoor arenas for basketball, volleyball and handball, a two-stadium hockey complex, a new velodrome and BMX track, and the Olympic Village, which can accommodate 17,500 athletes and officials. Elsewhere in London eight existing facilities were used to accommodate a range of other sports: the ExCel (Exhibition Centre for east London), for contact sports such as boxing; the new stadium at Wembley for football; Wimbledon for tennis; Lord's Cricket Ground for archery; Greenwich Park for equestrian events and the modern pentathlon (see below); Hyde Park for the triathlon and road cycling; Horse Guards

Parade for beach volleyball; and Earls Court for volleyball. Other facilities outside London were used for shooting (at Bisley, Surrey), rowing (at Eton Dorney, Berkshire), sailing (at Weymouth, Dorset) and football (at a range of football grounds, including Old Trafford in Manchester). These latter sites were part of a strategy designed to demonstrate how the whole of the UK would benefit from the Games. It could be argued that this was little more than tokenism, if not entirely cynical, given the earlier comments about London being the only viable bid for the UK to host the Games.

Greenwich Park

Some of the venue locations chosen for the 2012 Olympics were highly controversial. One that excited particular opposition was the decision to locate the equestrian sports and the modern pentathlon in Greenwich Park. The park is sited in east London but it is on the south side of the River Thames, London's historic and tidal river. As LOCOG noted, 'Greenwich Park is a site of unique historical, environmental and archaeological significance and important to local residents and users. Greenwich Park is also part of a World Heritage Site' (LOCOG 2009). They stated that the park was chosen for a number of reasons:

- The Park's close proximity to the Olympic Village ensures the Equestrian events are placed at the heart of the Games. Travel time for athletes will be kept to a minimum, enabling them to feel part of the action.
- It's cost effective. Modern Pentathlon takes place over one day in which the athletes need to access the fencing and swimming facilities in the Olympic Park and riding, shooting and running facilities close by. Holding Equestrian and Modern Pentathlon events in the same location in Greenwich Park removes the need to build duplicate facilities. This reduces costs and makes it easier for the athletes competing.
- Using a popular London location allows spectators to travel to the venue by public transport and ensures they enjoy the buzz of the city during the Games.
- New urban audiences have a chance to see elite-level Equestrian events at first hand.
- This iconic location showcases Greenwich and London to audiences worldwide. (Ibid.)

The project was endorsed by the Chief Executive of the Royal Parks, Mark Camley:

We welcome the opportunity to host the Equestrian and Modern Pentathlon events in Greenwich Park in 2012. Our priority is to protect the Park's historic and natural environment for the enjoyment of current users and future generations. We are working with LOCOG to ensure any impact to the Park and Park users is minimised and are assured that LOCOG has publicly committed to returning the Park to its pre-Games condition. (Ibid.)

Despite this, LOCOG was aware that the decision would be controversial and launched a consultation exercise accompanied by attractively presented publicity material. Among other things it identified benefits to the area that included worldwide awareness, improvements to the transport infrastructure and a sports legacy for Greenwich.

Notwithstanding this, there was much protest, symbolised by a poster produced by NOGOE (No to Greenwich Olympic Equestrian Events), a local community action group (see Figure 3.4).

In one of its newsletters NOGOE published the following letter:

The Olympic Equestrian Events in Greenwich Park

My family went for a walk in Greenwich Park this morning. It was a beautiful crisp day. The sun was shining and hundreds of people were out walking, running, exercising their dogs and enjoying the start of the year. The park with its ancient trees, undulations covering Saxon burial mounds, leaf covered ground, magnificent views and historic buildings was looking at its best. As I looked at the wonderful surroundings I thought that what the park really needs is:

- Three years of major building work.
- The removal of the branches of over 70 trees to a height of 11 feet.
- 6,500 extra lorry and 36,000 extra vehicle movements in the vicinity.
- The removal of tons of earth to make a billiard table flat surface in front of the Queen's House.
- The introduction of some 160 tonne cranes, 5 tonne mini excavators, bulldozers and JCBs.

Figure 3.4
Protest logo produced by NOGOE

Source: NOGOE 2010

- The erection of a nine foot high metal fence interspersed with 16 foot high poles carrying security cameras around large parts of the park.
- All the accompanying destruction and mess that this will make.
- The partial closure of the park for the next five years.
- 'Loss or partial loss of heritage features' in a World Heritage Site and 'Medium adverse damage' of the park according to your own organisation's review.

All this to be done on behalf of a minority elite sport of the wealthy in one of the poorest boroughs in London. At the end of the Olympic Games, all will be dismantled and only the legacy of destruction left behind with the locals picking up the pieces for the shattered park.

Meanwhile Hickstead, a pre-existing equestrian venue 35 miles from London which would happily receive the Games and the accompanying investment will be left with nothing.

How futile. How foolish. How destructive. Please reconsider and take the equestrian events elsewhere.

Patrick Wellington

(NOGOE 2010)

It appears from these extracts and other literature that there are two very different and apparently irreconcilable viewpoints about this temporary venue. Before looking at how such conflicts should be resolved, it is interesting to consider further the role of ethics in venue location.

Ethics and venue location

As indicated in earlier sections of this chapter, venue location is a political issue and, as NOGOE indicates, an issue of values. In a post-modern world many would argue that all sets of values have equal authority, although this can ultimately lead to a solipsistic position on every issue. In such a world all values are relative and none have an absolute quality. However, some moral philosophers disagree and argue that it is possible to rate some values more highly than others and that a social dimension exists beyond the individual. It is also true that some apparent absolute values prevalent in the past have changed, for example in terms of attitudes towards gender equality or homosexuality.

Pragmatically, if no set of values can be argued to have moral superiority, it is political power that will prevail. Ultimately, venue location decisions will be taken by those who have the power to do so. This can result in social injustice or environmental iniquity. Power will often lie with the executives of governments or their appointed quangos but ultimately it lies in western democracies with elected politicians at local, regional or national levels. Event practitioners with ambitions to locate future venues might benefit from the study of psychology and political science and hone their skills of networking and persuasion if they wish their venue preferences to prevail.

TASK

Review the Greenwich Park case study and research it further on the internet. Debate which sets of values prevailed (consider also the broader context of the capitalism which operates in the West) in this case and the consequences of that.

The Olympics – conclusion

The siting of an event as large and complicated as the Olympics is clearly a complex issue. Traditional location factors such as cost, access and land availability play a part as do more recent concerns such as environmental impacts and environmental sustainability. However, overlying these factors are issues such as perception, values and politics. Ultimately, as this case study has shown, these less tangible factors are often the ones that determine where venues of a variety of types, temporary and permanent, are located.

Improving environmental design

In recent years the construction industry has sought to improve its environmental performance and this has extended to the construction of venues. A significant development in this has been the establishment of LEED, founded by the US Green Building Council (USGBC) in 2000. LEED, or Leadership in Energy and Environmental Design, is an internationally recognised mark of excellence that provides 'building owners and operators with a framework for identifying and implementing practical and measurable green building design, construction, operations and maintenance solutions' (US Green Building Council 2011):

> LEED is transforming the way built environments are designed, constructed, and operated – from individual buildings and homes, to entire neighbourhoods and communities . . . LEED certification provides independent, third-party verification that a building, home or community was designed and built using strategies aimed at achieving high performance in key areas of human and environmental health: sustainable site development, water savings, energy efficiency, materials selection and indoor environmental quality. (Ibid.)

Case study: Confederation of Indian Industry Sohrabji Godrej Green Business Centre Building, India

The Confederation of Indian Industry Sohrabji Godrej Green Business Centre Building is a new building in Hyderabad, India. It was the first structure outside the United States to receive the prestigious platinum LEED rating from the USGBC. It is a building of 1900 square metres and comprises 'exhibition spaces, seminar halls, offices, meeting rooms, and a cafeteria. [It is] . . . a showcase for energy-efficient, eco-friendly architecture and an integration of centuries-old practices of sustainability with modern technologies' (Jadhav 2004).

The USBGC identifies a number of its key environmental credentials:

- construction combined ancient practices with modern architecture;
- energy-efficient lighting systems and extensive reliance on daylight;
- building layout ensures that 90 per cent of the spaces have daylight access and views to the outside;
- use of solar photovoltaic cells: a rooftop grid provides about 24 kilowatts or about 16 per cent of the building's electricity needs;
- additional energy savings are achieved by the facility's two wind towers;
- heavily insulated roof further reduces the cooling load;
- all wastewater generated by the building is recycled by 'root zone treatment';
- the use of low-flush toilets and waterless urinals ensures an additional 35 per cent reduction of municipally supplied potable water;
- 30 per cent of users use alternative modes of transportation: carpools, bicycles, and cars that run on liquefied petroleum gas, a low-polluting alternative to conventional gasoline and diesel;
- the documented reduction of harmful emissions achieved by the design, siting, and construction of the building is 62 per cent for carbon monoxide, and 63 per cent for hydrocarbons and nitrogen oxides;
- a large amount of energy – and pollution – was reduced in the production and transportation of building materials through sourcing them locally;
- its recycled timber louvres controlled by photovoltaic cells;
- 77 per cent of the building materials use recycled content in the form of fly ash, broken glass, broken tiles, recycled paper, recycled aluminium, cinder from industrial furnaces, bagasse (an agricultural waste from sugar cane), mineral fibres, cellulose fibres, and quarry dust; and
- all of the new wood was sustainably harvested. (Jadhav 2004)

As a building which has a significant event function, it provides a model for such buildings, one outside the traditional western world.

TASK

Investigate some local venues. Ascertain which environmentally friendly characteristics they display. What new features might they take advantage of?

Conclusion

The aims of this chapter were to:

- identify the different types of event venue;
- analyse their relationship to the environment;
- explain some of the key location factors in determining sites for venues, including those of a political and ethical nature;
- evaluate, through the provision of case studies, the venue decision-making process; and
- highlight some environmentally friendly practices in construction.

The chapter has examined the issue of venue location in relation to the environment. It has demonstrated that this is an interactive relationship – the environment influences the location of venues and the venues, in return, have an impact on the chosen environment. It has shown that there is a range of venue types and that their environmental relationships exhibit varying characteristics which are important when seeking sites for them. It has explained a range of location factors, both traditional and modern. It has also shown that decisions about location take place in a context that involves perception, psychology, politics and values and that these are at least as important in determining locations as traditional considerations that accepted embedded systems of decision-making.

In looking at a number of case studies it has identified issues that need to be evaluated when reviewing venue locations. It has shown that factors often operate at different levels, are often very complex, involve issues of social justice and varying impacts on different groups of people and ultimately are determined by prevailing forms of governance. Finally, it has indicated, with the aid of a case study, some of the environmentally friendly factors that can be incorporated into venue design.

Further reading

No single reference exists that covers all the material in this chapter.

Environmental impacts at the micro scale

Aims

The aims of this chapter are to:

- identify the range of environmental outputs, including pollutants, that emanate from events at a local scale;
- examine the impacts, both positive and negative, that these have on the local environment; and
- review some options for environmental auditing.

Introduction

Not all environmental impacts are negative. Positive effects are intended and manifested at a range of scales, from mega-events such as the Olympics, where the intended environmental legacy forms part of the bid, to community events that focus on cleaning up litter in local open spaces. In between are events such as the garden festivals that were held in Liverpool (1984) and South Wales (1992). These effects can be the focus of the event or a corollary of it. In either case the benefits can be significant and permanent, though little remains of the two festivals cited.

Environmental impacts do not exist in isolation from other types of impact – they are often intrinsically linked to each other. They may, for example, have knock-on effects on the economy, society and polity. Environmental damage can be expensive to clear up, may upset local residents and may embarrass politicians. Vandalism by attendees at events, for example, causes direct damage to the built or natural environment which may have to be repaired by the local council at a cost to taxpayers. Meanwhile, the desecration can offend the coterminous, permanent community and they in turn can vent their frustration and irritation on their elected representatives. Similarly, positive impacts, such as clearing up litter, can increase enjoyment of open spaces, not least by making them safer, with consequent social benefits. Thus, although identification of environmental impacts is a useful analytical device, it needs always to be aware of the synergy with other impacts in a wider context.

Environmental impacts are not new but they have changed in scale and nature. Mega-events, for example, take place on an unprecedented scale not only in the host city but worldwide through the conduit of multi-media. The supply chains for such events are complex and the use of resources extensive. Their ecological footprints are substantial, in particular their carbon footprints. The wastes they create are more complicated, varied and difficult to process, particularly in an era of increasing environmental legislation.

A number of authorities have sought to categorise the environmental impacts of events. The author's attempt at this can be seen in see Figure 1.2. While not exhaustive or precise, it does provide a useful framework and most of its content is discussed in this chapter and Chapter 5.

Some intrinsic problems in discussing event impacts

Before exploring the environmental impacts of events, it is necessary to discuss a number of problems regarding definitions and terminology. These relate to:

- the differences between micro and macro impacts;
- the relationship between positive and negative impacts;
- the delimitation of impacts due to events; and
- the differences between short-term and long-term effects.

Micro versus macro impacts

Distinguishing between macro and micro impacts is not straightforward. Many pollutants have impacts at both scales. Some exhaust fumes from vehicles can affect health at the micro level (breathing irritation for example) and global warming at the macro level. Chemical spillages can have a substantial local impact while also contributing to riverine and oceanic pollution levels at a global scale. The mobility of gaseous and liquid spillages is the reason for this. Solid wastes are less mobile, though some lightweight waste can be blown or floated into waterways to join the ever-increasing accumulation of debris in the oceans – plastic bags are examples, and can cause ecological damage far from the point of pollution through ingestion by birds and fish. Separating macro from micro can therefore be seen as an arbitrary exercise to some extent, but it is a useful one analytically as the nature of the impacts at the two scales is often different, as may be the treatment of those impacts. For the purposes of this chapter, micro impacts will be those that occur at the site itself, the immediate surroundings and any relevant catchment areas such as river basins or transport networks up to a distance of 25 km.

Positive and negative impacts

As noted above, events can have positive as well as negative environmental benefits. Indeed some events are designed specifically to promote or produce positive environmental impacts. Examples of this are neighbourhood litter clearances arranged by community groups, such as those found in parts of Basingstoke, Hampshire. Other events, such as the Olympics, aim to have positive impacts, although this is not their primary purpose. Overall, however, positive impacts in most cases are outweighed or severely mitigated by negative impacts – the impacts of travel alone are often enough to offset any benefits. There may be spatial inequalities in the impacts, however. Positive impacts will tend to be local while negative ones may be manifested at a global level.

Which environmental impacts result from events?

Distinguishing event impacts from other leisure and tourism impacts is not easy. Many event venues hold events daily or weekly. Football stadia are good examples. They may host two matches a week during the football season interspersed with one-off events such as pop concerts. Additionally they may host conferences and hospitality on a daily basis. In this respect they differ little from hotels that have event programmes in addition to their basic catering function, or cinemas, which could be said to be event venues as they have daily screenings. Some recreational facilities, such as golf courses, are in routine daily use but sometimes hold tournaments that are special events. More problematic is the use of rural paths for special events, for example. One or two fun runs a year may have a disproportionate impact on problems such as trampling. Separating out the impacts would require intensive research. This is not just a question of quantification of impacts – i.e. apportioning so many days to events – it is also a question of the nature of impacts. Staging a concert on a football ground will have different environmental effects – especially on the grass – from football matches. This problem also relates to the issue of short-term and long-term effects discussed below. It is of note that much of the academic literature, especially early studies, relating to impacts such as trampling does not distinguish between one-off events and regular use.

There is no simple way that the various impacts can be separately identified – it would require evaluation teams at every use of a venue or facility to compile such data, even if a failsafe definition of what constitutes an event could be established. This will not happen. This chapter will take a catholic view of the issue and include impacts that can occur at any venue capable of holding special or one-off events.

Short-term versus long-term impacts

A final issue concerns short-term and long-term effects. This relates to both positive and negative events. The clean-up events already mentioned tend to be short-term in their benefits: litter soon reappears. (This does raise the issue of whether such events should be replaced or supplemented by education programmes or the provision of more litter bins to prevent the littering in the first place.) The garden festivals also appear to have been short term: one of them at least appears to have had no long-term beneficial environmental impact. By contrast it is hoped that the provision of green spaces and trees linked to the 2012 London Olympics may be longer term.

Negative effects are variable. An annual fair in a local park may cause trampling but if not used for such intensive events for a significant period such sites recover their vegetation, especially in summer when plants grow more quickly. Many readers will have observed this for themselves. Even here, though, more permanent soil compaction may be taking place. If events take place too frequently, the vegetation will degrade for longer – football pitches for example – and need prolonged recovery and intensive care. Where this does not occur, damage may be permanent. In such cases appropriate management strategies should preclude permanent effects.

Positive impacts

The discussion of positive effects in this chapter may seem relatively short. This reflects partly the imbalance between positive and negative effects but it also reflects the coverage of environmental legacy in Chapter 6. This should be borne in mind when reviewing impacts overall.

The tourism literature has for long pointed out the positive effects of tourism (which includes tourism events). Page and Connell (2006: 384) cite three principal benefits: the conservation of redundant or historic buildings, the enhancement of local environments and the protection of wildlife. Many of their examples relate to routine tourism but some relate to events. They note that the Millennium Dome in London was an example of restoration of a brownfield site and was the result of a very specific event. The environmental legacies of events such as the Olympics and Commonwealth Games are other examples and are discussed in detail in Chapter 6. The enhancement of an area's appearance can be closely related to events, whether these are the visits of a monarch or statesman or the hosting of a stage of the Tour de France. The protection of wildlife is often considered in the planning of events but is rarely the cause for special designation – existing environmental legislation usually provides a framework for such planning. This is discussed in a later chapter.

The purpose of some events is to improve the environment. These range from local clean-up campaigns to conferences to promote good environmental practice. Others are designed to specifically improve a particular environment. Garden festivals are examples of these.

Case study: Liverpool Garden Festival

The Liverpool Garden festival is an interesting example of an event apparently designed specifically to provide positive environmental impacts. The Festival Gardens website states:

> In 1982, the largest reclamation scheme ever undertaken in the country at the time commenced on a former household tip site adjacent to the River Mersey. The site was transformed in 1984 into the country's first ever garden festival. Billed as 'a five month pageant of horticultural excellence and spectacular entertainment' the International Garden Festival was part of the now disbanded Government quango Merseyside Development Corporation's regeneration efforts for the city in the wake of the Toxteth riots and industrial decline. Running from May to October, the International Garden Festival attracted some 3.4 million visitors with its mix of 60 ornamental gardens from all parts of the world and the centrepiece Festival Hall which contained various floral displays.
>
> The success of the Liverpool show led to a number of other garden festivals in towns and cities around the world which tried to emulate the success of the

Liverpool show. The Festival finally closed its doors on October 14th 1984 and subsequently a large part of the site has been redeveloped into a new residential neighbourhood overlooking the river as per the original long-term vision. (Festival Gardens Liverpool 2012)

The site then had a number of uses – including use as a leisure park – but was eventually closed in 1997. Since then it has been neglected and has degenerated while various stakeholders have debated its future. The local authority has now come to an agreement with a local property company and a conservation trust that will see restoration of part of the gardens as a park and further residential development. The neglect has been ultimately beneficial, as the website notes:

In the gardens themselves, nature was left to take its course. Watercourses, pathways and open areas have been left to become overgrown and despite being secured, vandalism has left its unfortunate mark. The neglect has now become recognised in some senses as a blessing in disguise with nature being given a free rein for a quarter of a century. The gardens now boast an almost unique ecosystem with its mixture of flora and fauna. The job of the [restoration project] partnership is to slowly peel away the layers of overgrown weeds, carefully trim back trees and shrubs to allow the gardens to breathe again. The centrepiece pagodas in the oriental gardens are to be restored to their former glory along with opening up new access routes into the gardens which will allow better and safer access to the site than ever before.

This work is the first step in the regeneration of the site which will ultimately see new residential development sitting alongside the newly opened park. The creation of the park and the new residential community will finally deliver a long term sustainable scheme for this strategic site on a major gateway into the City. This new dawn for the Festival Gardens has been a long time coming and this restoration work represents a unique opportunity to ensure the future of this site is secured for the public to enjoy. (Ibid.)

Clearly, the long-term environmental impacts of targeted events can take some time to unravel. Premature criticism might need to be avoided in favour of long-term evaluation. In the interim, however, it is not surprising if scepticism prevails.

TASK

Research other garden festivals such as that in South Wales. How successful were they in achieving their short- and long-term goals?

Negative impacts

Negative impacts have received relatively limited critical scrutiny in the events literature until quite recently. Raj and Musgrave's book *Event Management and Sustainability* (2009), for example, devotes only one chapter to environmental impacts. In it L. David categorises environmental impacts into three groups:

- impacts on the natural environment;
- impacts on the man-made environment; and
- impacts on the ecosystem.

This classification is questionable. Many would argue that the ecosystem is part of the natural environment and that these two groups should be combined. In the first group David includes air quality, geological factors, water quality, depletion of natural resources, flora and fauna. No subcategories are identified for impacts on the ecosystem. The list is not exhaustive – the introduction of new species into an area (including diseases) is not discussed for example. However, David goes on to outline the general impacts in each of these categories and gives a specific example of the Sziget Festival in Budapest, though he gives little detail of the mechanisms involved.

A different approach to categorising impacts is adopted by Parks Canada in a study of event impacts in Cape Breton, Canada. This breaks down the various human processes involved in the event and identifies their specific impacts. The table below is an extract from the work showing how this is done and how various types of event relate to this breakdown. The Parks Canada paper goes on to outline possible mitigation factors and how these can reduce the environmental impact. The residual environmental effect is then classified. This approach is similar to some health and safety assessments.

TASK

Using the approach adopted by Parks Canada, analyse a small local event that you have been involved in. Identify the various activities involved in the event and indicate their environmental impacts.

Before reviewing the issue of mitigation, some of the mechanisms involved in environmental damage will be examined. Some of the issues are discussed elsewhere in this book, notably the depletion of natural resources, the impact of venue construction, the macro impacts such as global warming and the urban legacy of events – these will not be discussed here. Discussion will focus therefore on trampling and erosion, disruption to flora and fauna, localised air and noise pollution and the impact of liquid and solid wastes in the immediate area.

Table 4.1 Some environmental impacts caused by events in Cape Breton

Valued environmental components (VEC)	Project activities	Potential environmental effects	Applicable special event types					
			Concerts	Sporting and community events	Filming	Aquatic ecotourism	Terrestrial ecotourism	Encampments
	Installation/use/removal of generators	Damage to in-situ cultural resources	✓	✓	✓			✓
	Set up/use/removal of sound/lighting equipment	Damage to in-situ cultural resources	✓	✓	✓			✓
	Use of camera equipment	Damage to in-situ cultural resources			✓			✓
	Set construction/deconstruction	Damage to in-situ cultural resources			✓			
	Campfires	Damage to reconstructed buildings	✓			✓		✓
	People attending special event	Damage to reconstructed buildings	✓	✓	✓		✓	✓
	Use of special effects and/or black powder	Damage to in-situ cultural resources	✓		✓			✓
		Damage to reconstructed buildings			✓			✓

Vegetation type	Activity	Impact						
Forest and managed vegetation	Equipment/crew transportation (terrestrial)	Trampling/destruction of vegetation	✓	✓	✓	✓	✓	✓
	Equipment storage	Trampling of grass	✓	✓	✓	✓	✓	✓
	Mooring/parking	Trampling/destruction of vegetation	✓	✓	✓	✓	✓	✓
Forests and managed vegetation	Set up/dismantle temporary staging, fencing, tents, etc.	Destruction of grass	✓	✓	✓			✓
	Installation/removal of portable washrooms	Trampling of grass	✓	✓	✓		✓	✓
	Set up/removal of waste facilities	Trampling of grass	✓	✓	✓		✓	✓
	Use of vegetative props	Introduction of invasive species		✓	✓			
	Set construction/deconstruction	Destruction of grass		✓				
	Campfires	Destruction of vegetation	✓	✓	✓			✓
	People attending special events	Trampling of grass	✓	✓	✓		✓	✓
Bog and heathland vegetation	Equipment/crew transportation (terrestrial)	Trampling/destruction of vegetation		✓	✓		✓	
	Equipment storage	Trampling of vegetation		✓	✓			
	Mooring/parking	Trampling/destruction of vegetation		✓	✓		✓	
	Set up/dismantle temporary staging, fencing, tents, etc.	Destruction of vegetation		✓	✓			
	Use of vegetative props	Introduction of invasive species		✓				

Source: Parks Canada Agency 2011

Trampling and erosion

It is interesting that as recently as 2008 Jones *et al.* noted that 'impacts on ecosystems appear to be completely ignored in the events literature'. However, the study of trampling in relation to general recreation and tourism dates back many years. Much of this has focused on the impacts on paths and trails through areas such as national parks. In many cases the trampling is caused by long-term, routine walking supplemented by occasional special events such as cross-country running competitions. The principles involved, however, can be applied equally to short-term intensive use of natural sites.

Weaver and Dale (1978) looked at the impacts of motorcycles, horses and walkers on trails in meadow and forest environments. They noted that the existing literature had already come to a number of conclusions: first, that vegetation cover is damaged by trampling and that some plants and species are more susceptible than others; second, that trail width increases as slope angle, wetness of the soil, roughness and the number of users increases; third, that climate, soil type, vegetation characteristics, slope angle and user type affect the degree of erosion and compaction and thus the depth of the trial; and fourth, that soil compaction is greater in trampled areas than in untrampled areas. Their own study found that grassy vegetation was less susceptible to damage than shrubby vegetation and that damage got worse as slope angle increased. They also noted that the greater the number of transits (foot, motorcycle or horse) the greater the damage and suggested that carrying capacities should be set related to the type of damage caused.

Quinn and Morgan (1980) looked at the specific forces involved in trampling. Their results show that

> most damage to vegetation by walking arises from compaction by the heel in the early part of each step and shearing by the toe action at the end of each step. The shearing action is the most important, and, within the 5 to 20° range of slopes studied, has its greatest effect on the steeper slopes. The breakdown of the soil by trampling occurs whilst wear of vegetation is still in progress, and not, as previously thought, after the vegetation cover has disappeared. Thus, by the time there is visual evidence of declining plant cover, the critical period in which erosion is initiated is already past. (Quinn and Morgan 1980: 155)

Cole (1993) took a detailed look at conflict between recreation and the natural environment and notes that it is trampling by humans that has a major impact on soil and vegetation (see Figure 4.1). Most of the dead organic material in soil is concentrated in the upper layers, particularly in a surface layer that usually consists primarily of organic matter. He notes that the organic horizon (dead organic matter)

> is critical to the health of a soil because of the important role it plays in the soil's biological activity. The organic horizon also promotes good water relations by increasing the absorptive capacity of the soil, decreasing runoff, and increasing moisture retention. It is a source of nutrients critical to plant growth and can effectively cushion underlying mineral soil horizons, which are more vulnerable to the compacting and eroding effects of rainfall and recreation. Organic horizons are generally less vulnerable to erosion than mineral soil, but if organic matter is pulverized by trampling, they too can be eroded away, exposing the mineral soil beneath. (Cole 1993: 106)

Damage to the underlying mineral soil can reduce pore space and thus aeration and drainage. This in turn, can damage existing vegetation and reduce the chances of germination of new plants. Soil flora and fauna may be curtailed and their beneficial effects on vegetation mitigated. Physically, the infiltration capacity of the soil can be reduced. This means run-off is concentrated on the surface of the soil, leading to erosion. The movement of this material into streams and rivers can lead to increased siltation and the potential increased risk of flooding.

Cole addresses the direct impacts on vegetation:

> Trampling can crush, bruise, shear off, and uproot vegetation. Plants in trampled places may have reduced height, stem length, leaf area, flower and seed production, and carbohydrate reserves. . . . All of these changes lead to reduced vigour and less successful reproduction. Sometimes they lead to a plant's death. Consequently, vegetation in trampled places generally has less biomass, sparser cover, different structure (generally shorter stature), and different species than in undisturbed places. Species differ in their tolerance of trampling, and these differences are reflected in the mix of plant species-the floristic composition-found in an area. Tolerant species are apt to thrive with increased recreational use because they face reduced competition from intolerant species that are weakened or killed by trampling. Also favoured are those plants that can take advantage of the changes in microclimate – such as increased light and temperature – that result from trampling. (Cole 1993: 106)

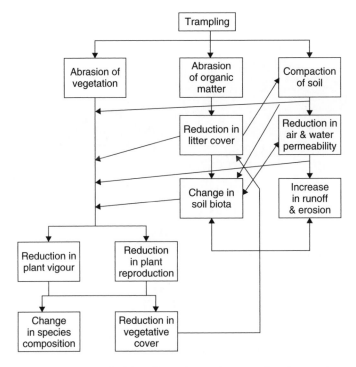

Figure 4.1 A conceptual model of the effects of trampling on soil and vegetation

Source: Cole 1993

Case study: trampling on Dartmoor

Dartmoor is a national park in south-west England. It is a wilderness area of great beauty characterised by extensive areas of moorland capped by very distinctive tors. It is an elevated area rising to over 600m and has a harsh climate with over 2000mm of rainfall in its western parts. The moorland is fragile but the area is popular with tourists and is host to a number of events, notably, in the past, the annual Ten Tors expedition. The National Park Authority has to deal with the erosive effects of trampling (see Figure 4.2). It deals with this in a number of ways: first, through the provision of educational materials; second, through physical measures; and third, through visitor management. In its educational materials it shows how the moorland can become degraded through trampling:

1   Trampling, by a variety of agents, at first causes a change in vegetation from taller plants e.g. gorse, heather and bracken, to shorter grasses.
2   Trampling, especially in extreme conditions, causes the mat of vegetation and roots to break up and expose the soil.
3   If the vegetation is not able to recover, then water run-off, combined with wind and frost begins to create gullies.
4   Further trampling combined with water, wind and frost action soon enlarges the gully and exposes the rocks beneath the soil.

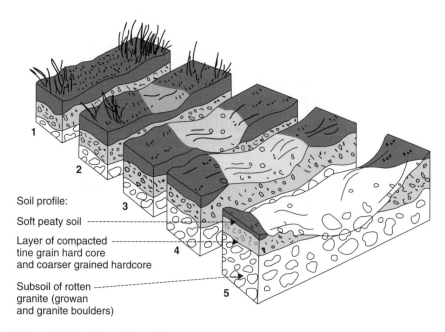

Soil profile:

Soft peaty soil

Layer of compacted
tine grain hard core
and coarser grained hardcore

Subsoil of rotten
granite (growan
and granite boulders)

Figure 4.2 The effects of trampling on Dartmoor

Source: Dartmoor NPA 2012

5   As the path becomes muddy and difficult to follow, people avoid the gully and the trampled area widens. (Dartmoor NPA 2012)

It identifies reasons why it is important to control erosion:

- it looks unsightly
- it can reduce the grazing value of the land
- it can permanently destroy habitats
- public rights of way and other routes can become impassable. (Ibid.)

The authority also outlines some of the techniques it is using to reduce effects of trampling at one of its most famous sites, Haytor:

- The exposed area soil appears to be fairly stable so it is not currently being managed but it is regularly monitored for change.
- Low grassed banks have been created beside the roads and in car parks.
- Large granite boulders are used to block off grass parking areas in the winter when the ground is soft and more vulnerable to damage from tyres. This both protects the grass and reduces the number of people using the area.
- These gullies have been filled in and the turf restored on the steeper parts of the path.
- Gorse clearance (burning and mowing) has been undertaken so as to widen or increase the number of paths and so spread the load of walkers walking between the two points. Some works have involved temporary diversions to allow vegetation to recover – accompanied by discreet signs explaining the reasons for the work and asking for people's co-operation. Grassed over, open drainage gullies have been created to divert rainwater away from the well-used paths and reduce the possible gully erosion.
- Granite paving slabs and rocks have been used to create a 'gateway' through the roadside banks and a solid base on a wet, boggy part of the path.
- Patches of bare earth have been restored with turf as well as reseeded with the Authority's moorland grass seed mix. Underground springs at some points continue to make this area vulnerable to damage.
- Currently the situation is being actively monitored and possible future works include placing of boulders, resurfacing and turf restoration.' (Ibid.)

Dartmoor and similar areas are particularly vulnerable to the effects of trampling and erosion but all vegetated areas are vulnerable to similar impacts through routine use or the occurrence of special events with large numbers of attendees.

Disruption to flora and fauna

Disruption to flora (vegetation) has already been discussed in connection with trampling and erosion. One aspect, however, needs to be mentioned. This is the introduction of weeds and other exotic species to areas as a result of visitors travelling to major events. At its most extreme this is a problem for international events where people come from many countries, and therefore many ecological environments. However, it can also occur at a more local scale. Jones *et al.* noted in their evaluation of nine events in Western Australia that:

> The introduction and spread of environmental weeds was identified as a key area of concern for the *Margaret River Pro* event. This was a major concern given the number of vehicles accessing the area and the pressure on parking facilities. This area of coastline embraces part of the Leeuwin-Naturaliste National Park. Measuring the environmental impact of this event in relation to the introduction and spread of weeds is problematic because the area is frequented by tourists/ recreationists all year round . . . The environmental impact of weed invasion in any area requires a longer term view – and can include a loss of agricultural production, loss of biodiversity, loss of landscape amenity and so on. (Jones *et al.* 2008: 51)

This quote reinforces the point already made that separating the impacts of events from those of general tourism can be problematic.

Seeds can be introduced in many ways. They can be on people's clothing or in the soles of their shoes. They may be in vegetables or fruit that have been carried to the event. They may be on vehicles or in the tyres of bicycles, motorcycles and cars. Although this is not the only mechanism for introducing exotics into an area – birds and winds are others – 'once in an area disturbed by recreation, exotic species often thrive because they favour the environmental conditions found there. The significance of this problem depends on the importance placed on maintaining strictly natural conditions as well as on the competitiveness of the exotic species' (Cole 1993: 107). In respect of natural conditions, note needs to be taken of the potential effect of climate change. In the past inhospitable climates in many areas will have limited the success of exotic species. Different climatic conditions in those same areas may, by contrast, encourage them. Their impacts can be considerable. Gardeners may have to cope with more weeds, some of them pernicious, such as the infamous Japanese knotweed. Farmers may have to spray more to curtail weeds or suffer loss of production. Vegetation in an area may become more diverse, particularly in the short term, but in the long term may become less diverse due to exotic species replacing native ones. This in turn can affect the fauna of an area if there is a loss of native feedstuffs. This may lead to animal migration. The combined effects of this can even lead to changes in the appearance of the landscape and its use.

Disturbance to animals is more extensive than that caused by habitat change due to the introduction of exotic species. Cole (1993: 108) notes a number of effects caused by recreation and summarises them in a useful diagram (see Figure 4.3). He identifies four types of impact which are summarised below (with additional comments by the present author in italics).

1. Animals can be harvested through hunting or fishing. *(This can result directly from an event such as a fishing competition.)*

2. Their habitats can be modified, either intentionally or unintentionally. Creating trails, for instance, can have pronounced impacts on populations of small mammals, birds, reptiles, amphibians and invertebrates in localised areas. An important characteristic of both soil and vegetation impacts is their highly concentrated nature. Most impact is confined to the specific place where the recreation occurs. *(Again such effects can result from specific events such as cross-country equestrian events.)*

3. Animals can suffer from pollutants, litter or food, left by recreationists. Discarded plastic six-pack rings or fishing line, for instance, can entangle birds. Less obvious, but more common, is the disturbance that results when animals are fed by recreationists or when animals eat food or garbage left behind. The significance of this problem is hard to assess. It has certainly been detrimental to bears in national parks. *(Additionally, the digestive systems of cattle and other ruminants can be affected by the ingestion of plastic bags. Food waste can attract rats, pigeons and other scavengers that may have impacts on native species. These issues are also referred to in a later section on waste – see below.)*

4. Direct disturbance may result when recreationists come too close to animals. This disturbance, sometimes called harassment although it is usually unintentional, is probably the primary means by which recreationists affect larger vertebrates –

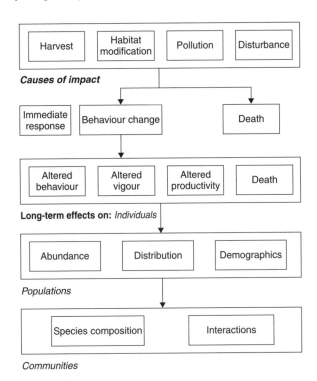

Figure 4.3 The impact of recreation on animals

Source: Cole 1993

birds and mammals. It can reduce the effective size and habitat quality of an area and even destroy a greenway's value as a migration corridor. The significance of harassment varies from place to place and from species to species. Unfortunately, our understanding of the problem is limited. (*Academic evidence in this respect is ambivalent. Some studies, such as those looking at the impact of tourists in Antarctica, indicate little impact on species such as penguins.*)

Clearly, the impacts on fauna are complex and, in respect of specific events, little studied, though many local authorities in countries such as Australia, Canada and the United States take animal disruption into account when granting licences for specific events.

Localised air and noise pollution

Air pollution is discussed more fully at the macro scale in Chapter 5. It also has localised effects which merit discussion. It results not only from activities at the site of any event but also from congestion in contiguous areas which results in vehicle emissions being concentrated locally.

Vehicle emissions are a pot pourri of unpleasant chemicals. They include carbon monoxide, carbon dioxide, various oxides of nitrogen, and particulates. They are all toxic to a degree, carbon monoxide being fatal in concentrated doses. Under certain meteorological conditions the effects of some of these gases are exacerbated. In areas which commonly experience high-pressure conditions (inversions), exhaust fumes can lead to the creation of photochemical smog. This produces a brownish layer in the lower atmosphere and confines pollutants to the air close to the ground. In places such as Los Angeles, where the local topography concentrates pollutants further, the effects can be intense. Exposure to the chemicals can cause eye irritation and difficulties in breathing which can be serious for people with compromised immune systems and chronic conditions such as asthma. If smoke particles, resulting from activities such as coal burning in domestic and industrial premises, combine with fog, they can produce smog. Again, they can distress vulnerable people and in some cases kill them. This was the case in the famous London smogs of the 20th century that occurred before the Clean Air Acts were introduced.

Vehicle emissions are not the only sources of air pollution at events. Campers' fires, which occur at many festivals, contribute smoke and other chemicals. Generators, cooking facilities and human flatulence also contribute. At some events, the nature of the event itself is a major cause of air pollution, firework displays, Formula One racing and air shows being good examples. As noted in Chapter 5, air pollution caused by events is one of the most intractable problems that the industry faces as so much travel to events is by vehicles using internal combustion engines. Additionally, such use is also contributing to the depletion of scarce energy resources.

Noise pollution is another adverse atmospheric phenomenon that can result from events. This can range from the short-term anxiety caused to cats and dogs from firework displays to the more sustained discomfort brought about by high decibel activity such as open-air concerts, motor racing and air displays. Licensing authorities are aware of these problems and often try to limit the impact of noise pollution. At a low level it can be irritating, for example, the low-level vibration that can be transmitted through the ground over considerable distances. At a high level, it can be dangerous. Evidence now exists to show that standing close to high-powered amplifiers for prolonged periods can cause not only temporary deafness but long-term effects as well. The author recalls sitting close to an amplifier at a concert in 1971 and not being able to hear properly for three days afterwards. He also wonders if the frequency range of his hearing has been permanently compromised by too much activity of this sort when young.

Light pollution is a further problem little appreciated by many event attendees. In urban areas the light impacts of events are often absorbed or concealed in the overall high light output of towns and cities. Even here, though, concentrated light effects such as sports stadia floodlighting and laser beam displays can be disruptive to some people, such as those who have difficulty getting to sleep. In rural areas the problems can be more acute. Animals and human inhabitants are used to dark skies at night and can find concentrated light sources disturbing, especially as they can often be seen at considerable distances.

Congestion

Congestion is a regular impact of events. In many cases the management of it is built into the design of venues, such as the Stade de France, which has excellent public transport facilities. It is not easy to define congestion. Crowded streets and full public transport are tolerated at sports events and concerts on a regular basis throughout the world. However, when motorways grind to a halt, fans are late to an event and 'innocent' motorists are affected, the impact is more serious and can prompt government action, as the following case study shows.

Case study: Robbie Williams concert at Knebworth House, 2003

Knebworth is a village close to Stevenage, 47km north of London and close to the A1(M) motorway. It has a stately home, Knebworth House, which has been home to the Lytton family since 1490. Its website describes the house as 'Britain's most accessible stately home!' (Knebworth House 2012). It had held concerts for some time and in August 2003 hosted three concerts featuring Robbie Williams. The first, on a Friday, created traffic chaos however. Thousands were caught up in huge traffic jams and missed the Hertfordshire gig, while others spent five hours trying to leave the car park afterwards' (BBC News 2003a). The problems centred on a 16km stretch of the A1 in Hertfordshire from Baldock to Stevenage and were blamed by AA Roadwatch on Friday night traffic and bad weather. Chief Superintendent Wright of Hertfordshire Police commented:

> We sympathise with those that were unable to get to the concert on Friday evening due to the heavy congestion. Many people chose to leave for the concerts later because of the poor weather which combined with heavy rush hour and holiday traffic aggravated the situation on the roads. However, people heeded our advice to leave plenty of time for their journeys on Saturday and Sunday and both days passed with few traffic problems en route to Knebworth Park. (BBC News 2003b)

Not surprisingly many fans were disappointed, others angry. The BBC reported the anguish of many:

> Robbie Williams fan Paul Glover said he was 'gutted' after paying £40 to hear a muffled version of his favourite song, Angels, from the hard shoulder.
>
> The 31-year-old from Kent set off at midday with five friends to watch his pop idol perform live but the group spent nine hours stuck in traffic on the A1 between junctions six and seven.
>
> Mr Glover, a company director, said: 'We got to the roundabout that leads to Knebworth about five minutes after the concert had ended so we listened outside our cars on the hard shoulder to three or four of his songs.
>
> 'We could actually see the stage, the lighting and at the end a few pyrotechnics and fireworks, so not only did we hear a muffled version of Angels we could also see the lights we should have seen up close.'
>
> He said hundreds of cars with fans from across the country were stuck on the motorway, including children, with home-made posters of the pop star on the windows.
>
> There were also delays for those who saw the gig.
>
> One fan told BBC Radio Five Live he finally got out of the car park at 0400 BST on Saturday, five-and-a-half hours after the concert finished.
>
> Police are reviewing their handling of the traffic for the weekend concerts.
>
> 'Certainly there is a plan that is being reviewed and revised in co-operation with the traffic management consultants,' a Hertfordshire Police spokesman said.
>
> The spokesman said the 'sheer volume of traffic' descending on the venue caused the chaos. (BBC News 2003a).

The BBC noted that 'Robbie Williams . . . flew in by helicopter' (Ibid.).

It is important to note that the concerts were musically successful, but the congestion had ramifications, not least of which were complaints to the local authorities. One was to the Chief Executive of North Hertfordshire Council, which elicited an extensive response from Chris Evans, the Chief Environmental Health Officer. It included the following:

> For the concert to take place at Knebworth a traffic management plan was agreed between the Police, the Highways Partnership, the Highways Agency and a traffic management consultant for the promoter. The traffic de-brief covered a number

of events which took place well outside the traffic management area and some inside which all combined to cause a problem on the Friday. On Saturday and Sunday concertgoers were asked to arrive early and there were no serious problems on the roads. However, the experience of the Friday could well affect planning for future workday events at Knebworth. (Safe Concerts 2004)

A further concert at Knebworth in 2005 also caused problems.

Following similar congestion at other concerts, national government looked at the problem. The Auditor General, Sir John Bourn, produced a report which said that 'event organisers should be obliged to warn highways chiefs in advance' (Craig 2004). Discussing hold-ups on motorways, he noted: 'The agency has not been aware of some major sporting and entertainment events – and has therefore not been well prepared to deal with them' (ibid.). He also noted that the Highways Agency had 'been too cautious in bringing in measures to ease congestion. Sir John said that incident signalling systems had been introduced on the M1 and M6 in the north and Midlands, but not the crowded south east' (ibid.).

The Knebworth incidents were also cited in a Public Accounts Committee Report to the House of Commons.

Most cases of congestion are less noteworthy or dramatic but have a regular impact on the population living close to event venues.

Case study: air quality at the Beijing 2008 Olympics

The Sydney Olympics had been described as the green games. While critical scrutiny of such claims reveals some weaknesses in the environmental performance of the Games, they did set a standard against which future Olympics would be judged. This was a particular challenge for China when hosting the Beijing Games in 2008. China has a massive population and has been rapidly industrialising over the past decade. Rapid industrialisation tends to produce significant amounts of pollution. Before the Games Beijing had a reputation for poor air quality. Improving air quality was an aim of the bidders for the Beijing Games and many measures were undertaken. These included improvements to domestic heating systems, power generation, public transport infrastructure and controls on industrial pollutants:

> Overall, Greenpeace believes that the environmental efforts of BOCOG and the Beijing municipal government have created a positive legacy for the city of Beijing. Beijing did more than Athens and should be commended for its efforts in using the Games as an opportunity to upgrade and improve city infrastructure as well as to integrate leading energy saving technologies in Games venues. Many of Beijing's environmental initiatives have set a good example for other Chinese cities to follow. However, in part due to inadequate transparency and engagement with third party stakeholders, Beijing's green Games efforts do not meet the comprehensive approach of the Sydney Government before and during the 2000 Games. In addition, the International Olympic Committee (IOC) has an important role to play in ensuring that all Olympic host cities meet some minimal

environmental standards and should require the use of independent verifiers for large-scale Games venues to encourage the best environmental legacies for all Olympic Games. (Greenpeace 2008)

However, in terms of air quality Greenpeace remained concerned:

Although Beijing adopted a number of long-term measures to improve air quality in the city, they nevertheless had to introduce temporary measures, such as drastically reducing vehicle numbers and shutting down industrial production in order to ensure that air quality meets standards during the Games. Beijing could have adopted clean production measures more widely across the municipality to speed up the improvement of air quality and to ensure that standards are met for the whole year. (Ibid.)

The United Nations carried out its own report on Beijing (UNEP). It commented on air quality:

Air quality was by far the most prominent environmental issue the Olympic organizers and the Beijing municipal authorities had to manage. Indeed it has been an issue for several previous Olympic Games, including Los Angeles and Athens. The report notes that 'significant efforts before and during the Games were focused on improving Beijing's air quality' and that 'as a result, air quality improved significantly'. Studies show that the special measures taken for the Olympic Games – in conjunction with weather conditions in August – led to reductions in carbon monoxide (CO) by 47 per cent; nitrogen dioxide (NO_2) by 38 per cent; volatile organic compounds (VOC) by 30 per cent; particulate matter (PM10) by 20 per cent; and sulphur dioxide (SO_2) by 14 per cent. The Games also 'greatly increased public awareness of air quality' in Beijing, leading the public to press for continued efforts to sustain the improved quality of life experienced during the Games.

However, the report notes that 'there remains significant room to improve Beijing's air quality' – the PM10 standard in the city remains a challenge. Future air quality challenges in Beijing are likely to focus on the smaller particles . . . which are not currently subject to standards in China but raise health issues. (UNEP 2009)

At the time of writing Beijing continues to experience problems with its air quality and there is controversy over the accuracy of data relating to its levels of air pollution. In January 2012 BBC News commented:

Beijing residents have become increasingly concerned at the way the government measures air quality – something that was exacerbated when the US embassy began publicising its own pollution readings. The embassy readings have frequently been much higher than the official ones. The discrepancy is because the US embassy measures particles under 2.5 micrometres (PM2.5), while most local authorities including Beijing monitor particles under 10 micrometres (PM10). Health experts warn that the smaller particles can move further into the lungs, causing respiratory problems.

Beijing is now preparing to release real-time monitoring data of PM10, sulphur dioxide and nitrogen dioxide on the environment bureau's website before the Chinese New Year. At the same time, PM2.5 monitoring data 'for research purposes' will also be made available for reference, says the statement published on Friday. Real-time PM2.5 data will eventually be made available 'pending new national standards and relevant monitoring criteria'. The new measure is expected to be welcomed by environmentalists in China. However, Wang Qiuxia, an air pollution expert with Chinese group GreenBeagle, warned that cleaning up Beijing's air would be a long process. 'According to some assessments it will take 20 years before we see an improvement in Beijing's air quality, provided that proper measures are adopted,' she is quoted by the AFP news agency as saying (BBC News 2012).

This does raise questions about the long-term effects of the measures undertaken by the Beijing Olympic authorities and the ability of major events to make significant, permanent improvements to the environment.

TASK

Bearing in mind the comments made about the 2008 Olympics, review the proposals of the London 2012 organising committee in respect of air quality. This information is available online on the 2012 website.

The impact of liquid and solid wastes

Events create a large range of liquid and solid wastes. These include sewage, formal and informal, cosmetics including suntan lotions, cleaning products, hydrocarbons and litter, including heavy metals, plastics and glass. Some of these, such as food waste, paper and cardboard, are biodegradable. Many are not. The amount of waste created at events can be very large. The 2008 Glastonbury Festival, for example, created 1651 tonnes of waste.

Waste is a problem for many reasons:

- many attendees do not dispose of their litter in appropriate ways and this requires large numbers of staff to collect and back up the rubbish;
- some litter, if not properly collected, can be dangerous – cigarette ends and glass can start fires and plastic bags can be fatal to animals;
- liquid wastes, including urine and hydrocarbons, can seep directly into the ground and contaminate the water table, and the effects of these can vary from increased toxicity to eutrophication of nearby waterways; and
- much of the waste will finish up in landfill sites, which are increasingly scarce and expensive to maintain, or incinerators, which even if highly specified not to pollute are unwelcome in most neighbourhoods.

Many of these problems would be reduced if the behaviour of attendees improved. However, despite the provision of educational materials, extensive signage and incentives such as the provision of plastic bin bags to arrivals, much undesirable waste is still created, as the mini case study below illustrates.

Mini case study: a cautionary tale from the Reading Festival

The following information is anecdotal and has to remain anonymous for obvious reasons. Personal experience at earlier festivals by the author confirms the detail and many readers will recognise its veracity from their own experience.

At a recent Reading Festival a group of students camped on the official campsite. Their tents were some distance from the stages and the nearest toilet facilities. To enhance the enjoyment of the event much alcohol was drunk, much of this being beer, with its well-known diuretic effects. After the concerts were over and the group had returned to its tents the levels of intoxication tended to militate against long journeys to the toilets when the need for micturition became urgent. Nearby was a small clump of vegetation with a slight hollow at its centre. This provided a handy spot for urination, particularly for the males present. As a result the area became slippery. Inevitably one of the students fell into the mess on one of his visits to the site. With his clothes contaminated, his return was not welcomed by his colleagues and he became a social outcast among them. His clothes were all subsequently destroyed and urgent visits to washing facilities were necessitated. Apart from the potential damage to the environment, the individual concerned did not enjoy the remainder of the festival.

Although the precise environmental outcomes of this incident are not known, mass urination (urine contains nutrients) can lead, like the application of fertilisers in agriculture or on golf courses, to eutrophication,

> a process whereby water bodies, such as lakes, estuaries, or slow-moving streams receive excess nutrients that stimulate excessive plant growth. The plants can be algae and/or nuisance plant weeds. This enhanced plant growth, often called an algal bloom, reduces dissolved oxygen in the water when the dead plant material decomposes and can cause other organisms to die. Nutrients can come from many sources, such as fertilizers applied to agricultural fields, golf courses, and suburban lawns; deposition of nitrogen from the atmosphere; erosion of soil containing nutrients; and sewage treatment plant discharges. (US government definition, cited in CIOSS 2005)

Higher level organisms are those that may die leading to a loss of fish in waterways.

To compound this particular environmental felony, the group left their cheap tents and sleeping bags at the site for others to clean up and dispose of.

Assessing the overall environmental impact of events: approaches from Australia

In recent years a number of attempts have been made to assess the overall environmental impact of given events. One such attempt was carried out by Jones and others (2008) for the Sustainable Tourism Cooperative Research Centre. They looked at nine events in Western Australia. For each they began by describing the event. The Avon Descent, for example, is a time trial event for paddle and power craft spread over two days and beginning in the town of Northam, north-east of Perth in Western Australia. It involves about 25,000 spectators, around 2500 family and friends and an additional 2500 volunteers to assist with tasks such as traffic management, rescue services and the provision of food. This is a two-day event, commencing in Northam. The event involves peripheral activities such as parades, festivals, fairs and fireworks in Northam and other towns along the route.

The assessment moved on to look at how the event was approved and the conditions that the authorities impose on the event to promote good environmental practice. For the Avon Descent this involves consultation with local councils and the state government. The organisers have to complete a traffic management plan for approval and abide by environmental conditions for camping that include 'the proper use of toilet facilities provided, the non-disposal of waste water near or in the Avon River, avoidance of damage to areas of natural bushland or disturbance of wildlife and rules relating to the storage and use of fuels' (Jones *et al.* 2008: 37).

The assessment process then turns its attention to the environmental impacts and direct costs relating to the event, beginning with surface transport – traffic, parking and public transport. In the case of the Avon Descent traffic congestion was not identified as a major area of concern although some roads were closed for a few hours. This is mainly because the 30,000 people involved were spread over a large area, there was ample hard surface parking, signage was generally good and additional staff assisted with traffic management.

On the negative side, Jones *et al.* did note 'some damage to tracks, roadsides and natural vegetation from what is probably a small number of four-wheel drive owners' (Jones *et al.* 2008: 37)

The issue of noise was then addressed. At the Avon Descent this was not a significant problem, although there was excessive noise at some of the campsites.

Energy and water provision were then reviewed, but not much information was available for the Avon Descent so little comment was made.

Litter and general refuse were then reviewed. The number of additional bins for the Avon Descent was noted to give an idea of the volume of waste involved. Litter was limited, however, mainly to the roadsides leading to the designated campsites. The type of litter found at these locations was mainly beer bottles. The organisers used volunteers to assist with the clean-up of litter at campsites along the Avon River. The worst litter problem was that created by illegal campers – drink cans, paper, food and sweet wrappers. The litter was found primarily at the campsites. Elsewhere litter problems were largely related to food packaging and food scraps. In conclusion Jones *et al.* noted that 'NADA [Northern Avon Descent Association] has responsibility for the collection of litter, although according to the City of Bayswater Environmental Health officer, NADA often underestimated the amount of litter that would be generated' (Jones *et al.* 2008: 38).

The review then identified the degree of waste minimisation and recycling. In the Avon Descent there was an absence of kerb recycling and observed that there were 'also no banners, signs and/or other media encouraging people to recycle, as there are at many other events' (Jones *et al.* 2008: 38). Regarding waste water (grey water), there were few serious problems and compliance with regulations was high, although disposal of water from the temporary spas might have been approved.

Toilet facilities were the final aspect of the impact assessment. No significant issues were identified at the Avon Descent, the permanent facilities being complemented by additional temporary chemical toilets.

The review process then turned to the issue of minimising environmental damage. A number of problems were identified in the Avon Descent:

- Damage to areas of natural vegetation by four-wheel drive vehicles which could be reduced by closing some access roads.
- The erosion of river banks (especially in areas where banks are already degraded) by the wash from power boats. Minimisation of this is problematic as it is unlikely that there would be much support for a significantly reduced speed limit along stretches of river most prone to bank erosion. A photographic monitoring program has been suggested to identify riverbank damage and the need for remediation of damage caused by the event.
- The potential impact of craft and participants on the river bed at times of low flow when competitors have to carry their vessels across the exposed bed – the organisers can identify less sensitive crossing points to minimise this damage.
- The potential impact of participants and spectators on the river banks.
- The potential impact of spectators on the river floodplain. (Jones *et al.* 2008: 39)

Jones *et al.* observe that these potential environmental impacts are included within a comprehensive environmental checklist for the event compiled by the organisers.

Before concluding the reviews with a commentary, attempts at promoting environmental awareness were discussed. In the case of the Avon Descent these amounted to stakeholder consultation and a donation of $2000 from the organisers to the volunteer group Friends of the River for river restoration work.

The concluding commentary on the Avon Descent focused on the issue of whether environmental checklists would improve the environmental outcomes of the event. The compilation of such a checklist was one of the aims of the authors. Views differed among the various authorities but most were relaxed about the adequacy of the present arrangements. Jones *et al.* concluded that:

> the fact that there is an *Avon Descent* Environmental Management Plan demonstrates that . . . [the organisers and authorities are] . . . perhaps more engaged in environmental impact assessment than the other events organisers (and hosts) and works closely with the relevant councils and agencies. This is most likely a reflection

of the highly sensitive nature of the Avon River environment and the active involvement of DEC [the Department of Environment and Conservation] in working in partnership with landowners to undertake river restoration work such as the restoration of riparian vegetation.' (Jones *et al.* 2008: 40)

TASKS

- Using the internet or an atlas find out where the Avon Descent takes place.
- Review the article above and access the report online (see references). Do you think the event organisers are doing all they can to minimise negative environmental impacts?
- Using a similar format of headings, interview the event organisers of an event close to you and produce a report on their environmental performance.
- Do you think a checklist is a useful framework for event organisers to use in planning the environmental aspects of their events? When you have read the later chapters in this book you may reflect on your views at this stage.

Conclusion

This chapter set out to achieve the following aims:

- identify the range of environmental outputs, including pollutants, that emanate from events at a local scale;
- examine the impacts, both positive and negative, that these have on the local environment; and
- review some options for environmental auditing.

It has shown that the range of environmental outputs is extensive. Some of these are minimal in their impact but others can have serious effects. Environmental impacts can be positive as well as negative and some events are targeted at improving the state of the environment. However, overall it would appear that events have more negative than positive impacts. Fortunately there is a growing awareness of the environmental impacts of events and research has begun to assess the overall environmental performance of particular events. Further discussion regarding the mitigation of negative environmental impacts will be found in later chapters.

Further reading

Much of the discussion of environmental impacts is found in books on geography, environmental science and tourism. One particular report, however – by Jones *et al.*, and published by the Cooperative Research Centre for Sustainable Tourism in 2008, is worth reviewing and is available online.

5 Environmental impacts at the macro scale

Aims

The aims of this chapter are to:

*   identify some of the principal pollutants that are causing problems at a global scale and investigate their causes and impacts;
*   examine the extent to which human activity is changing planetary systems, in particular the climate system; and
*   assess the contribution of the event industry to these pollutants.

Introduction

Like much economic activity, the event industry not only impacts on its local environment, but also on the global environment. Some of this relates to pollutants that affect the local area before becoming more widely diffused, such as sewage, increased run-off, oil and other liquid discharges. Much of it relates to gaseous discharges. These are more mobile than solid and liquid wastes and are usually discharged directly to the atmosphere. If warmer and/or lighter than air, they rise. The ascent may be many thousands of metres. At all levels of the ascent they can be easily carried away by winds. Even heavier gases can be blown away by ground-level winds. The gases get caught up in the general circulation of the atmosphere and can be carried around the globe and throughout the various layers of the atmosphere. Various factors such as the prevailing wind directions at different altitudes can result in the gases becoming concentrated in parts of the world far from the source of the pollution. Examples of this are the chlorofluorocarbons (CFCs) that led to the breakdown in the ozone layers over the Arctic and Antarctic, and the acid rain (resulting from CO, CO_2, SO_2, SO_3 and NO_3 emissions) that has damaged forests in Scandinavia and central Europe. Other gases become universally distributed, such as the so-called greenhouse gases.

These pollutants are important because they not only threaten our way of life but our very existence on the planet. Unchecked global warming has the capacity to alter the ecosystems on which we depend to such an extent that we will be unable to feed ourselves. We have some ability to mitigate climate change but that depends on our understanding of it. This is controversial partly because there are limitations to our understanding of the mechanisms involved but also because there are philosophical differences in how to approach the problems and vested interests that have a stake in maintenance of the status quo. The extent to which man-made (anthropogenic) pollution is responsible for climate change will be discussed later in this chapter.

The event industry is not the only industry that contributes to these emissions but because of its intrinsic nature it is a significant polluter. The intrinsic nature relates to the activities involved in events such as motor racing and, most important, to the travel to the events. As events are mainly about people coming together, travel to events is a major challenge to the event industry's ability to become more environmentally friendly. The remainder of this chapter will look at some of the major pollutants, how they are caused and how they are affecting the environment. It will then look at the contribution of the event industry to this pollution with reference to some case studies.

Global pollutants

There are many types of pollution that have an impact at the macro or global scale. Some of these are mentioned above. In a book of this scope it is only possible to focus on a few of these. Discussion here will therefore focus on three major pollution issues:

- acid rain and its impacts;
- the impacts of depletion of the ozone layers; and
- greenhouse gas emission and its impact on climate change.

Rainfall acidification and its impacts on forests

Acid rain has been known about for a long time. Middleton (1995: 114) suggests that awareness of it dates to 1852 and the observations of R.A. Smith that rainfall in Manchester was unusually acidic. Its causes and impacts are well researched. Smith suggested that in Manchester it was connected to the emission of sulphur dioxide in coal-burning factories. He was partly right. Natural rainfall is slightly acidic due to carbon dioxide and sulphur dioxide in the air that results from volcanic eruptions, rock decay and biological activity. These gases when dissolved in water create carbonic and other acids.

Fossil fuel burning has massively increased the amount of carbon dioxide in the atmosphere (see the section later in this chapter on global warming) and it has also added to the presence of sulphur and nitrogen gases in the atmosphere. These are dissolved to form sulphurous and sulphuric acids from sulphur dioxide and sulphur trioxide and nitrous and nitric acids from nitrogen oxide and nitrogen dioxide. Fossil fuels are not the only sources of these gases. Industrial processes such as smelting and agricultural practices such as use of ammonium-based fertilisers also contribute. Barrow (2006: 299) suggests that by 1988 half the sulphur in the earth's atmosphere could be attributed to human activity. It may be argued that events play no part in this. This is not true. Fossil fuel burning provides much of the energy use of the event industry and metals and other chemicals are part of its supply chain. It even makes use of fertilisers in events such as golf tournaments, cricket, football and horse racing.

One of the characteristics of acid rain is that it is transported by winds. It may thus be deposited far from the areas in which it was emitted. This often involves movements across national boundaries, so the impacts of acid rain can be experienced in countries other than the principal polluters. Middleton (1995) cites figures from the European Monitoring and Evaluation Programme relating to the deposition of wet and dry sulphur in Norway and Sweden in 1991–2. Sweden and Norway were responsible for 10.7% of the pollution. Germany, however, was responsible for 16% and Great Britain for 15.5%. Acid rain is clearly an international problem which cannot be resolved unilaterally.

The terrestrial impacts of acid rain are complex. Some are beneficial. Both sulphur and nitrogen are vital to vegetation and increases in areas where these are deficient can be beneficial to a certain extent if they enter the ecosystem in a way that enables them to be absorbed. Sulphur dioxide particles may also help to deflect solar radiation and act as a damper on global warming. However, acid rain is not a calibrated dose of fertiliser and uncontrolled amounts are thought to be damaging to vegetation, forests in particular. Likewise the global warming effect is not one that is part of a managed mitigation system.

The negative effects are considerable. Barrow (2006: 299) has identified six types of damage. These, and some examples of the damage they cause, are:

1. they cause direct damage to plants and animals – e.g. respiratory disease in humans;
2. they alter soil chemistry or structure – e.g. leech or displace vital minerals out of the soil, thus depriving plants of micro-nutrients;
3. they alter plant metabolism – e.g. damage to leaves of trees or to certain types of coral;
4. they alter the metabolism or species diversity of soil micro-organisms – e.g. changes in fertility or soil chemistry;
5. they damage man-made and natural structures – e.g. the erosion of limestone buildings such as cathedrals or houses; and
6. they mobilise compounds in soils, waste dumps and water (notably phosphates, heavy metal and aluminium) – e.g. the release of toxic chemicals into the water supply.

The aggregate effects of these types of damage can be considerable.

The depletion of the ozone layer

The ozone hole is one of many environmental problems to which the event industry has contributed, along with many other industries, over the past hundred years. The problem was discovered by the British Antarctic Survey (BAS). It produced many accounts of this including that in an education pack on Antarctica (Foreign and Commonwealth Office 1999). The author of this book contributed to the writing of this and much of the following is based on that publication.

Ozone is a gas found naturally in the atmosphere. It is formed by the action of ultraviolet (UV) light on oxygen which converts the gas molecules from two to three atoms, a process more prevalent in the tropics than elsewhere due to the higher incidence of solar radiation there. However, winds sweep the gas towards the poles so that the maximum thickness of the ozone layer is over the poles. Overall it is a trace gas in the atmosphere with a maximum concentration of 0.001 per cent, or one in every 100,000 molecules of air compared to normal oxygen's 21 per cent. It has interesting properties. It is a bluish gas and chemically very active. Contrary to the old wives' tale that inhaling a dose of ozone is good for you, it is actually toxic and particularly harmful to asthmatics and others with breathing difficulties. Physically, ozone absorbs UV radiation, a property of considerable significance to life on earth as it protects it from excessive doses of UV with their deleterious effects. Significantly, it is also a greenhouse gas that contributes to global warming.

The first sign of damage to the ozone layer was reported in 1985 by scientists at BAS who had been measuring ozone levels over the Halley Research Station in Antarctica since the 1950s. In the early 1980s the scientists noticed that each year during the month of October ozone was almost completely destroyed over Antarctica. They had discovered what became known as the 'ozone hole'. The decline in the ozone concentration can be seen in Figure 5.1.

Destruction of ozone occurs naturally in the atmosphere and until recently this was in balance with the rate of its creation. Natural events, such as volcanic eruptions, could upset the balance temporarily but the losses identified in the 1980s were too great to be explained by these events. Research indicated that a range of man-made chlorine- and bromine-based gases, such as CFCs, were responsible for ozone depletion. The increase in CFC releases is shown in Figure 5.1 plotted against the declining levels of

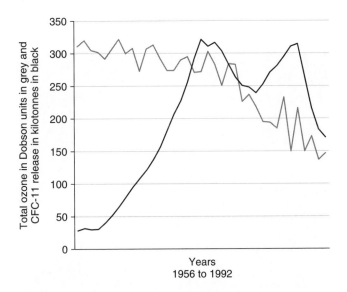

Figure 5.1 Ozone concentrations over Antarctica and levels of CFC-11 release from 1956 to 1992

Source: BAS data

ozone over Antarctica. CFCs were widely used in fridges, air-conditioning units, fire retardants and aerosol sprays. These uses were widespread throughout society and the event industry was one of the many contributors to the problem. CFCs are very stable compounds and can remain in the atmosphere for over a century. These gases do not break down in the lower atmosphere but are destroyed by UV radiation in the stratosphere leading to the release of free chlorine, which then acts as a catalyst in the destruction of ozone. For complex reasons to do with air temperatures, lack of sunlight and wind directions this destruction of ozone became concentrated over Antarctica in the southern hemisphere spring (see Figure 5.2).

The impacts of ozone depletion

Although the impacts of ozone depletion are limited at present, they could, if the depletion is unchecked and spreads beyond the polar regions, have the potential to be serious. Humans have natural defences against UV radiation, but prolonged exposure to UV light can have serious effects on human health, notably sunburn in the short term. Over longer periods exposure can lead to the immune defences of the skin breaking down. This makes the skin more susceptible to infection, premature ageing, disorders and even melanoma, a cancer that is often fatal. Plants can react to UV-B by changing their pigment or growing in shaded positions. However, prolonged exposure may cause serious damage by lowering resistance to disease. This could lead to lower crop yields. Failure of crops for whatever reason or reduced cover leaves soils exposed and thus susceptible to erosion. This in turn increases run-off and the likelihood of flooding in times of high rainfall. Sediment can increase in rivers and disrupt their flow and silt up dams. In lakes or the sea UV-B can penetrate to a depth of 20m. This may be harmful

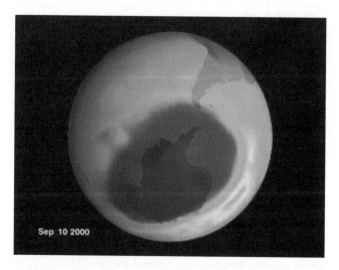

Figure 5.2 A satellite image of the ozone hole over Antarctica

Source: NASA/Goddard Space Flight Centre Scientific Visualization Studio

to phytoplankton (minute marine vegetation), plankton and the larvae of fish. This, in turn, could impact on climate change. Phytoplankton fixes (i.e. absorbs) a substantial amount of carbon from the atmosphere, thus reducing carbon dioxide levels. If primary productivity fell as a result of ozone depletion this could lower the amount of carbon fixing, which could lead to higher levels of carbon dioxide and further climate change.

UV causes many building materials such as paints and plastics to deteriorate and natural and artificial dyes to become faded and bleached.

Action to combat the loss of ozone

After the discovery and potential implications of the ozone hole emerged governments began to react to it and in 1987 the Montreal Protocol on Substances that Deplete the Ozone Layer was signed. It aims to control the production and consumption of ozone-depleting substances. Its original aim was to halve the use of CFCs by 1999. It is a significant agreement, as it was the first international treaty to embody the preventative (or precautionary) principle. It was designed on the basis of scientific evidence to prevent, rather than to cure, a global environmental problem. It could provide a model for other legislation designed to address environmental problems. It has been amended since, partly to alleviate the problems of less developed countries. The European Union has also implemented measures. However, trade in illegally produced CFCs has been a problem, with a vigorous black market in existence. It has been suggested that illegal shipments of CFCs may amount to some 20 per cent of former production levels. This could undermine the attempts of the Montreal Protocol nations to attain pre-1970 ozone levels by the year 2050. There is also a problem of time lag. Even if the world stopped using these substances immediately it would still take around 50 years for the ozone hole to disappear, as the ozone-depleting gases break down slowly and remain in the upper atmosphere for decades after release.

The problem of the ozone layer is an interesting one for event students to study. The event industry is only one of many that has contributed to the depletion of ozone but nonetheless it has been a contributor. In some parts of the world it may still be so. In the protocol nations it must now be compliant with the treaty's requirements (and those of subsequent EU legislation). This has had an effect on the materials it uses and the cost of CFC and halon substitution. This is a significant issue in tackling pollution problems – resolving them often involves costs. The problem also shows that resolution can only be achieved at an international level. Gaseous pollution is mobile and no respecter of national boundaries. Finally, it illustrates the need to combat problems with a sense of urgency as it takes a long time to resolve them and restore environmental equilibrium. This is particularly applicable to climate change which will be discussed next.

Greenhouse gases and climate change

There can be few reading this who are unaware of the debate over global warming. While the majority of the world's scientific community – according to the IPCC (Inter-Governmental Panel on Climate Change) reports – is in little doubt that the climate is warming, a persistent minority maintains that it is not. Some who believe in climate change do not ascribe it to human action. Many with vested interests, including politicians, remain sceptical for obvious reasons. It is confusing for the general public who are unsure what to believe, not least because, for a while in the 1960s, it appeared that the climate might be cooling. This section will attempt to answer three questions:

- Is the climate warming?
- If it is warming, what is causing it?
- Are the causes the result of human activity?

The final section of the chapter will investigate the extent to which the event industry is contributing to human activity that is altering the climate.

Is there climate change – is it warming?

The climate has changed throughout the history of the earth. If it had not we would not be alive today. This raises the question as to what climate scientists mean by climate change. In essence climate change refers to a statistically significant variation in either the mean state of the climate or in its variability, persisting for an extended period (typically decades or longer). Climate change may be due to natural internal processes or external forcings (natural causes), or to persistent anthropogenic (human-induced) changes in the composition of the atmosphere or in land use. Some authorities distinguish between climate variability (natural causes) and climate change (humanly caused) but as climate change is used so widely to discuss both, this chapter will adopt the more catholic usage.

If scientists are to demonstrate climate change they need to show significant statistical change. To mathematicians significant change has specific meaning. This section will avoid this and present evidence from a number of sources. First, the UK has the Central England Temperature record dating back to 1659. Inspection of these data reveals the following:

- since 1700 mean annual temperatures have risen by $0.7°C$;
- since 1900 mean annual temperatures have risen by $0.5°C$;
- warming has occurred in all seasons but is most pronounced in autumn and summer (November 2011 was the second warmest on record for England);
- the changes are comparable to other northern hemisphere changes on land; and
- three of the four warmest years have occurred since 1980.

These trends can be seen in Figure 5.3.
The IPCC cites further suggestive data:

- global records indicate a rise of $0.6°C$ + or − $0.2°C$ since the late 19th century, mostly from 1910 to 1940 and 1976 to present
- in N hemisphere 20th century warming appears to be greater than at any other time since 1000 AD

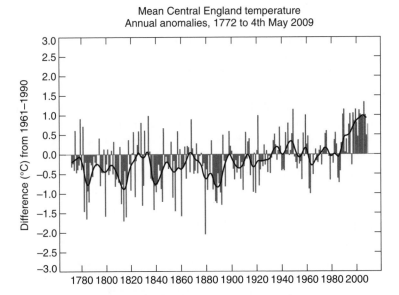

Figure 5.3 Differences in temperatures between 1961 and 1990 in Central England records (note the sharp positive rise after 1980)

Source: Met Office 2012

- 1990s appear to have been the warmest decade of the millennium
- 1998 was the warmest year. (IPCC 2007a)

There is also evidence of warming in the extreme regions of the planet, such as Antarctica. During the first decade of the present century BAS noted a rapid warming of the Antarctic peninsula – 2.5°C over the previous 50 years. This has impacted on the ice cover, with 75 per cent of the peninsula glaciers showing retreat and massive ice ledges breaking up, such as the 3200km² Larsen B in March 2002

The UN, using data from the IPCC, notes a number of ancillary features that suggest climate change:

- Mean sea level has risen 10 to 20 cm due largely to thermal expansion – this is consistent with a 0.6°C rise. This is complicated by ice melt/accretion and land movement (isostasy).
- Snow cover in high latitudes of N hemisphere has fallen 10% since 1960s.
- Arctic sea ice has thinned 40% in late summer/autumn and its extent declined 10–15% in spring/summer.
- There is a 2% increase in cloud cover in N hemisphere per decade.
- There has been a 0.55 to 1% increase in precipitation in N hemisphere per decade – elsewhere there have been declines though e.g. sub-Saharan Africa.
- There is anecdotal evidence of increased extreme weather. (UN Framework Convention on Climate Change 2012)

There are many other pieces of evidence that support the idea of significant climate change. Although some of the data have been challenged, scrutiny of the suspect data does not contest their basic validity. Indeed by 2007 the IPCC, set up by governments to investigate climate change, concluded that 'warming of the climate system is unequivocal, as is now evident from observations of increases in global average air and ocean temperatures, widespread melting of snow and ice, and rising global average sea level' (IPCC 2007b: 30: fig SPM.3 3.2, 4.2, 5.5). Although debate continues, fuelled no doubt by skilful public relations from interested parties, the key organisation investigating the problem has no doubt that global warming is occurring. Figure 5.4 shows the trend for the past 150 years graphically, along with rises in sea temperatures and the contrasting falls in snow cover in the northern hemisphere.

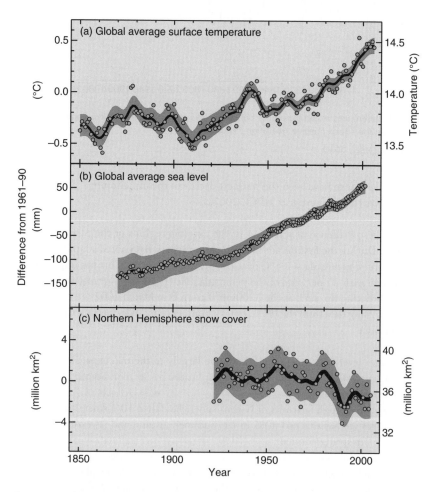

Figure 5.4 Changes in temperature, sea level and northern hemisphere snow cover

Source: IPCC 2007b: 31

What is causing the warming?

There are many possible causes of climate change, some natural, some anthropogenic (caused by human activity). Possible natural changes include:

- volcanic eruption – aerosols, gases and heat;
- solar input
  - o   variations in solar output – sunspot cycle
  - o   variations in earth's tilt/axis
  - o   wobble
  - o   variations in earth's orbit (and thus distance from the sun);
- volume of biomass, on land and in the sea;
- oceanic/air gaseous exchange (temperature dependent); and
- changes in oceanic circulation – the thermo-haline circulation.

All have been investigated as potential causes of the sudden upward trend in global temperatures. Some have clearly contributed to climate change in the past and some may still be contributing now. However, the IPCC, in its *Second Assessment Report* (SAR), concluded that on the basis of careful analyses 'the observed change in global mean, annually averaged temperatures over the last century **is unlikely to be due entirely to natural fluctuations of the climate system**' (IPCC 2005).

If natural forces cannot explain all the change, what anthropogenic causes might there be?

The following are possibilities:

- fossil fuel burning – discharge of gases and aerosols caused by energy use and manufacturing processes related to industrial, domestic and transport use;
- changing farming practices – use of fertilisers, mechanisation and increasing animal production;
- forest clearance; and
- urbanisation.

These may contribute to global warming because they either emit greenhouse gases or reduce the capability of primary producers (vegetation including phyto-plankton in the oceans) to absorb greenhouse gases. Greenhouse gases collect in the upper atmosphere. There are several of them including water vapour, nitrous oxide, methane and ozone but the principal one is carbon dioxide. These gases are transparent to incoming solar radiation (principally light) but they are less so to outgoing long wave radiation emitted by the earth. The net effect of this is that outgoing heat is trapped by the upper atmosphere leading to a rise in atmospheric temperatures. This is a similar process to that which operates in a greenhouse, thus the name greenhouse gases. The more greenhouse gases that are present in the atmosphere, the greater the retention of heat. There are offsetting factors such as reflection by sulphate particles, smoke and ozone depletion but these appear to be outweighed by the increase in carbon dioxide in particular.

There is clear evidence that carbon dioxide levels have been rising since the industrial revolution, as Figure 5.5 shows. It will be noticed that the hockey stick shape of this graph is very similar to that in Figure 5.4, which plotted the rise in global temperatures. It is the apparent correlation between these two sets of data that provides one of the central arguments suggesting that carbon dioxide is a principal cause of global warming. Given that the gas can be demonstrated to have a greenhouse effect the evidence seems strong.

Even if the greenhouse gases are largely responsible for global warming, their increase in the atmosphere might be natural. Evidence from a range of sources, notably ice cores in Antarctica, shows substantial variations in carbon dioxide levels over geological time and these are related to past climatic change. Scientists have tested for natural emissions in carbon dioxide over the past 1000 years from sources such as volcanoes and changing vegetative patterns. However, natural sources do not appear to explain all the climate change. By contrast, patterns of greenhouse gas emissions appear to correlate well with the temperature rises shown in Figure 5.4.

By the time of the 2007 IPCC report the panel had concluded that

> most of the observed increase in globally averaged temperatures since the mid-20th century is *very likely* due to the observed increase in anthropogenic greenhouse gas concentration . . . Discernible human influences now extend to other aspects of climate, including ocean warming, continental-average temperatures, temperature extremes and wind patterns. (IPCC 2007a SPM4, table SPM5 9.4, 9.5)

The evidence is not 100 per cent certain, but it is overwhelming, and few climate scientists now doubt that human activity is contributing to global warming. Nearly all governments now accept this, though some are reluctant to implement measures that may mitigate the change, as the wrangling over the Kyoto Protocol demonstrates. At present greenhouse gas levels in the atmosphere are still rising. The IPCC predicts that temperatures will rise with them. Some scientists, such as James Lovelock, believe that we have already passed a threshold in temperature rise that prevents the earth's natural systems from dampening down the changes. Such scientists believe that the resultant climate change could be catastrophic for human survival.

Possible human impacts of global warming

Some climate change sceptics maintain that the impacts may be beneficial: for example, northern Europe may become like the Mediterranean. Even if that were true, more cloud cover and rain and possibly colder winters are also possible. The impacts on the Mediterranean or the Sahel may be prolonged drought in the former and desertification in the latter.

The list of potential impacts is massive. Those wishing to examine them in detail should review the IPCC reports.

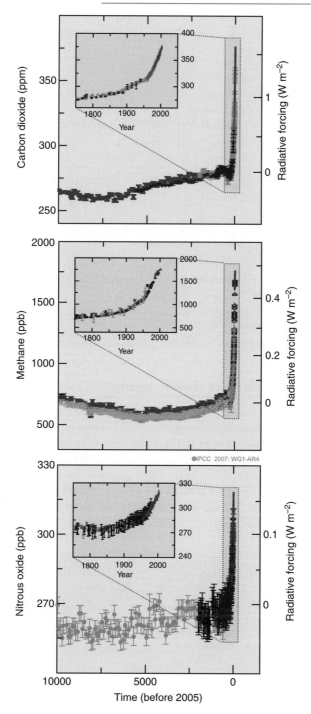

Figure 5.5 Changes in greenhouse gases from ice core and modern data

Source: IPCC 2007b: 38

TASK

Investigate the IPCC reports online at www.ipcc.ch/publications_and_data/publications_and_data_reports.shtml.

List all the potential impacts of climate change and suggest whether they are detrimental or beneficial. A few of these are included in the chart below.

Then consider the impact on the event industry worldwide, and complete the chart. You can add more impacts if you wish.

Potential impact	Impact on the event industry
Reduced snow cover	
Reduction in sea ice	
More extreme climatic events e.g. hurricanes	
Sea level rise by up to 0.59m by 2100	
More droughts in water-scarce areas	
Retreat of many glaciers	
Spread of tropical diseases and pests toward the temperate regions	

Mitigating the effects of climate change

Many scientists believe that the adverse impacts of climate change can be mitigated, that is, made less damaging, if governments take action to reduce greenhouse gas emissions and adapt our lifestyles to likely changes. At a global level conferences in Kyoto, Copenhagen and latterly Durban have had mixed effects. While there is a consensus that there is a problem, there is less agreement about the measures needed to reduce emissions and the pace at which any measures should be implemented. Many countries, including the UK and much of Europe, are already taking steps to reduce the output of greenhouse gases.

TASK

Working in groups, consider some local events – perhaps ones in which you have been involved.

In what ways could they reduce their energy use? Consider issues in the supply chain as well as the event itself.

Adapting to climate change

In addition to mitigating climate change through reduction of greenhouse gases, many organisations are combining this with plans to adapt to the changes. One such organisation is Hampshire County Council.

Case study: Hampshire County Council

Local governments have been asked to draw up Local Climate Impacts Profiles so that they are able to model the potential effects of climate change in the future. This should allow them to draw up plans for the adaptation and mitigation of their services and attach potential costs to them. It is important to distinguish between adaptation and mitigation. In Hampshire's terminology adaptation is preparing for the impacts and effects of climate change such as intense rainfall and consequent flooding, storms and resultant wind damage, heat and its effect on human health and new pests and diseases with their impacts on agriculture and health. Mitigation relates to action to reduce greenhouse gas emissions.

The county has used data from the United Kingdom Climate Projections available on the Defra website (Defra 2012). Use of these data shows that Hampshire may, on the higher warming assumptions, experience warmer, wetter winters (with anything up to 30 per cent more rain and more of this falling at high intensity), hotter, drier summers (up to 5°C warmer and with 50 per cent less rainfall) and more extreme sea levels. The Hampshire profile goes on to note some meteorological events in the county since 2000 along with some of their impacts:

- in the winter of 2000/01, there was rainfall of over 150 per cent of the seasonal average, leading to river flooding, groundwater flooding, damage to property and landslides;
- in the summer of 2003, temperatures of 2.2°C above the seasonal average led to deaths from heat and localised drought; and
- in the autumn of 2006, temperatures of 2.6°C above seasonal average led to severe storms, tornadoes, intense rainfall and damage to property.

Looking to the future the authority tries to anticipate some of the impacts and identifies three types of impact: the physical environment, human health and the economy.

The physical environment

With regard to the physical environment, impacts include drought (hosepipe bans and severe water shortages), flooding (groundwater, fluvial damage and landslides) and rainfall intensity impacts (damage to property, loss of life and water storage issues for drier months).

Anticipated summer temperatures of up to 40°C will necessitate buildings being adapted to reflect solar radiation and reduce absorption to the urban heat island effect.

This would apply not only to new buildings but also to existing ones, requiring planning authorities to adjust their policies.

Hampshire has an extensive coastline. Increased storminess and sea-level rises may lead to coastal flooding, coastal erosion, and saline intrusion into water supplies. To protect against this, existing sea barriers may need to be renewed (as many are nearing the ends of their lives) or new ones may have to be built to protect vulnerable areas.

Rising temperatures present a mixed bag for Hampshire's biodiversity and agriculture. They will probably result in some species suffering, and migrating north, while others will become more dominant. New species may also migrate to Hampshire from mainland Europe. It may be possible to grow new crops. The biggest threat to biodiversity and agriculture lies with the sea. Rising sea levels will squeeze coastal habitats and penetration of salt water into the water system will ruin farmland. Agriculture will be especially vulnerable to reduced availability of water.

Human health and welfare

Many of the impacts on the physical environments will have effects on human health and wellbeing. The effects on food, water and fuel supply are obvious. We will have to learn to live with less water and be more efficient with its use. The types of gardens we have may have to adjust. Figure 5.6 shows the predictions for summer rainfall in the UK in the mid-21st century (all areas are likely to have less rain in the summer). The balance of our diet may have to change. Less obvious is social disruption caused by road and rail closures. There may be difficulties in getting to work and isolated communities may suffer from temporary loss of medical and social services.

The economy

The economy is already being hit by regulations aimed at mitigating the effects of climate change through reduced use of fossil fuels. The insurance sector could assist in this by setting economic barriers on developments. In any case, the sector needs to be prepared for more and more weather-related claims.

County, district and city councils will face increasing risks as a result of the impact on the physical environment. For example, Portsmouth City Council can expect to see 72 per cent of its industrial sector in danger of flooding unless flood defences are extended. Indeed flooding probably poses the greatest risk to Hampshire, at least in the medium term.

Cost

Hampshire County Council has reviewed the costs of weather events between 2000 and 2008 to give an indication of the possible costs of adapting to climate change. The number of incidents is shown in Table 5.1. The total cost of these events exceeded a staggering £17,245,319 (Hampshire). Clearly, adapting to climate change may be a very expensive process.

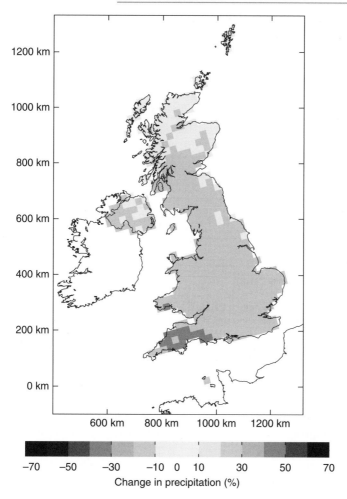

Figure 5.6 Summer rainfall predictions for the 2050s at 50 per cent probability level

Source: Defra 2012

TASK

Take the role of the board of a medium-sized events company operating in Hampshire. Review your operations over the next five years and, using the information given in the case study, estimate some of the impacts of climate change that you may have to adapt to. Consider what measure you might take to manage these.

Table 5.1 Extreme weather event frequency in Hampshire (including the city of Portsmouth), 2000–2008

Heavy rainfall	169
Snow	32
Tornado	8
Ice	12
Hail	2
High temperatures/heatwave	48
Cold temperatures	13
Severe weather– storms and gales	77
High winds	20
High tides	5
Lightning	14
Hurricane	0
Other	10

Source: Hampshire County Council

(Thanks are expressed to Hampshire County Council and their staff for the information used in this case study.)

The contribution of the event industry to macro-scale pollution

It is very difficult to measure the contribution of the event industry to global pollution. There are a number of reasons for this. First, there is little agreement on what the event industry comprises. A labour market review of the industry points out that it:

> is extremely diverse and fragmented . . . [and] . . . it is difficult to calculate the total number of businesses and employees that make up the events industry for the following reasons:
>
> • The industry is extremely diverse and difficult to define
> • There is overlap with other industries (for example hotels)
> • Only part of the industry is covered by official government Standard Industrial Classification (SIC) codes. (People 1st 2010)

It is thus very difficult to define the scope of the industry and thus what should be included in any attempt to calculate the amount of pollution it generates.

Second, there is limited agreement on what should be included in any inventory of pollution. This is difficult enough when looking at greenhouse gases alone. As the Sustainable Event Alliance website notes:

> It is . . . fraught with controversy and confusion as there are no clear direction or agreement on how far down the line a GHG [greenhouse gas] emissions calculation

should go. Each event will have a certain set of circumstances which make it unique and that makes creating a one-size-fits all directive or methodology quite impractical and almost impossible for our industry. (Sustainable Event Alliance 2011)

The alliance goes on to describe how the Greenhouse Gas Protocol applies in Australia:

Scope 1 emissions are those from sources that are owned or controlled by the event – 'direct' emissions. Energy generated onsite at an event would include mobile power generators, bottled gas, fuel used in site plant, equipment and vehicles, and vehicles owned by the company and used offsite. If waste is disposed of at the event site and emissions are estimated to be generated (i.e. methane from buried waste) these are also included in Scope 1.

Scope 2 emissions from 'indirect' sources – purchased heat, steam or electricity used by the event. For example mains supply and mains gas supply. . . .

[The] event industry as a whole does not have a determination on what should be included in emissions calculations over and above Scope 1 and 2 emissions.

Scope 3 emissions are 'other indirect' emissions – these are emissions that occur because of an event's activities but occur at sources owned by others. This includes transport of employees (including all paid contractors, talent, and crew), hotel nights for event production (crew, talent, staff, and contractors), significant additional freight impact of equipment, goods and services required by the event or waste produced by the event, and hired transportation (shuttle buses, taxis, limos, boats, aircraft).

And then going deeper, emissions embodied in the products and materials purchased by the event, transport of products and equipment for the event, energy used or emissions created in processing waste (liquid and solid), transport of waste (liquid and solid) and energy and transport to produce and supply water. Finally there is attendee travel – the single GHG contributor for many events – and hotel nights of attendees (for example delegates at a conference/convention). (Adapted from Sustainable Event Alliance 2011)

Clearly organisers have latitude in what is included in their inventories and this makes comparative studies difficult to conduct and aggregate statistics difficult to amass.

Third, research seems to have focused on individual events rather than the industry as a whole. This is probably explained by the relatively short history of research and the difficulties outlined above.

Research on individual events, however, does give an insight into the scale of the pollution involved. To give an example of the scale the 2010 World Cup can be cited. Greg McManus, managing director of the Heritage Environmental Rating Programme, suggests that 'based on existing resource consumption patterns for tourists to South Africa, the additional international tourist are expected to consume an additional 2.50 billion litres of water and 420,000 megawatts of power and create almost 23,000 tonnes of waste in just fourteen days. The duration of the mega event will be four weeks in total' (cited in Otto and Heath 2009: 175). This excludes any carbon footprint, which can be calculated as 180,000 tons of CO_2 for internal travel and additional electricity generation alone during the four week duration of the cup. Travel to South Africa, mainly by air, needs to be added to that (Case 2011: 362).

Case study: carbon footprint of the London 2012 Olympics

A recent study for the London 2012 Olympics looked at the event's likely carbon footprint and 'estimated [it] to be 3.4 million tonnes of carbon dioxide equivalents ($3.4MtCO_2e$)' (LOCOG 2010a: 27).

As Figure 5.7 shows, the total is split between four broad categories: venues, spectators, operations and transport infrastructure. Although there are 250 elements that contribute to the total, most of the emissions are the result of what LOCOG calls the big hitters. These are shown in Figure 5.8.

Most of the carbon emissions will occur pre-Games. These arise from the construction of venues, the delivery of the transport infrastructure, and the fitting out and 'dressing' of the venues and Olympic Park. Most of the remaining operational activities and emissions attributable to spectators occur at Games-time (LOCOG 2010a: 27).

LOCOG's decision to publish this report could be seen as brave. It will be interesting to see how the actual carbon footprint has matched the anticipated one.

It is useful to put this figure in perspective. In 2008, the carbon footprint of the UK central government was approximately 65 million tonnes of CO_2 equivalent (CO_2e), an increase of 12 per cent since 2000. Carbon emissions peaked in 2004 at almost 70 million tonnes of CO_2e. This accounts for approximately 7 per cent of the total UK carbon footprint. In the same year the total CO_2 emissions in the manufacturing sector

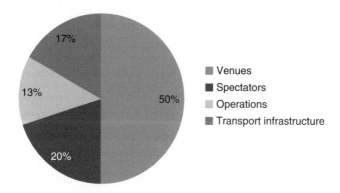

Figure 5.7 Total London reference footprint by component in ktCO$_2$e

Source: Data from LOCOG 2010a

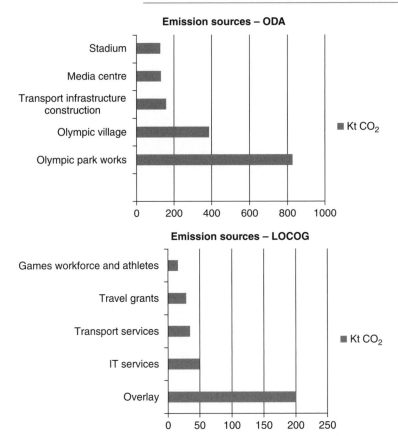

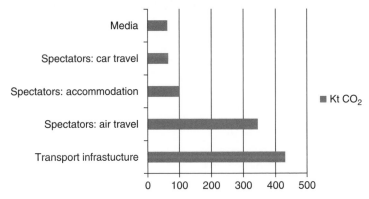

Figure 5.8 London 2012 reference footprint: 'top five' emission sources for the ODA, LOCOG and 'others' (includes shared and associated)

Source: Data from LOCOG 2010a

were equivalent to 140 million tonnes of carbon dioxide. This demonstrates that the carbon footprint of an event such as the Olympics is very large indeed and indicates the scale of the problem that the event industry faces in reducing its impact on the global environment.

TASK

Using the data provided above, calculate the likely percentage contribution of the Olympics to the UK's total carbon emissions in 2012. You will have to make some assumptions about what proportion of the Games' emissions is new.

Case study: the Sydney 2000 Olympics

After a period in which the Olympic Games had been criticised for its poor environmental impacts it began to focus on improving its performance during the 1990s. The first Summer Games to venture the label of 'green games' were those in Sydney 2000. The organisers involved Greenpeace in their preparations. As Kearins and Pavlovich (2002: 157–69) noted, the non-governmental organisation (NGO) had both 'planning and monitoring roles' and just before the Games awarded them a bronze medal for their environmental performance. Following the Games Greenpeace audited them and 'issued a positive report' (Toyne 2009: 233). However, as this author notes elsewhere:

> this verdict requires qualification. Not all environmental organisations were as enthusiastic as Greenpeace. A coalition of five national and state groups had established a Green Games Watch 2000. Their final analysis was that the Games 'could at best be called the "half green" or "light green" games, in that many environmental initiatives were adopted, but much more could have been achieved'. (Case 2011)

Green Games Watch 2000 (cited in Kearins and Pavlovich 2002: 166) listed the main green wins as:

- public transport access;
- solar power applications;
- building material selection;
- recycling of construction waste;
- progressive tendering policies;
- energy and water conservation; and
- wetland restoration.

The main green losses it identified were:

- the failure of most sponsors to go green;
- poor quality Olympic merchandising;

- environmentally destructive refrigerant selection;
- loss of biodiversity in some projects; and
- failure to clean up contaminated Homebush Bay sediments in time for the Games.

Kearins and Pavlovich go on to suggest that the 'Olympic Games are inherently unsustainable' (ibid.) and that green event management raises a number of issues, notably the difficulty of getting all stakeholders to give equal priority to the environment when there are cost and other burdens associated with it. Such a conclusion is not encouraging for the event industry.

TASKS

- Review the wins and losses identified for the Sydney Games. Which of them relate to global as opposed to local issues?
- Review LOCOG's Sustainability Plan at www.london2012.com/documents/locog-publications/london-2012-sustainability-plan.pdf. Has it addressed the losses identified above?

Conclusion

The aims of this chapter were to:

- identify some of the principal pollutants that are causing problems at a global scale and investigate their causes and impacts;
- examine the extent to which human activity is changing planetary systems, in particular the climate system; and
- assess the contribution of the event industry to these pollutants.

It has achieved the first by identifying a number of significant pollutants and focusing on how CFCs, acidic gases and the so-called greenhouse gases affect the earth's systems at a global scale. It has achieved the second by illustrating the impacts of these pollutants, in particular by outlining the effect on climate change. It has shown some of the dangers of global warming and how the effects of this can be mitigated and adapted to. Finally, it has discussed the role of the event industry in contributing to global pollution while acknowledging the difficulty of quantifying its contribution at an aggregate level. It has also indicated the potential scale of the problem by looking at the greenhouse gas contributions of selected mega-events.

Further detail on the mitigation and management of pollution caused by events will be provided in later chapters.

Further reading

An extended essay on events and sustainability can be found in this author's chapter in Page and Connell's *The Routledge Handbook of Events* (Case 2011). For an introductory account of the planet's environmental problems, *The Global Casino* is a useful start (Middleton 1995).

6   Urban regeneration

Aims

The aims of this chapter are to:

- explore the history of urban regeneration in the domain of events and assess why it has received so much attention relative to other environmental impacts;
- examine the nature of event-stimulated urban regeneration; and
- evaluate the success of such regeneration with respect to selected case studies.

Introduction

In the recently published *Routledge Handbook of Events* (Page and Connell 2011) there is a chapter on events and sustainability that addresses a whole range of environmental impacts and the issue of sustainability. There is a separate chapter on urban legacy. Whole books have been written on the subject of Olympic cities and their urban legacies. A Google search on 'event driven urban legacies' yields 3.5 million results. Recent Olympic bids feature the topic substantially. The question inevitably arises as to why this issue receives such prominence.

Thomson *et al.* note that 'within the sport and event management context, legacy has emerged as an important justification for public sector involvement and investment since the late 1980s' (Thomson *et al.* 2010: 1), but as Baim (2009) observes in respect of the modern Olympics, mega-events have acted as agents of urban development since the 19th century. Using a model predicated on work by Preuss, he identifies five aspects of urban investment: sports facilities, housing, transport, urban culture and the environment. He produces a table that summarises the history of the host cities in investing in these various aspects. Urban culture could be said to be a category outside the remit of this book, but it includes the provision of parkland and other leisure facilities and could be expanded to incorporate cultural institutions such as art galleries and museums. The other four are very much aspects of urban regeneration that relate directly to the environment. Baim argues that investment in sports facilities dates back to the 1896 Athens Games; housing to the 1932 Los Angeles Games; transport to the 1920 Antwerp Games; and environmental investment to the 1960 Rome Games. An amended version of his table, which is updated to include 2008 Beijing and the legacies expected of 2012 London, is shown in Table 6.1.

The potential impacts on urban regeneration were major reasons why London bid for the 2012 Games and why it was successful in gaining them. The trend continues. As Matheson notes in a paper on the Glasgow Commonwealth Games, scheduled for 2014, 'The bid was symptomatic of a trend utilising events within place marketing and urban regeneration strategies, following deindustrialisation and economic restructuring . . . As part of this, legacies have become fundamental to major event hosting and/or bidding' (Matheson (2010: 10). Similar trends can be seen in the FIFA World Cup, the Rugby World Cup and other international mega-events. They can also be seen in

Table 6.1 History of urban investment by sector: Olympic Games, 1896–2004

Year	Host	Sports facilities	Housing	Transport	Urban culture	Environment
1896	Athens	Y				
1900	Paris					
1904	St Louis					
1908	London	Y			Y	
1912	Stockholm	X			Y	
1920	Antwerp	X		X	Y	
1924	Paris	X			Y	
1928	Amsterdam	X			Y	
1932	Los Angeles		X		Y	
1936	Berlin	X	X			
1948	London				Y	
1952	Helsinki	X	X		Y	
1956	Melbourne	X	X		Y	
1960	Roma	X	X	X	X	X
1964	Tokyo	X	X	X	X	X
1968	Mexico City	Y				
1972	Munich	X	X	X	X	
1976	Montreal	X	X	Y	X	
1980	Moscow	X	X	Y		
1984	Los Angeles			Y		
1988	Seoul	X	X	X	X	X
1992	Barcelona	X	X	X	X	
1996	Atlanta	X	X		X	
2000	Sydney	X	X	X	X	X
2004	Athens	X	X	X	X	X
2008	Beijing	X	X	X	X	X
2012	London	X	X	X	X	X

X = Major commitment
Y = Minor commitment

Source: Poynter and MacRury 2009

competitions such as those to become European Cultural Capitals and hosts to World Fairs. They can be seen on a smaller scale too, as cities promote and/or subsidise the development of new sports stadia or iconic cultural institutions. An example of the former is the success of St Mary's, a run-down area in the docklands of Southampton, in gaining the new football ground for Southampton Football Club (see Chapter 3). An example of the latter is Bilbao's development of the Guggenheim Museum.

The reasons for this trend are complex. First, many of the older industrial nations such as the United Kingdom and France have seen their economies move from the secondary manufacturing sector to the tertiary and quaternary service sectors, in a process described by Pacione as a 'shift from a post-war Fordist paradigm to a post-Fordist regime of flexible accumulation' (Pacione 2011: 385). Shipping has been transformed by containerisation and the growing size of ships. Both trends have resulted in large swathes of many industrial cities and ports becoming derelict, with attendant population loss. Both central and local governments have found it difficult to secure the investment necessary to regenerate these areas, though they have experimented with a range of strategies including public–private partnerships and the provision of incentives to the private sector such as tax relief and grants. Second, the hosting of events is seen as internationally prestigious, gaining massive media coverage for the country/city concerned. Third, and linked to this, is the promotion of the city as a tourist centre for both leisure and business purposes. Fourth, large-scale investment in urban infrastructure is expensive whatever its purpose. Fifth, less developed countries see the potential of events to hasten their own development.

It is not surprising, therefore, that governments at both a local and national level have seen the hosting of international mega-events as an opportunity to address many issues in a timely and economical manner. Although hosting such events is expensive, governments expect investment to see an economic return through tourism, the potential to hold further events, investment from entrepreneurs and stimulation of the economy. In particular governments will see such events as accelerating development that might otherwise take decades. In focusing on run-down areas, as London has done for the 2012 Olympics, there is potential for a double benefit – economic development and urban regeneration. As later discussion will show, the benefits to the environment have not always outweighed the problems. Much of the infrastructure created for earlier Olympics remains underused or unused. The environmental costs, such as the demolition of existing buildings and the displacement of local inhabitants, often receive little coverage.

Thus, while the focus on urban regeneration can be easily explained, the efficacy and efficiency of using events to improve urban infrastructure may be questioned. The remainder of this chapter will review the history of the topic in more detail and look at a number of case studies to evaluate the success of events in driving positive urban development.

How events create urban regeneration

Baim's identification of five components of physical urban regeneration will be adapted to provide a framework for discussion of how events create urban regeneration. The five aspects – sports facilities, housing, transport, urban cultural institutions and the environment – will be discussed in turn.

Sports facilities

New sports facilities have been transforming towns and cities since Greek times. The original Olympia and Colosseum in Rome have already been referred to. These were egregious examples, but such stadia were widespread. Rome, for example, had several. Many provincial cities, both in Italy and abroad, had their own arenas, racecourses and amphitheatres. Examples include Pompeii and St Albans (Verulamium). These stadia had considerable environmental impacts. Negatively, they produced unpleasant wastes and litter referred to elsewhere in this book (see Chapter 1) and noise and congestion. Positively, however, they became foci for service development. The streets around a stadium were often crowded with shops selling food and liquor and other products likely to enhance a sporting day out.

Following the decline of the Roman Empire, building of new stadia was rare until the 19th century when sports such as football and cricket began to develop on a large scale. By the beginning of the 20th century many of the famous sporting venues, such as Old Trafford, Highbury, Anfield and Lord's, were already in existence. As noted above, 1896 saw the construction of the first modern Olympic Stadium in Athens. Many more Olympic stadia were to follow, with the new London stadium being the latest. Some of the stadia have not survived and others have been little used since the Games for which they were built finished. Some have become notorious, such as Berlin, a monument to the power projection of Adolf Hitler, and Munich, a site of a famous act of terrorism in 1972. Some have become tourist attractions in their own right, such as the stadium in Beijing. The future of some is in doubt, for example the 2012 London stadium, which was to have become the home of West Ham Football Club. Following the threat of litigation from other football clubs, however, the exact future of the stadium was uncertain at the time of writing. This perhaps illustrates the potential political and commercial importance of such structures.

Such stadia have both direct and indirect impacts on the environment. Directly, they occupy physical space that previously might have been parkland, housing, derelict land or had some other use. They have a visual impact on the area – evaluation of this will depend to some extent on individual sensibilities. In use they may create noise and light pollution, though measures are often taken to minimise this. Attendees will create congestion around the stadium and on principal transport routes to it. Street vendors will occupy spaces on approaches and the dropping of litter is likely to be widespread. There may be vandalism leading to graffiti and other defacement of buildings in the area. There is also an environmental opportunity cost – what environmental enhancement might have been achieved through different use, such as an inner-city park?

Housing

The provision of housing in association with events is somewhat ambivalent. Although some of the Olympic villages have been designed to be converted to housing after the

Games, this has not always happened. Evaluation of this issue is made more difficult by the fact that the creation of Olympic infrastructure often involves the displacement of existing residents. In an article in 2009 Libby Porter notes that:

> Displacement is a defining feature of the mega-event: those major sporting and cultural events that roam every few years to a new venue, and a new city. This is the legacy of such events that goes almost unreported publicly. It is considered either unimportant, or the unfortunate but necessary by-product of the urban redevelopment needed to make a successful event. (Porter 2009: 395)

She goes on to cite a report from the Centre on Housing Rights and Evictions (2007) which concludes that 'the Olympic Games and other mega-events are often catalysts for redevelopment entailing massive displacements and reductions in low cost and social housing stock, all of which result in a significant decrease in housing affordability' (ibid.: 396). Even the apparently sustainably conscious 2012 London Games resulted in the displacement of people in the East End of London.

Shang-Chun Ma, in a review of the World Games in South Korea, writes:

> The main considerations for constructing new facilities for the Games were to meet the requirements of the standards of international federations, to develop transportation and to make suitable land available, rather than to secure future use of the facilities by the host population. There were also issues of social equality and inclusion together with the relocation of some of the host population. In this research the host population identified a failure of communication prior to the Games concerning all these potential impacts on the local population.' (Ma *et al.* 2010: 9)

The difficulties over housing illustrate that there are significant spatial issues of social justice involved in the creation of infrastructure for major events. The displaced are often poor; the new residents are often affluent.

Transport

Improved transport and other communications infrastructure is a common outcome from the hosting of events. The 1964 Tokyo Olympic Games saw 'the development of the high speed *shinkansen* rail network . . . important improvements were also made to the subway system within the city itself such as the *Marunouchi* line, the *Haneda* monorail and a number of lines that connected suburbs with the centre' (cited in Cybriwsky 1998: 96). The Rome Games saw the building of a new railway terminus and new roads and the Barcelona Games saw new ring roads and improvements to the airport. The heavily criticised Athens Games saw improvements to the Metro, new tramlines and over 100km of new roads. The Beijing Games saw the completion of a new high-speed rail link to the airport as well as a host of other public transport improvements.

Cultural infrastructure

The creation of cultural infrastructure can come about in a number of ways. First, new venues can be created. These may be full-time event venues or cultural institutions which run significant event programmes. The O2 arena is an example of the former and the Guggenheim Museum in Bilbao an example of the latter. Second, the hosting of major cultural events such as the European City of Culture can lead to a range of environmental improvements. These include refurbishment of existing venues, transformation of derelict buildings into new venues, renovation of cultural monuments, the creation of temporary attractions and improvement to streetscapes in urban areas. Psychologically, these may lead to the improvement of the image of an area and foster future heritage tourism. If successful this may attract migrants to the town and 'yuppification' of the housing and commercial infrastructure of an area. This in turn improves the environmental quality of an area and may in some circumstances lead to a virtuous circle of improvement. Separating out the role of events from other factors in such complex transformations is difficult but it is possible to suggest that parts of Edinburgh (resulting from the festival) and Glasgow (resulting from its status as a European City of Culture) have benefited in this way.

Environmental improvement

Some aspects of environmental improvement have already been discussed in previous paragraphs. In this section attention is drawn to features such as the creation of new parks, cleaning of buildings and improvements to the streetscape. As discussed below, the 2004 Athens Olympic Games aimed to achieve significant results in this area; the outcomes, however, were very variable.

Evaluation of urban regeneration

Many papers have attempted to evaluate the success of events in effecting successful urban regeneration. Many bids for such events have outlined in detail how these legacies are to come about in theory. Evaluation of environmental impacts alone is rare – most reviews look at the combined effects on environment, culture, local communities and the economy. Governments often carry out their own cost–benefit analyses of projects before they bid for an event. The United Kingdom government did this for the 2012 Olympics.

Cost–benefit analysis is an interesting technique as it attempts to quantify all the positive and negative outcomes from any given project. It usually attempts to put an economic figure on each of the outcomes, though this can be very difficult in some cases. A simple example relating to a potential new stadium in the UK is shown in Table 6.2.

It is possible to be quite ingenious in devising ways of putting economic values on a range of tangible and intangible impacts. The task below invites you to do this yourself.

Table 6.2 Theoretical approach to a cost–benefit analysis of a new sports stadium

	Benefit	Cost
Planning phase	Hire of designers, architects, planner etc. in £	Planning blight leading to lower housing values in £
Construction phase	Earnings of construction workers in £	Loss of earnings in closed businesses in £
	Profit to property developers in £	Disruption to traffic – lost working hours in £
Operating phase	Expenditure of attendees in £	Displacement of other income opportunities on the site in £
	Purchase of food in local shops in £	Cleaning up litter by street cleaners in £
	Increased profit to traders through price inflation in £	Increased cost of living to local population in £
	Increased tourism leading to more occupation of hotel rooms in £	Temporary migration of local population during events leading to additional accommodation costs for those concerned in £

TASK

Consider the following potential impacts of events and suggest ways in which an economic cost could be put on them:

- noise pollution;
- light pollution;
- graffiti;
- lower air quality;
- attendance by celebrities; and
- fighting outside the stadium.

Putting an economic value on impacts has been a traditional way of evaluating impacts. However, in an age of environmental problems such as global pollution, global warming and resource depletion, it may be more suitable to assess the impacts in terms of their sustainability or their environmental value. Some researchers have begun to adopt this approach. Shang-Chung Ma *et al.* looked at the Kaohsiung 2009 World Games and suggested some specific criteria for sustainable development in sports mega-events. Their suggestions in terms of the physical environment are shown in Table 6.3.

Table 6.3 Specific criteria for sustainable development in sports mega-events

Protection of natural resources and cultural heritage	(1)	To protect conservation areas, cultural heritage and natural resources
	(2)	To minimise the environmental impact of the infrastructure
Sports facilities	(1)	To use existing sports facilities
	(2)	To design facilities to fit in with the surrounding natural or man-made scenery
Transport	(1)	To encourage use of public transport
	(2)	To encourage walking or cycling for short distances
Energy	(1)	To promote the use of renewable energy sources and energy savings
Water management	(1)	Not to jeopardise general water supplies in order to satisfy the needs of a sports activity
	(2)	To avoid contaminating underground or surface water
Management of hazardous products, waste and pollution	(1)	To take advantage of the organising of major events to remediate contaminated sites
	(2)	To build upon successful practices and technologies used in previous events
	(3)	To maximise the recycling of the products used
Quality of the biosphere and maintenance of biodiversity	(1)	To avoid giving rise to unnecessary or irreversible contamination of air, soil or water
	(2)	To avoid jeopardising biodiversity or endangering plant or animal species
	(3)	To avoid contributing to deforestation or being prejudicial to land conservation

Source: Ma *et al.* 2010, reprinted by permission of Taylor & Francis Ltd

It is possible to develop this approach and create a cost–benefit table that relates to sustainability issues. Table 6.4 is an example of this in relation to a new stadium.

When reviewing the following case studies such an approach may be borne in mind.

TASK

Research an event driven urban regeneration scheme using the internet. Has it been evaluated? Was it evaluated economically and/or in some other way? Attempt an environmental evaluation of the scheme.

Two case studies will illustrate that the urban legacies of events can be very variable. One appears to have an excellent legacy in terms of urban regeneration while the other appears to have been, in the short term at least, very disappointing.

Table 6.4 Some indices that can be used in a sustainability evaluation of a new stadium

	+	−
Uses less energy than predecessors or comparable stadia		
Uses renewable energy		
Travel is mainly by public transport		
Creates less food waste than predecessors or comparable stadia		
Utilises anti-graffiti construction materials		
Utilises noise insulation techniques		
Is aesthetically pleasing		

Case study: the Athens 2004 Olympics

Hopes for the 2004 Athens Olympics were high. A return to the country of origin of the Games provided Greece with an ideal opportunity to showcase the positive impacts that such an event could create. The Games organisers had ambitious plans:

> the city of Athens sought to use the Games as part of an overall regeneration strategy. The city's chaotic growth after the civil war which followed the Second World War and the subsequent period of military dictatorship which ended in 1975 had made it relatively squalid by EU standards, and after the entry of Greece into the EU efforts were made to plan and structure urban growth in a less destructive way. A Master Plan for urban development, and a complementary Environmental Protection Plan, tried to set the planning standards for the city's future. (University of East London 2007: 86)

The Athens Organising Committee followed Sydney in consulting environmental NGOs such as Greenpeace and the World Wide Fund for Nature (WWF). They set out a number of environmental principles, cited by UEL:

- The siting of all new Olympic venues was to be in full alignment with the existing land use and sustainability plan for the city of Athens.
- In all areas with Olympic venues, the post-Olympic use excluded the construction of hotels, offices, private houses, casinos and night clubs or restaurants. This provision was included in special legislation (Law 2730/1999) on the design and integrated development of the areas hosting Olympic construction, and in full knowledge that such a provision would mean that the self-funding of the projects would therefore not be feasible.
- All temporary constructions for the Games were to be removed within six months of the completion of the Paralympic Games. Again this was among the legal provisions – Law 2819/2000 – passed during the construction period. (Ibid.: 85)

The urban regeneration plans included many ambitious projects. Most of the categories identified by Baim (2009) were included. There were to be new sports venues and new housing would result from the creation of the athletes' village. Transport infrastructure was to be substantially improved, with 120km of new roads, six major new highway interchanges, the development of the Attica peripheral highway, a 23km two-line tram system, an expanded Metro system with upgrading of old stations and a new suburban rail link between the Metro and the airport.

Improvements to the urban culture and general environment included cleaning of much of the city's rich architectural heritage and the removal of many unsightly advertising billboards. Additionally, the city centre was to be provided with new walkways and parks which were to be planted with low water demand vegetation (only to be expected in a Mediterranean location).

Delays in the completion of many of these projects attracted much publicity. Criticism had begun well before the Games started. The delays in construction meant that some projects were not completed and others were completed to less environmentally satisfactory specifications, such as some of the parks which were planted with water-demanding species. Unsurprisingly many of these plants were dead within a few years. Greenpeace and the WWF both produced reports which compared Athens unfavourably with Sydney. The WWF in particular was very uncomplimentary about the environmental performance of Athens. As the UEL report notes, '"When the lights of the 2004 Olympic Games fade out", asked the WWF report in conclusion, "when the Games are over and the athletes and visitors go, what will Athens inherit?"' (University of East London 2007: 86):

The report identified only four (*sic*) gains:
- Improved mass transport system
- A city centre free from huge advertisements
- Refreshed building facades
- New pavements and a network of pedestrian walkways
- Information and awareness material against littering and in favour of water saving.

While there were nine negatives:
- Fewer free, undeveloped spaces
- One ecologically significant area which will have undergone irreversible damage
- Huge sports complexes without definite post-Olympic use and provision for maintenance
- One new town at the foothill of the Mount Parnitha National Forest
- A city that will have expanded and encroached at the expense of the natural and agricultural landscape
- No improvement in the environmental profile of Greece's energy sector
- No introduction of new water management and saving technologies
- No improvement in the waste management system
- No progress in the area of environmentally friendly construction technologies.

The overall score offered by the WWF report was a damning 0.77 out of 4. (Ibid.: 98)

Not all these criticisms relate directly to urban regeneration but several of them do. Some commentators are less critical. Tziralis *et al.* comment that:

> the sustainable impact of the Games . . . in the sphere of the environment was also of great significance. Especially on the issue of transport networks, the Games served as a strict pressure factor that finally resulted in a massive re-engineering of the public transport system and the road network. The underground railway network grew by a factor of 1.74, a new railway and bus lanes network was constructed and 200km of rather new or upgraded motorways effected a significant decrease of stationary traffic contributed to a reduction in air pollution. (Tziralis *et al.* 2006)

Criticism was not limited to academe and NGOs. The press was full of adverse comments about the construction projects. As Panagiotopolou notes:

> press reports focused monotonously on the question of whether Athens would be ready in time to host the games. Such on-going negative reports tend to damage the image of Olympic cities, especially when the host city belongs to a small country that does not have a powerful international lobby with a capacity to counter such stories. (Panagiotopolou 2009: 157).

He goes on to comment that neither the organising committee nor the Greek government 'managed to come up with an effective communications strategy to reduce these overall negative press reports though eventually some more positive reports began to appear. Despite this, even four years later the following comment could be found in *The Independent* newspaper:

> the best Olympics regenerate neglected districts, inspire children to take up sport and leave a city furnished with world-class venues and rolling in Olympic dollars – Barcelona is a good example of this. The worst are poisoned chalices that leave a nation in debt and a city overrun by white elephants – look no further than Athens. (Usborne 2008)

The *Daily Mail* Online was equally dismissive:

> The Olympic 'legacy' – the favourite buzzword of London's Olympic planners – was meant to be visible to all, transforming the chaotic Greek capital as if Apollo, the god of harmony and civilisation, had smiled on it. That has not happened. A staggering 21 out of 22 venues lie abandoned since an event lasting just three weeks was held, and the magnificent stadiums are now over-run with rubbish and weeds. (Malone 2008)

The negative press was probably one of the factors that led to a fall in tourism in Greece throughout 2004.

Although the physical legacy of the Athens Games is often cited as poor, Panagiotopolou suggests that this evaluation may change over time as it was 'widely acknowledged that the sporting venues of Athens were among the best constructions of their sort' (Panagiotopolou 2009: 159). However, a debate continues over their use:

> The government has repeatedly said that it does not seek to sell the venues. However, most of them are expected to be leased by companies from the private sector for a long period, because the government wants to avoid the operating and maintenance costs of the venues as well as to find sources of funding to pay off the huge public debt. The maintenance and operation of such costly facilities cannot be undertaken by the various Greek sporting federations. Clearly, such problems arising in the post-games period demonstrate that the original bid was constructed in a haphazard way, without plans for the post-Olympic use of the installations after the games. (Ibid.: 150)

There is a clear message here. If positive legacy effects are to be maximised then they need to be meticulously planned. This appears to be the case with the 2012 London Olympics. However, just as evaluation may become more favourable over time, it can also do the reverse.

Case study: the Barcelona 2000 Olympics

In a report anticipating the legacy of the 2012 London Olympics, the OECD remarked:

> The Olympics were the foundation for Barcelona's transformation. They gave the city the opportunity to execute a plan for its modernisation. The scale of the Olympic project and the immovable nature of its associated deadlines allowed Barcelona to deliver what ordinarily would have taken several phases of development to achieve. The Olympic project also delivered five major outcomes which have supported the internationalisation and increased quality of life and competitiveness of the city for nearly 20 years. (OECD 2010: 75)

The OECD identified the five outcomes as:

- the branding impact;
- the tourism impact;
- the infrastructure, land use and economic development platform impact;
- the civic pride impact; and
- the public–private partnership impact. (Ibid.)

While all these outcomes relate directly or indirectly to urban regeneration, it is the third that is particularly pertinent in the context of this chapter. The OECD notes that:

> the infrastructure legacy of the Olympic Games has perhaps been of greater importance to Barcelona than to any other recent Olympic city. Barcelona used the

Olympics to accelerate the fulfilment of an urgent and perpetual need for significant infrastructure investment. Almost the entire infrastructure required for the delivery of the Games also delivered a long-term dividend for the city. (OECD 2010: 77)

The report identifies a number of significant areas of regeneration and it is of value to cite from it at length. First:

> the Olympics catalysed the construction of two new telecommunication towers in Barcelona . . . essentially designed to support the growth of the city's post-Games economy. Today, the telecommunications installed during the Olympics is a fundamental support to the city's knowledge-based businesses. (Ibid.: 76)

Second:

> to ensure the rapid movement of athletes and Olympic officials between venues and facilities during the Games, Barcelona needed to build new ring roads. In this way, the Olympics accelerated the construction of infrastructure which would ease traffic congestion in the city over the long-term. Today, the ring roads re-route traffic away from the city centre. As a result, traffic congestion has eased and the retail sector has benefitted from an increase in footfall and a decrease in air and noise pollution. (Ibid.: 77)

Third:

> The Olympics also required that Barcelona's small, congested airport was renovated to cope with the increase in Games-related traffic. [This has] been critical to the growth of Barcelona's post-Games economy. (Ibid.)

Fourth:

> the decision to locate the Athletes' Village near to the city centre rather than a cheaper location in Metropolitan Barcelona has proven decisive. By constructing this piece of essential Olympic infrastructure in an area of old rail infrastructure and factory buildings, the city was able to reconnect itself to its seafront and begin the development of a new neighbourhood adjacent to the city centre. The displacement of the railway lines did two things. First, it kick-started the development of the city's seafront. The delivery of a new Leisure Port (which was the Olympic Port during the Games) and the creation of five kilometres of urban beaches produced the right environment to support the post-Games growth of the local neighbourhood which is now emerging as high quality, middle class residential location. Second, the displacement of the railway lines opened 1 000 000 square kilometres [*sic* – should read square metres?] of under-utilised and dilapidated land near the city centre known as Poblenou. Following the Games, city planners and economists decided the best use for this land was for it to remain

designated as industrial but to add to it the necessary infrastructure to support the growth of knowledge-based firms. In 2000, the area was designated as the 22@ Innovation District and by 2009 1502 knowledge-based firms had relocated to the area which now supports 44 600 new jobs. (Ibid.: 77–8)

The report concludes its evaluation of Barcelona's urban regeneration by stating that:

> the creation of infrastructure with the dual purpose of both delivering a successful Olympics and supporting the growth of the city after the Games kick-started the most profound transformation that Barcelona has experienced for many years. Each of the infrastructural improvements and the decisions taken to leverage the impact of the positioning of them, built a platform for a successful phase of economic growth and development in Barcelona that has only recently ended. As a result, from a de-industrialised, declining city in the early 1980s, the Barcelona of today has a diversified and dynamic knowledge-based economy which delivers a high quality of life for its residents. (Ibid.: 78).

It is not only the OECD that has praised the achievements of the Barcelona Games. In a report carried out by the University of East London for the London Assembly the impacts of the Barcelona Games, among others, were assessed. In noting the environmental impacts the report focused on the urban regeneration:

> the improvements were suffused, as they were with most of the Games held before 2000, within a more general regeneration project which has successfully transformed the city from an inward-facing industrial town to a vibrant international centre for business and leisure tourism which has continued to develop as such in the fifteen years since the Games helped to bring it to world attention. While fifteen new venues were built, the Barcelona Games' competition centre, including the main competition stadium, was developed around the existing facilities at Montjüic Park, which had originally been built for an international exposition in 1929. But the building of an Olympic village on the site of former industrial warehouses, together with the rerouting of railway lines, the transformation of the seafront into beaches by the importation of sand, the building of a new marina and new public parks, the construction of new roads and the control of river pollution, can also be said to have given the city a net environmental benefit. The Barcelona Games' success is generally acknowledged – as the decennial celebration of the event, held in the city in 2002, signals. The city has expanded considerably in population while maintaining a can-do attitude which makes it one of Europe's most desirable destinations for work or play. The post-Olympic recreation and business areas of the Forum are part of the longitudinal regeneration legacy of the 1992 Games, and also of its environmental legacy. (University of East London 2007: 88)

Brunet evaluates the Games in an economic context but identifies the importance of physical urban regeneration in achieving economic prosperity for the city. He notes that the Barcelona Games can be seen as a model in three respects, for organisation, for economic impact and as 'a model for urban transformation, improved attractiveness and strategic positioning' (Brunet 2009: 114). He concludes that 'thanks to the Olympic Games, Barcelona is now a different city. The organisation was optimum, fostering massive investment in infrastructure. Thanks to the correct use of the Olympic legacy – increased capital investment and improved attractiveness – the urban development process has continued long after 1992' (ibid.).

Conclusion

The aims of this chapter were to:

- explore the history of urban regeneration in the domain of events and assess why it has received so much attention relative to other environmental impacts;
- examine the nature of event stimulated urban regeneration; and
- evaluate the success of such regeneration with respect to selected case studies.

It has addressed the first aim by showing that event driven urban regeneration has a long history dating back to Greece and Rome. It has argued that the topic receives much attention because of the economic and political imperatives attaching to government bids at a range of scales to host events. It has shown that urban regeneration is a complex matter that relates to the economic history of an area. Finally, it has looked at a number of case studies of such regeneration. Some have been very successful, such as the 1992 Barcelona Olympic Games; others have been much less successful, such as the 2004 Athens Olympic Games. There appears to be a consensus that the former represents, in many ways, a model of the ways in which the hosting of events can be used to effect successful urban regeneration. It is clear that the organising committee for the 2012 London Olympics is very aware of this model and it is worth concluding by quoting from the OECD report on London 2012. The report itself concludes by citing the lessons that can be learnt from Barcelona. They are:

- The smart positioning of venues and event-related facilities can unlock 'hidden' land parcels within the city, which may be developed to maintain the impact of the event legacy over time.
- A major event offers the opportunity to deliver infrastructure that has the dual function of both delivering a world class event and supporting the growth of the expected post-event economy.
- A major event may not leverage the finance to deliver all of the plans made. The major event impetus can be maintained beyond the event, however, if authorities commit to realising unfulfilled plans within a reasonable timescale.
- The impact that a renewed sense of civic pride and confidence can bring should not be underestimated. Every effort should be made to communicate to the people of the city or area in which the event is hosted that it is for them.
- The intensification of activities creates a critical mass for success by providing high levels of accessibility, clustering benefits and proximity to markets. The spatial

sharing of the benefits of major events is obviously desirable, but it is more effectively delivered through the rippling outward of positive effects from a central hub or a number of hubs of activity. (OECD 2010: 79)

Further reading

Poynter and MacRury's 2009 book, *Olympic Cities: 2012 and the Remaking of London*, is a valuable resource on this subject. Pacione's chapter in *The Routledge Handbook of Events* (2011) provides an insightful overview from an urban geographer. The OECD's report *Local Development Benefits from Staging Global Events: Achieving the Local Development Legacy from 2012* (2010) provides a useful summary of a number of Olympic legacies.

Environmental legislation and standards

Aims

The aims of this chapter are to:

- explore key aspects of the environmental legislation that exists at a number of levels, global, regional, national and local; and
- examine key aspects of the standards that have been developed for the event industry to manage its environmental performance in a sustainable way.

Introduction

Although environmental legislation has a long history, it is only relatively recently that it has become both extensive in its scope and widespread in its application. In the second half of the 20th century, after 150 years of western industrialisation with its associated air, land and water pollution, public attitudes began to change and demand government action. This era of protest was ushered in by the 1962 publication of Rachel Carson's *The Silent Spring* (Carson 1962). This book catalogued the effects that the indiscriminate use of chemicals was having on our environment. Carson's chapter headings, such as 'Rivers of Death' and 'No Birds Sing', were often emotive and crafted to cause a sense of alarm. During the 1960s a number of environmental catastrophes emerged, such as Minimata and the *Torrey Canyon*, and these fuelled the growth of the protest movement. As Case has noted:

> the early seventies [saw] the publication of *Blueprint for Survival* (Goldsmith 1972) and *The Limits to Growth* (Meadows 1972) [that] created a doomsday atmosphere which dissipated, to some extent, in the self-seeking 80s. However, by the late 80s even governments were becoming publicly concerned with the possibility of global warming and the IPCC was set up to advise governments (or as some cynics saw it, delay any action). Environmental NGOs, such as Greenpeace, were taking direct action and publicising issues such as the adverse impacts of the Olympic Games. Changes in public attitudes were reflected not only in the actions of global NGOs but also locally, as residents increasingly protested at the impacts of mega-events. As a result the IOC eventually added environmental criteria to its bidding process.

Resource shortages resulting in price rises (e.g. petrol) brought home to the public the wider environmental concerns as did the increasing coverage of extreme meteorological events. There can be few, especially in the media dominated western world, who can be unaware of environmental problems even if they contest their causes and fail to alter their lifestyles appropriately. (Case 2011: 366)

As governments responded to environmental problems, and the political issues associated with them, a wealth of legislation began to emerge, particularly in the western world. This occurred not only at the national level but also at the regional level, such as the European Union, and the global level with the United Nations. The result is a mass of complex legislation which affects what we can and cannot do with the environment. The event industry has to comply with this legislation.

In parallel with legislative developments, there have been attempts by the industry to develop standards to govern its own environmental behaviour. At an international level these have included the ISO 14000 series of standards. At a national level these have included the UK event industry's development of BS 8901. The scale and detail relating to the legislation and standards are so great that they cannot be encompassed in a chapter of a few thousand words. The remainder of this chapter will therefore be necessarily selective and provide pointers to the various types of legislation and a range of standards so that students can investigate these further for themselves. The intention is to make students aware of the legal environmental context in which the event industry works.

The legislative framework

The international level

The principal agent of environmental legislation at the international level is the United Nations Environmental Programme (UNEP).

UNEP was established by the UN General Assembly in 1972. Its mission is 'to provide leadership and encourage partnership in caring for the environment by inspiring, informing and enabling nations and peoples to improve their quality of life without compromising that of the future generations' (UNEP 2012):

Since its establishment, environmental law has been one of the priority areas of UNEP, in line with the mandate accorded by the UN General Assembly Resolution 2997 (XXVII) and subsequent decisions of the Governing Council of UNEP. UNEP's Environmental Law activities are carried out within the framework of strategic Programmes for the Development and Periodic Review of environmental Law (The Montevideo Programmes) approved by the Governing Council every ten years.

UNEP aims at promoting the coherent implementation of the environmental dimension of sustainable development within the United Nations system. Agenda 21 designated UNEP as the principal United Nations body in the field of the environment. Among the priority areas identified in Agenda 21 on which UNEP should concentrate, are the following:

- Further development of international environmental law, in particular conventions and guidelines, promotion of its implementation and coordinating functions arising from an increasing number of international legal agreements, inter alia, the functioning of the secretariats of the Conventions; (Agenda 21, Chapter 38 – chap. 38.22 (h))
- Provision of technical, legal and institutional advice to Governments, upon request, in establishing and enhancing their national legal and institutional frameworks, in particular, in cooperation with UNDP capacity-building efforts; (Agenda 21, Chapter 38 – chap 38.22 (l). (Ibid.)

The organisation has brought about dozens of global environmental agreements, some of them binding, some of them not. Many of them would appear to have had little impact directly on the event industry. However, the industry and its supply chain are affected by them. For example, the refrigerants and fireproofing materials it uses are constrained by the Montreal Protocol which aims to eliminate the use of chlorofluoro-carbons (CFCs), which deplete the ozone layer in the upper atmosphere. Without the ozone layer we should all be prone to higher levels of ultraviolet radiation with their potential to cause sunburn and skin cancer. The Kyoto Protocol aims to limit the amount of carbon dioxide that can be emitted into the atmosphere. All countries that have signed up to this, including the United Kingdom, have introduced a wide range of measures, many of them exhortatory, to reduce the use of fossil fuels. The Ramsar Treaty limits the use of wetlands worldwide and would constrain, if not prevent, any event scheduled to take place in them.

Many of these protocols are made effective by national legislation. Thus, while the United Nations' agreements may seem remote from the activities of an individual event manager, they may well provide the context for what can be permitted in any local environment.

Case study: events in Antarctica

Antarctica is a continent but it is not a country. Many states lay claim to parts of it but they have agreed to suspend these claims and govern the continent through an international agreement known as the Antarctic Treaty System (ATS). This is a unique form of governance. Antarctica has a very fragile environment that is easily damaged. As the climate is severe any degradation of the environment can take many years to repair.

Antarctica remains the last great wilderness on earth. In the past the continent was protected by its remoteness and inaccessibility. Thanks to modern technology this is no longer the case and Antarctica is receiving an increasing number of visitors. Some of the activities in which visitors engage are events, such as expeditions to reach the South Pole or the running of marathons on the 'seventh continent'. International concern over the conservation of the continent led to the Antarctic Treaty nations adopting the Protocol on Environmental Protection to the Antarctic Treaty in 1991, which came into force in 1998. The Environmental Protocol provides for the comprehensive protection of the Antarctic environment, and sets out mandatory regulations governing human activities in the region.

Antarctica is now protected by one of the toughest sets of environmental regulations found anywhere in the world. In summary, the Protocol:

- designates Antarctica as a 'natural reserve, devoted to peace and science';
- sets out principles for environmental protection;
- bans mineral resource activity (other than scientific research), with a mechanism to review the ban after 50 years, or before if all Treaty nations agree;
- requires the Environmental Impact Assessment (EIA) of all activities before they can go ahead. (Foreign and Commonwealth Office 1999)

The UK enacted domestic legislation to enforce the Protocol through the Antarctic Act 1994. The Act introduced a permit system, administered by the Foreign and Commonwealth Office (FCO), for all British activities in Antarctica. This means that permits are required for all British expeditions to Antarctica, as well as all British-registered aircraft and vessels operating south of latitude 60° S. Thus any event taking place in the region is carefully scrutinised before it can proceed. The International Association of Antarctica Tour Operators (IAATO) provides advice for all tourists visiting the continent, some of which is listed in Figure 7.1 on pp. 117–18.

TASK

Antarctica is clearly a difficult environment in which to hold events.

Develop an idea for an event to be held in Antarctica. Provide a justification for it being held there. Outline how your event would safeguard the environment.

Many of the suggestions in the IAATO guidelines would be sensible for environments outside Antarctica. Suggest some of the difficulties in implementing such advice in the Peak District or similar national park.

Regional legislation

There are many political unions around the world where groups of countries work together on a wide range of themes. This includes environmental legislation. Prominent among these unions, in terms of the environment, is the European Union. It produces a substantial number of directives relating to a range of issues. As the Environment Agency notes, 'European directives require member states to achieve specific environmental objectives. Each directive is translated into UK law through a set of regulations'

(Environment Agency 2012a). At the time of writing the Environment Agency lists nineteen directives and provides guidance on each of them.

Like the United Nations legislation, many of these directives do not appear to have an immediate impact on the event industry. Closer examination however, reveals the relevance of many. The Groundwater Directive, for example, aims to protect groundwater from pollution and cites (in chapter 4) some of the liquid wastes that can find their way into the soil and thence to groundwater supplies. The EU Habitats Directive aims to protect the wild plants, animals and habitats that make up our diverse natural environment, and illustrates (again in chapter 4) a number of ways in which event activity can affect wild plants and animals. This ranges from the effects of trampling through to the introduction of alien species; the latter are becoming an increasing threat to the biodiversity of our environment. The Landfill Directive is designed to bring about a change in the way we dispose of waste in this country and is a challenge for the event industry. The Glastonbury Festival, among others, makes much of its attempts to recycle materials and reduce the amount of waste from the festival going to landfill. This is in line with a national objective to limit landfill.

National legislation

As noted in the previous sections international and regional agreements and directives are made effective through national legislation. In addition to that nations can design their own legislation and make provision for legislation at a local level. The Environment Agency holds extensive information on this legislation and categorises it under the following headings:

- English air legislation
- English chemicals legislation
- English conservation legislation
- English energy legislation
- English environmental permitting legislation
- English land legislation
- English noise and statutory nuisance legislation
- English pesticides and biocides legislation
- English radioactive substances legislation
- English waste legislation
- English water legislation. (Environment Agency 2012b)

The agency tries to simplify access to this information by providing guides for particular sectors of industry. Unfortunately, there is no section on the event industry as such. The closest section is the leisure and tourism industry, the mobile section of this in particular. It describes this as:

guidance is for hospitality, leisure and tourism businesses without a fixed operating location including:

- fast-food vans
- ice cream vans

Guidance for Visitors to the Antarctic

Protect Antarctic Wildlife

Taking or harmful interference with Antarctic wildlife is prohibited except in accordance with a permit issued by a national authority.

- Do not use aircraft, vessels, small boats, or other means of transport in ways that disturb wildlife, either at sea or on land.
- Do not feed, touch, or handle birds or seals, or approach or photograph them in ways that cause them to alter their behaviour. Special care is needed when animals are breeding or moulting.
- Do not damage plants, for example by walking, driving, or landing on extensive moss beds or lichen-covered scree slopes.
- Do not use guns or explosives. Keep noise to the minimum to avoid frightening wildlife.
- Do not bring non-native plants or animals into the Antarctic such as live poultry, pet dogs and cats or house plants.

Respect Protected Areas

A variety of areas in the Antarctic have been afforded special protection because of their particular ecological, scientific, historic or other values. Entry into certain areas may be prohibited except in accordance with a permit issued by an appropriate national authority. Activities in and near designated Historic Sites and Monuments and certain other areas may be subject to special restrictions.

- Know the locations of areas that have been afforded special protection and any restrictions regarding entry and activities that can be carried out in and near them.
- Observe applicable restrictions.
- Do not damage, remove, or destroy Historic Sites or Monuments or any artefacts associated with them.

Respect Scientific Research

Do not interfere with scientific research, facilities or equipment.

- Obtain permission before visiting Antarctic science and support facilities; reconfirm arrangements 24–72 hours before arrival; and comply with the rules regarding such visits.
- Do not interfere with, or remove, scientific equipment or marker posts, and do not disturb experimental study sites, field camps or supplies.

Figure 7.1 Guidance for visitors to the Antarctic

Source: IAATO 2012

Be Safe

Be prepared for severe and changeable weather and ensure that your equipment and clothing meet Antarctic standards. Remember that the Antarctic environment is inhospitable, unpredictable, and potentially dangerous.

- Know your capabilities, the dangers posed by the Antarctic environment, and act accordingly. Plan activities with safety in mind at all times.
- Keep a safe distance from all wildlife, both on land and at sea.
- Take note of, and act on, the advice and instructions from your leaders; do not stray from your group.
- Do not walk onto glaciers or large snow fields without the proper equipment and experience; there is a real danger of falling into hidden crevasses.
- Do not expect a rescue service. Self-sufficiency is increased and risks reduced by sound planning, quality equipment, and trained personnel.
- Do not enter emergency refuges (except in emergencies). If you use equipment or food from a refuge, inform the nearest research station or national authority once the emergency is over.
- Respect any smoking restrictions, particularly around buildings, and take great care to safeguard against the danger of fire. This is a real hazard in the dry environment of Antarctica.

Keep Antarctica Pristine

Antarctica remains relatively pristine, the largest wilderness area on Earth. It has not yet been subjected to large scale human perturbations. Please keep it that way.

- Do not dispose of litter or garbage on land. Open burning is prohibited.
- Do not disturb or pollute lakes or streams. Any materials discarded at sea must be disposed of properly.
- Do not paint or engrave names or graffiti on rocks or buildings.
- Do not collect or take away biological or geological specimens or man-made artefacts as a souvenir, including rocks, bones, eggs, fossils, and parts or contents of buildings.
- Do not deface or vandalize buildings, whether occupied, abandoned, or unoccupied, or emergency refuges.

Source: IAATO available at http://iaato.org/c/document_library/get_file?uuid=022e237f-740e-4e7a-b952-a8acfe5d45c8&groupId=10157

- doughnut sellers
- mobile entertainment. (Environment Agency 2012c)

It could be argued that the last category includes many events, and the previous categories are often present at events in any case. For this sector of industry the agency draws attention to the following environmental legislation:

Air and noise
- Air quality
- Noise and vibration from hospitality, leisure and tourism businesses

Materials and equipment
- Waste electrical and electronic equipment
- Refrigerators and chiller units

Packaging
- Packaging

Transport
- Vehicle emissions from hospitality, leisure and tourism

Waste
- Fly-tipped material
- Hazardous/special waste
- Sanitary waste disposal
- Waste reduction, reuse and recycling
- Waste storage and transport
- Your waste responsibilities

Water
- Discharges to water and sewer. (Ibid.)

Each of these categories can be interrogated further. For example, the vehicle emissions section contains the following advice:

Emissions from vehicle exhausts are a significant source of air pollution. Air pollutants in vehicle emissions include:
- carbon dioxide
- carbon monoxide
- fine particles, e.g. PM10, PM2.5
- nitrogen oxides
- unburnt hydrocarbons.

You should try to limit the vehicle emissions produced by your business as they may:
- lead to ill health, such as respiratory problems, in your staff and the public
- cause a nuisance to your neighbours

- contribute to roadside pollution levels in urban areas
- contribute to climate change.

WHAT YOU MUST DO

Meet requirements for your vehicles

Make sure that your vehicles comply with **emission limits** and **weight regulations**. The Vehicle and Operator Services Agency (VOSA) carries out roadside checks to enforce these standards.

Ensure your vehicles comply with **exhaust emission standards** as specified in the:
- Ministry of Transport (MOT) test scheme for motor vehicles
- Heavy Goods Vehicle (HGV) scheme, or
- Public Service Vehicle (PSV) scheme.

These schemes are operated by:
- Vehicle and Operator Services Agency (VOSA)
- Driver and Vehicle Agency (Northern Ireland): Vehicle testing

Check if you drive in low emission zones or air quality management areas

Your local council monitors air quality in your area. If the air quality exceeds a certain threshold, it may declare an area to be an **Air Quality Management Area**. Often these areas are declared due to emissions from transport.

Some local councils are introducing **low emission zones** to reduce pollution in urban centres. These are areas where you may have to pay a daily charge if your vehicle doesn't meet certain emission standards or qualify for an exemption. Check with your local council to find out if there are any low emission zones or air quality management areas in your area.

You can also search for air quality management areas on the Defra website.

You must turn off your engine if your vehicle is stationary to reduce exhaust emissions and noise. You can be prosecuted or fined by some local councils if you leave your engine running while stationary for more than a few minutes.

Good practice

When buying new company vehicles, select models with **low carbon dioxide** (CO_2) emissions and high **fuel efficiency**.

You can find out the fuel efficiency of a vehicle from the Vehicle Certification Agency (VCA) or Society of Motor Manufacturers and Traders Ltd (SMMT).

You can benefit from tax breaks by buying low emission vehicles.

You can reduce your vehicle emissions and possibly reduce running costs by using **alternative fuels,** such as gas or electrical hybrids.

You can fit **older vehicles** with devices that reduce their emissions. This can be a cheaper alternative to upgrading engines.

HM Revenue & Customs (HMRC) reward businesses that use cleaner, more fuel-efficient cars. Road tax and National Insurance Contributions (NICs) are linked to the car's exhaust emissions, particularly its CO_2 emissions. You can get more details from the HMRC.

Service all your vehicles regularly.

Make sure tyres are correctly inflated and remove roof bars and boxes when they are not needed.

Remove any **excess weight** by only carrying what you need.

Keep speed down. Driving at 50–60 mph produces the lowest emissions. Driving over 70mph rapidly increases vehicle emissions. It can cost up to 15% more in fuel to drive at 70mph compared with 50mph.

Keep the vehicle moving if possible. Starting and stopping uses more fuel than a vehicle moving steadily.

Use **air-conditioning** and other electrical devices sparingly as this increases fuel consumption.

Monitor your **fuel consumption** to help detect problems early.

Pre-plan delivery routes to maximise the efficient use of vehicles.

Avoid using vehicles for **short journeys**. Encourage your staff to use public transport, cycle or walk.

Reduce the impact of necessary journeys by using less-congested routes, avoiding peak travel times and encouraging car sharing. (Environment Agency 2012d)

TASK

Access the Environment Agency website. Find the advice it gives about air pollution for the leisure and tourism industry (mobile). Reflect on an event that you have been to recently. How might the advice on air pollution have been relevant to that event?

Case study: special events in the national historic sites of Canada in Cape Breton

One of the environmental protection measures enacted by governments concerns the use of environmental assessment before projects or events take place. Canada is a country with such legislation relating to sensitive environmental areas. The Canadian Environmental Assessment Act ensures that the environmental effects of projects involving the federal government are carefully considered early in project planning. Parks Canada is a Federal Authority that issues a licence of occupation granting authority to conduct special events at a National Heritage Site (NHS) within the Cape

Breton area. Parks Canada must ensure that an environmental assessment is completed before issuing a licence to enable the project to be carried out. As many of the special events that take place in the area are routine, repetitive events with predictable and mitigable environmental effects, Parks Canada has developed what it calls a Replacement Class Screening (RCS) which enables the environmental assessment process to be streamlined while ensuring the uniform approach remains consistent with existing legislation, policies and procedures. Aspects of this have already been mentioned in Chapter 4. The RCS approach means that groups of similar activities can be approved by one assessment and can go ahead without further approval providing they come within the coverage of the assessment. The types of activity must meet six criteria:

1. *Well-Defined Class of Projects:* Special events at the Cape Breton sites are based on several common characteristics. The sites . . . have similar environmental settings . . . and share many activities, such as the setup of temporary staging, lighting/sound equipment, portable washroom facilities, etc. and have predictable, mitigable environmental effects.

2. *Well-Understood Environmental Setting:* Parks Canada began acquiring responsibility for the Cape Breton Field sites in 1925 and is familiar with each site's environmental setting. Events generally take place on paved and/or gravelled areas, therefore keeping the environmental settings relatively constant between properties. The slight variations in wooded area and water sources at each site are taken into consideration.

3. *Unlikely to Cause Significant Adverse Environmental Effects, Taking into Account Mitigation Measures:* Based on previous experience with special events, no significant adverse environmental effects are likely to occur. Minor environmental impacts have occurred during the past and were successfully mitigated to ensure protection of ecological values and commemorative integrity. There is no evidence of significant cumulative effects to date and none are expected due to the short duration of the special events and limited environmental effects that result.

4. *No Project-Specific Follow-Up Measures Required:* Project-specific follow-up programs are not required as there are no expected variations in predictions or effects to be monitored. A Parks Canada official must verify, however, that the property is returned to its natural state following a special event. This is applicable to all special events, regardless of the site.

5. *Effective and Efficient Planning and Decision-Making Process:* Special event projects involve activities that are straightforward and routine in nature, so event planning is uncomplicated and Parks Canada is usually the only authority involved in the assessments.

6. *Public Concerns Unlikely:* Projects conducted over the past 50 years have not elicited any major public concerns. Given the residential setting of many of the

NHSs, community residents have been unhappy with any increase in noise and traffic associated with special events or limited access to them. However, mitigation measures are outlined in the RCSR [Replacement Class Screening Report] to minimise public disturbance. As a general rule, the public welcomes special events as they usually have a positive impact on the local economy. (Adapted from Parks Canada 2011)

The screening process covers a number of issues:

- researched past land use at the Cape Breton NHSs during special events and the environmental settings of each site;
- described project activities associated with each type of special event and location;
- determined Valued Environmental Components (VECs);
- identified potential environmental effects, mitigation measures, and residual
- environmental effects associated with each type of special event and location; and considered possible cumulative effects. (Adapted from Parks Canada 2011)

This scrutiny is followed by public consultation and review before the report is approved. The types of activity vary between special events, though all share common elements. Six groups of special events are identified for the purpose of identifying activities associated with each type of special event. Two of these groups, concerts and sporting/community events, are shown in Table 7.1.

The approach of Parks Canada can be seen as a sensible response to environmental legislation. It respects the need for conformity with the legal need to protect fragile environments, while minimising the bureaucracy involved by treating whole groups of event activity under one heading. It is not therefore necessary for each event to go through the environmental assessment process. This approach could provide a template for procedures in other countries which fear that increased environmental scrutiny of proposed events could lead to unnecessary red tape.

Local legislation

Local legislation is very significant for many event organisations. To build new venues planning permission has to be obtained and to run them there must be compliance with a range of local bylaws and regulations. Event organisers may well have to gain permissions to run events and these may also have to comply with local environmental legislation.

Standards

As well as environmental legislation at a range of levels, event organisers have a number of standards with which they can comply. These are set by organisations such as the British Standards Institute (BSI) and the International Standards Organisation (ISO). Over the past 20 years, they have produced standards on quality management and environmental management. These include the British Standard BS 5750 (ISO 9001)

Table 7.1 Project activities associated with special events at national historic sites in the Cape Breton Field area, by event type and phase

Event type	Event phase	Equipment/crew transportation (both terrestrial and aquatic)	Equipment storage	Mooring/parking	Set up/dismantle temporary staging, fencing, tents, etc.	Installation/removal of portable washrooms	Prepare/remove stands/promotional displays	Food preparation, sales, and clean-up; merchandise sales	Set up/removal of waste facilities, waste generation and waste removal	Install/use/removal of generators	Set up/use/removal of sound/lighting equipment	Use of camera equipment	Use of props	Set construction/deconstruction	Campfires	Special event (performances, sporting event, etc.)	Use of special effects and/or black powder	Attendance between 0–500	Attendance between 0–2000	Attendance between 0–10000
Concerts	Site preparation	✓	✓	✓	✓	✓	✓		✓	✓	✓									
	Event	✓	✓	✓	✓	✓	✓	✓	✓	✓	✓	✓				✓	✓			✓
	Site restoration	✓	✓	✓	✓	✓	✓		✓	✓	✓									
Sporting and community events	Site preparation	✓	✓	✓	✓	✓	✓		✓	✓	✓									
	Event	✓	✓	✓	✓	✓	✓	✓	✓	✓	✓					✓			✓	
	Site restoration	✓	✓	✓	✓	✓	✓	✓		✓	✓									

Source: © Parks Canada Agency

which relates to the former and BS 7750 (ISO 14001) which relates to the latter. Both these standards applied to industry in general and had significant effects on the way many companies managed themselves.

In 2007 the BSI introduced BS 8901 A *Specification for a Sustainable Event Management System with Guidance for Use* (BSI 2007). This was a significant development within the event industry and is discussed in this chapter and Chapter 8. Here the emphasis is on its role as a standard, whereas in the following chapter the emphasis is on its role in the development of thinking on sustainability and the evolution of ISO 20121.

BS 8901

BS 8901 has an interesting history. According to David Stubbs, Head of Sustainability for the London Organising Committee of the Olympic Games and parallel Paralympic Games:

> It all started with a chance encounter over a glass of red wine. The occasion was a London 2012 bid promotion to business leaders in the City of London at the Mansion house one day in 2004. Seb Coe and Mayor of London, Ken Livingstone, were at front making the pitch. Other big team colleagues and I were working the rest of the room.
>
> And so I came across Arnold Pinder of the BSI. Well what do you say to a standards man about bidding for the Olympic and Paralympic games? If it had been any of my other colleagues, probably not a great deal. However, I had a bee in my bonnet about making events more sustainable, but I was stymied by the then lack of any formal systems or standards that applied in this field . . .
>
> My musings about sustainable events that night at the Mansion House obviously struck a chord with Arnold and the BSI. After we won the bid to host the 2012 Games, my dialogue with the BSI continued and I was obviously delighted with their interest in this field, which led to the subsequent development and launch of BS 8901, in November 2007. (David Stubbs, cited in Cumming and Pelham 2011: ix–x)

The standard set out the requirements for planning and managing sustainable events of all sizes and types, supplemented by guidance on how to meet, and surpass, these requirements. It was the first standard to specify a sustainable management system for industry and was designed specifically for the event industry. Given the event industry's relative neglect of environmental issues for many years, it is a great credit to the industry that it became a pathfinder in the quest to manage in a more environmentally friendly way. BS 8901 specifies the requirements for a sustainability management system for the entire range of events, from school fetes, through conferences and festivals, to mega-events such as the Olympic and Paralympic Games. It was aimed at a range of users that not only included event organisers and venue managers but also organisations and/or individuals in the supply chain:

BS 8901 is a management system standard. A management system is defined as a system to establish policy and objectives and to continually achieve those objectives. BS 8901 requires organisations to understand the sustainability issues relevant to their event(s) and to put in place measures to control and minimise these impacts. It requires organisations to aspire to continually improve their sustainability performance in relation to the management of events.

It is foreseeable that many event clients, particularly corporations and local authorities will demand that event organisers, venues and suppliers to the industry adopt the standard. Indeed, the London 2012 Olympics are requiring organisations to be working towards implementation of BS 8901. (Sustainable Event Solutions 2012)

BS 8901 follows the traditional Plan>Do>Check>Act model (discussed in Chapter 10) associated with many management systems and is about process – the way things are managed. It does not guarantee the quality of the output but the way the output is achieved. In theory, a disappointing event could be compliant with the standard, similar to the IT concept GIGO – garbage in, garbage out.

The standard has a number of stages (see road map in Figure 7.4):

- **Identifying the scope of the implementation**: Organisations need to decide whether there are any limitations on the scope of their implementation. Some may choose for only parts or specific divisions to introduce the standard in the first instance.
- **Determining the purpose and values:** Organisations must identify the reasons why they are implementing the standard. In establishing the purpose and values of implementation, along with the scope, it is useful for an organisation to effect a review of its existing management practices and, if any, sustainability policies.
- **Establishing the sustainability policy:** Obviously organisations have to develop a sustainability policy. An example of this, the sustainability policy of Positive Impact Events, is shown in Figure 7.2. Positive Impact is a not-for-profit-organisation whose vision is an event sector inspired to have a positive impact on its economic, environmental and social surroundings. They are helping to make this vision a reality by providing education, resources and change support.
- **Identifying key issues:** Any organisation needs to identify key issues with respect to sustainability. Positive Impact Events, for example, identifies the following issues:
  - o   Demonstrate best practice
  - o   Deliver a return on investment
  - o   Improve supplier engagement and education. (BSI 2012)
- **Establishing objectives, targets and plans:** Once a policy is established, it is necessary to develop objectives and targets for implementation. These ought, ideally, to be SMART: specific, measurable, achievable, realistic and time-limited, as shown in Figure 7.3. They should also be incorporated into a project plan against which progress can be precisely measured.

Positive Impact Events

Positive Impact Events understand that our event management operations and processes impact both positively and negatively on the environment, social and economic issues.

Our purpose and mission is to promote and support the development of sustainability in the event industry.

We are committed to show sustainability leadership within all of our event management operations and processes.

Our core principles and values are honesty and integrity, professionalism, leadership, a partnership approach, positivity and productivity.

We are committed to upholding these principles and values in all of our event management operations and processes.

We strive to continually improve and develop to leave a positive legacy.

We recognise that event management can have positive long-term social, environmental and economic impacts and therefore sustainability is core to the foundation of all our event management operations and processes, including products and services.

We will ensure that this policy is communicated to all our stakeholders and supply chain with regards to our event management operations, products, services and processes which includes the whole event life-cycle from events conception to post events review.

We will ensure we listen and record any feedback from stakeholder engagement and our end users.

Positive Impact Events will ensure that we adhere and comply with all applicable legal and other requirements to which Positive Impacts Events subscribes.

The Positive Impact Events sustainable objectives are to:
• grow income levels to allow sustainable growth;
• provide unique leadership for the implementation of sustainability;
• develop our way of working structure to maximise potential.

These objectives address actual issues of business growth and improving industry training.

Figure 7.2 Sustainability policy of Positive Impact Events

Source: Saunders 2012

- **Setting roles and responsibilities:** For the standard to be implemented successfully is essential to set out clear roles and responsibilities. It is helpful if a senior member of the management team can have overall responsibility assisted by suitable champions, who are enthusiasts for the project. If staff detect a lack of commitment from management, the project can wither on the vine. It is helpful if the role of all members of staff is clearly established – this needs to be linked to the overall goals of the organisation.
- **Engaging stakeholders:** All organisations should be aware of their stakeholders. These range from suppliers through to clients and also include all the employees in the organisation itself. The engagement of stakeholders is particularly important when implementing standards because their co-operation is essential to success – for example, if a particular supplier has no interest in sustainability issues it can undermine the attempts of your organisation to be sustainable. It will be wise for an organisation to consult with its stakeholders in advance of implementation so that they are on board from the outset.

TASK

Working either on your own or in a group, think of an event that you have been involved in. Identify all the stakeholders in that event. What might their perspectives be on sustainability?

You might find mind melding (brainstorming) a useful technique to help answer this question.

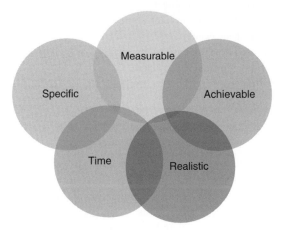

Figure 7.3 SMART objectives and targets

Source: LearnMarketing.net 2012

- **Resourcing the implementation:** It is essential that the implementation is properly resourced. This may include a number of aspects – finance, appropriate staff, training and promotion. As noted above all it requires management commitment, without which implementation can be lacklustre and destined to failure.

- **Auditing – monitoring and evaluating the implementation:** If the objective setting has been SMART it should have identified the ways in which progress can be measured. These will be individual to particular organisations and will depend on the targets established. It will be useful to have specific individuals responsible for the collection of the relevant data. Use of spreadsheets can be useful in recording the results. Individual measures will be variable but could include things such as:

  o   lower energy use;
  o   reduced use of water;
  o   lower food miles;
  o   reduced volumes of waste; or
  o   increased recycling.

  Audit needs to be systematic and regular. The data need careful evaluation (see next section) and divergences from targets need to be identified. Where these are negative it may be necessary to revise aspects of the implementation. If they are positive, however, milestones have been reached and should be celebrated.

- **Management reviewing:** Finally, management must review the success of implementation to establish whether targets have been met and whether the implementation has been BS 8901 compliant. Positive Impacts Events, for example, put into place an event debrief post-event which identified whether the sustainability objectives were achieved. The results showed that Positive Impact achieved the following in relation to their objectives:

  o   Delivered a BS 8901 compliant event
  o   Benchmarked the event
  o   Demonstrated best practice
  o   Engaged and educated supply chain
  o   Educated delegates on how to minimise the impact of future events. (BSI 2012)

ISO 20121

BS 8901 was first published on 30 November 2007. It was revised and reissued in September 2009. It has now evolved into a new international standard, ISO 20121, launched in the summer of 2012 (after the completion of this manuscript) to coincide with the London Olympic Games. This is the first international standard for sustainability management systems and will replace BS 8901 after a transition period of two or three years, although organisations certified against BS 8901 will be able to achieve certification against the international standard by having a transition audit.

According to the company SGS, ISO20121 will, like BS8901, have commercial benefits. They argue that it will:

Road map for implementation of BS 8901

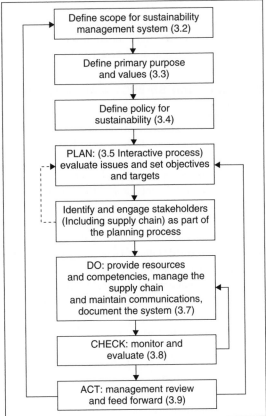

Figure 7.4 Road map for implementation of BS 8901

Source: Cumming and Pelham 2011: 10

- provide assurance to stakeholders, customers and anyone else involved, that the event has been planned and implemented in a sustainable manner;
- help differentiate an organisation from its competitors, helping to win new business, improve reputation and brand image;
- help to reduce carbon emissions and waste and improve resource efficiency of the entire event supply chain; and
- improve relationships with the employees, local communities, suppliers and other relevant stakeholders. (SGS 2012: 2)

Its applicability includes:

- Tier 1: Event owner – anyone who commissions and is responsible for the overall management of an event;

- Tier 2: Event organiser – anyone with overall responsibility for managing the delivery of an event;
- Tier 3: Suppliers to the event – any organisation providing products, services or facilities such as stand builders, lighting engineers, sound engineers, printers, caterers, venue owners, couriers and printers. (Ibid.)

Case study: implementing BS 8901 – Manchester International Festival

The inaugural Manchester International Festival (MIF), the world's first international festival of original, new work, ran from 28 June to 15 July 2007.

Drawing from the city's pivotal role in music, the Festival programme focused on new music – premiering work by established and emerging international musicians – but also, in step with Manchester's history, aimed to address the important issues and stories of our time through debates and new commissions.

Recognizing that sustainability is at once both an urgent issue of our time and an important requirement for the long-term success of the Festival, a series of links with sustainability experts were formed. One of these links was with Organise This – a Manchester-based event management company which produces events designed to have a positive impact on the environment and the local community. Out of this arose the opportunity to trial an implementation of BS 8901 across four events during the 2007 Manchester International Festival.

These were deliberately chosen to provide a range of event size, style and settings:

- Manchester Dines, a series of free, communal dinners showcasing the best of Manchester's international cuisine;
- The Cunning Little Vixen, a fusion of music, theatre and film set in an established concert hall with accompaniment from the Hallé Orchestra and a local children's choirs;
- Unknown Pleasures, a site-specific open-air showcase of emerging bands at The Quays;
- Festival Futures, a public debate about The Future of the Planet. (BSI 2007)

External consultants, Organise This, worked closely with internal management in implementing the standard, which involved three phases – pre-event planning, events monitoring and post-event development. 'The first step was to draft and agree a Sustainable Development Policy' (BSI 2007). This was then circulated among stakeholders for discussion and feedback. Key objectives and performance indicators were identified along with plans for evaluating the event's impacts. These included 'indicators of waste, energy, community involvement, economic impact and cause of carbon emissions and was monitored across all the constituent elements of venue, accommodation, food and drink, transport, marketing and communications, and back office' (ibid.). The trial established that the standard was found

> to be equally applicable to all four events assessed, highlighting its generic nature
> . . . An important point is that implementing the standard does not necessarily

deliver a 100 per cent sustainable event. Rather, it provides a framework to work towards continuously improving the levels of sustainability. So, while the trial highlighted where Manchester International Festival was successful in its sustainability goals it also flagged up where the future challenges lie. (Ibid.)

One interesting aspect of the exercise was a survey of 100 attendees, all of whom agreed 'that the Festival should demonstrate sustainability' (BSI 2007). This may indicate that the event attendees were more aware of the need for sustainability than some of the event organisers. The organisers expected that

> independent evaluation of the Festival is also expected to highlight that sustainability is increasingly important to public and private funders, partners and suppliers. Organizations that can demonstrate commitment to improving their sustainability may well see a competitive advantage and as no other country has a comparable standard, BS 8901 also presents an opportunity to lead on best practice internationally. (Ibid.)

While the BSI might be expected to be positive in its reporting of this trial, it is evident that much was achieved during this exercise. Readers will be pleased to know that the Manchester International Festival continues to thrive.

Conclusion

This chapter aimed to:

- explore some of the environmental legislation that exists at a number of levels, global, regional, national and local; and
- examine some of the standards that have been developed for the event industry to manage its environmental performance in a sustainable way.

It has achieved the former by establishing that environmental legislation has a significant history and arose from increasing awareness that the planet was becoming seriously degraded as a result of environmental pollution and overexploitation of the earth's natural resources. It has shown that the legislation is now extensive and continues to grow, operating at a range of levels from the global to the local, and that event organisers need to be aware of this legislation if they are to deliver the events legally. Help and support exists for them to do this.

The chapter has achieved the second aim by looking at some of the standards that have emerged. It looked in particular at BS 8901 and how it emerged in conjunction with the sustainable management of the 2012 London Olympic Games. It noted the development of the new ISO 20121 standard published in the summer of 2012 (after the submission of the manuscript of this book).

Further reading

For further reading on BS 8901 readers should investigate the BSI website at www.bsigroup.com.

8 Sustainability: its nature and development as a concept and emergence in event management

Aims

This chapter is the first of two looking at sustainability and sustainable management. It looks at the more theoretical and developmental aspects of the term while Chapter 9 focuses on practicalities, though there is an inevitable overlap. This chapter aims to:

- examine the development of ideas on sustainability and their political, cultural and social context;
- trace the evolution of the idea within event academe and the event industry;
- note the strand of green meetings;
- explore the scope of sustainable protocols, principles and policies; and
- evaluate aspects of the implementation of BS 8901 in the UK.

Sustainability – a contested idea

Sustainability is a popular term. Carter claims that 'sustainable development has rapidly become the dominant idea, or discourse, shaping international policy towards the environment' (Carter 2007: 208). However, there is no clear consensus about exactly what it means or how its associated terms of sustainable development and sustainable management are differentiated. Confusingly, the terms are often used interchangeably. Johnston *et al.* have noted that 'sustainable development has proven conceptually elusive, however, it has provided a focal point for discussion and debate in the chaotic realm of global change' (Johnston *et al.* 1994: 611). Most writers on sustainability cite the Brundtland Report (1987) when they seek to define the term though it has a significant antecedence probably dating back to the 1960s and 1970s. Specific publications such as Meadows *et al.*'s *The Limits to Growth* and Goldsmith and Allen's *Blueprint for Survival*, both published in 1972, created major debates and called for urgent action to avoid environmental catastrophe. While their ideas were readily taken up by acolytes, they also stimulated sceptics who queried their assumptions. This led to an era of debate and uncertainty until the UN established the World Commission on Environment and Development in 1983. It produced its final report in 1987, published as *Our Common Future* (WCED 1987) but better known as the Brundtland Report after its chairman, a former Norwegian prime minister.

Famously, the report defined sustainable development as 'development that meets the needs of the present without compromising the ability of future generations to meet their own needs' (WCED 1987: 43). One might query how present, let alone, future needs can be known or defined and how 'compromising' should be defined. Significantly, it implies the idea of the inevitability and necessity of economic growth, an assumption not accepted by many environmentalists and recently some economists. However, in 1992 Principle 12 of Agenda 21 (see case study below) noted that national environmental policies should not be used as a 'disguised restriction on international trade' (UNCED 1992, cited in Hay 2002: 213). Hay comments that it 'was apparent to most people in the environment movement that the goal of "sustainable development" had been thoroughly subverted . . . [and that the term] was thought by many to be an oxymoron' (Hay 2002: 213). Hay goes on to note that for others 'the formulation was a cynical exercise to accord a fake legitimacy to full-on, business-as-usual global environmental rapine' (ibid.). Hay notes that the many definitions of sustainable development can be classified as 'weak' (like the Brundtland definition) or 'strong' like that adopted in *Caring for the Earth*, which describes it as 'improving the quality of life while living within the carrying capacity of supporting ecosystems' (WCU/UNEP/ WWFN 1991, cited in Hay 2002: 214).

However, it would appear that the Brundtland approach has prevailed. Its catholic principles, which incorporate a concern for 'human welfare and the exploitation of nature in preference to an ecocentric interest in protecting nature for its own sake' (Carter 2007: 212) are reflected, for example, in the sustainability goals of the 2012 Olympics. Appraisal of the concept probably depends on beliefs as much as evidence. As Carter also notes, 'sustainable development, like beauty, is in the eye of the beholder' (ibid.). While it could be argued that the term sustainable development has provided a banner under which a range of protagonists of varying viewpoints can march in apparent unison, it needs also to be remembered that it is a contested concept that requires constant challenge when loosely used.

The social, cultural and political context of sustainability

The nature of sustainability needs to be set against a background of changing public attitudes and an increasing political awareness of environmental issues, brought about by resource crises such as the supply of food and increasing evidence of environmental degradation such as atmospheric pollution. This has been encouraged by an environmental movement that can be traced back to at least the age of enlightenment. The Romantic Movement in the 18th century, with its focus on nature – the Lakeland poets are perhaps the most egregious examples – was an early manifestation of this. In the US the movement was developed by the likes of Emerson and Thoreau and their concern for wilderness. As wilderness in the US became increasingly threatened, organisations began to emerge such as the Sierra Club, founded by John Muir. Pressure for preservation created by such groups prompted the establishment of the first national park, Yellowstone, in 1872. In the UK national intervention in preserving wilderness came about somewhat later, for a variety of geographical, cadastral and cultural reasons. Britain was smaller, had less genuine wilderness and most of the land was privately owned. Although the National Trust, a charity, was founded in the 19th century, it was not until the late 1940s that the Peak District was designated as the first national park. This had been prompted by actions such as the mass trespass on Kinder Scout and the later Dower Report, and can be seen as part of the development of the welfare state under the Attlee government. The UK national parks are very different from those in the US and Australia. They tend to be more populated, less remote and largely privately owned.

There followed a lull in environmentalism in the 1950s. The year 1962 saw the publication of Rachel Carson's *The Silent Spring*, which acted as a wake-up call. As noted in Chapter 7, a series of environmental disasters and the emergence of a number of often alarmist environmental publications were facets of the 1960s and early 1970s. At the same time there was growing public protest over environmental issues. Governments began to respond in a number of ways, notably by establishing the United Nations Environmental Programme (UNEP) in 1972 (see Chapter 7).

After the publication in 1987 of *Our Common Future* (the Brundtland Report) the IPCC (Inter-Governmental Panel on Climate Change) was set up to investigate the problem of global warming. Perhaps the most notable political development relating to sustainability was the Rio Summit of 1992 which was a major event in its own right, leading to the Rio Declaration and Agenda 21, discussed below as a case study. The Johannesburg Summit ten years later (see Chapter 9 case study) led to the Johannesburg Declaration on Sustainable Development. A further conference on sustainable development, the Earth Summit, is scheduled to be held in Rio in 2012. Its objectives are:

- to secure renewed political commitment to sustainable development;
- to assess progress towards internationally agreed goals on sustainable development; and
- to address new and emerging challenges.

The Summit will also focus on two specific themes: a green economy in the context of poverty eradication and sustainable development, and an institutional framework for sustainable development (UN 2012a).

Case study: the United Nations Conference on Environment and Development in Rio, 1992

The United Nations Conference on Environment and Development (UNCED) was held in Rio de Janeiro on 3–14 June 1992. It was a follow-up to the UN Conference on the Human Environment held in Stockholm in 1972 and was unprecedented in size and scope for a UN conference. There were 178 governments participating, 108 of which were represented by heads of state or government; 2400 NGO representatives also attended.

> The Summit's message – that nothing less than a transformation of our attitudes and behaviour would bring about the necessary changes – was transmitted by almost 10,000 on-site journalists and heard by millions around the world. The message reflected the complexity of the problems facing us: that poverty as well

as excessive consumption by affluent populations place damaging stress on the environment. Governments recognized the need to redirect international and national plans and policies to ensure that all economic decisions fully took into account any environmental impact. And the message has produced results, making eco-efficiency a guiding principle for business and governments alike. (UN 2012b)

The UN identified a number of environmental outcomes:

- Patterns of production – particularly the production of toxic components, such as lead in gasoline, or poisonous waste – are being scrutinized in a systematic manner by the UN and Governments alike;
- Alternative sources of energy are being sought to replace the use of fossil fuels which are linked to global climate change;
- New reliance on public transportation systems is being emphasized in order to reduce vehicle emissions, congestion in cities and the health problems caused by polluted air and smog;
- There is much greater awareness of and concern over the growing scarcity of water. (Ibid.)

Above all the two-week Earth Summit was the climax of a process that led to the adoption of Agenda 21, a wide-ranging blueprint for action to achieve sustainable development worldwide. Its preamble sets a high moral tone:

Humanity stands at a defining moment in history. We are confronted with a perpetuation of disparities between and within nations, a worsening of poverty, hunger, ill health and illiteracy, and the continuing deterioration of the ecosystems on which we depend for our well-being. However, integration of environment and development concerns and greater attention to them will lead to the fulfilment of basic needs, improved living standards for all, better protected and managed ecosystems and a safer, more prosperous future. No nation can achieve this on its own; but together we can – in a global partnership for sustainable development. (UNCED 1992)

Middleton and O'Keefe have described Agenda 21 as an 'ambitious programme for sustainable development: both a guideline for governments, INGOs and multilateral agencies, and a basic document for local initiatives, particularly among municipal authorities. It has led to the foundation of over 2,000 groups throughout the world known as "LA21s" (Local Agenda 21)' (Middleton and O'Keefe 2003: 8). Local initiatives have had an impact on the event industry with some local authorities developing plans which affect how they deliver events.

The summit also saw the signing of two agreements, the Framework Convention on Climate Change and the Convention on Biological Diversity. They have had mixed fortunes, the former leading to Kyoto, but the latter being 'a sorry affair' (Middleton and O'Keefe 2003: 8). However, as Middleton and O'Keefe note, 'both conventions have prompted some movement, no matter how minimal, in those wealthy states least in thrall to their lumpen right. They also become points of departure for that contemporary phenomenon of widespread, single issue political protest' (ibid.).

There has been extensive criticism of the Rio Summit, but it was a significant event in the history of sustainability. As Dernbach and Feldman have noted:

> Environmental degradation has been considered a price that we necessarily pay for this progress. The concept of sustainable development changed this definition of progress by incorporating environmental protection and even restoration into the definition of development. Instead of making progress in conventional development at the environment's expense, or protecting only the environment, the idea is to work toward both conventional development and environmental protection at the same time. That concept is the irreducible core of Agenda 21 and the Rio Declaration. (Dernbach and Feldman 2003, cited in Rechkemmer 2005)

Protests against the event industry

The protests against environmental degradation extended to the event industry, notably over the impact of the Olympic Games at Albertville, and this eventually led to the IOC introducing environmental criteria to their award of the Olympic Games to bidding venues. This has culminated in the 2012 Olympic Games in London, which has been anticipated as the most sustainable ever. A social, cultural and political consensus now exists whereby events on a large scale, and indeed often a local scale, cannot take place without consideration of their environmental impacts or the nature of their sustainability.

Event academe and the event industry

Until relatively recently the event industry has not been prominent in the push for sustainability. This has also been true of much of the educational community studying event management at advanced and degree levels. There may be some intrinsic reasons for this. First, and most critically, events, by their nature, usually involve movement of people to venues. Where these events are local the resulting carbon and ecological footprints may be modest, but where the events are large the footprints may also be very large indeed, especially if air travel is involved, as it tends to be in mega-events. This can engender a feeling of helplessness even when organisers try to be sustainable in other aspects of their management.

Second, the number and scale of events is rising, even though the post-2009 economic recession appears to be having some effect, for example on ticket sales for festivals. However, by contrast, the 2012 Olympics were a sell-out though this may reflect prioritisation for a one-off UK event. This growth in events may result from consumerist societies becoming sated with material products and seeking experiences instead to satisfy their leisure desires and enable the self-actualisation identified by Maslow in his hierarchy of needs (Maslow 1968). As James has noted, societies in many countries, particularly in the more developed world, are becoming subject to an 'affluenza' virus that 'entails placing a high value on acquiring money and possessions' (James 2007: vii). Events facilitate an alternative form of acquisition.

Third, many event organisers are small-scale enterprises or individuals who may not have the training to be aware of all the environmental issues or the resources to adopt good environmental practices. Academic degrees in event studies are of relatively recent origin (see Getz 2007: 1–8) and have not always prioritised issues such as environmental impacts or sustainability. Where they have, such an emphasis has not always been popular with students. More recently most courses have been incorporating elements of sustainability and it is now possible to study events and sustainability at masters level. As the courses have developed this has been reflected in the textbooks provided for study. Bowdin *et al.*'s popular *Events Management* was published in 2001. It included a chapter on event impacts, of which three pages are on physical and environmental impacts – this includes a brief review of the Sydney Games. However, the term sustainability does not appear in the chapter headings or the index. By contrast the revised edition, published in 2010, trumpets its focus on sustainability.

Sustainability in academe

Early academic interest in sustainability tended to focus in subjects such as geography, ecology and environmental science. As Getz (2007: 50–125) notes, it was perhaps human geography, in particular, that helped spawn the study of tourism, leisure and heritage. It was out of such secondary subjects that many event courses emerged from the 1990s onwards. In shaping the event discipline, Getz notes that, among other things, human geography contributed the study of 'human-resource interactions, especially spatial and temporal patterns of human activity including impacts on the environment' (ibid.: 214). To this may be added an interest in sustainability. Many early tourism academics had geographical backgrounds, so it is not surprising that tourism began to generate books on sustainability. What was happening in the tourism industry helped drive this, as mass tourism began seriously to damage destination environments and the attractions that drew tourists to them in the first place.

As noted earlier, an emerging cognisance of global environmental issues such as climate change and energy supplies provided research opportunities for academics. Numerous books on tourism began to incorporate the words sustainability, environment or geography in their titles: 1994 saw the publication of *The Earth as a Holiday Resort: An Introduction to Tourism and the Environment* (Boers and Bosch 1994), 1998 saw Mowforth and Munt's *Tourism and Sustainability*, a fascinating study of how these issues applied to the Third World, and 2000 saw *The Development of Sustainable Tourism* (Aronson 2000) and *Environment and Tourism* (Holden 2000). More specialist texts focusing on issues such as ecotourism began to appear, such as *Ecotourism: A Sustainable Option* (Cater and Lowman 1994), *Ecotourism and Sustainable Development* (Honey 1999) and *Ecotourism* (Page and Dowling 2002). Generalist textbooks incorporated major sections on impacts and sustainability, such as *Global Tourism* (Theobold 1994) and *Tourism: A Modern Synthesis* (Page and Connell 2006). Non-academic texts also emerged, such as *The Good Tourist* (Wood and House 1991) and

Preserve or Destroy: Tourism and the Environment (Croall 1995), while the youth market was targeted with titles such as Solway's *Sustainable Tourism* (Solway 2009).

Leisure literature saw a similar progression. 1994 saw the publication of *Leisure and the Environment* (Spink 1994), which does not feature sustainability in its index, and 2004 *The Geography of Sport and Leisure* (Terrell 2004), which does have a chapter on environmental impacts but none on sustainability. Where the environment was discussed in leisure texts, it was often with reference to examples from tourism. Torkildsen's attempt to produce a comprehensive guide to leisure and recreation management, first published in 1983 (Torkildsen 1983), had no chapters on impacts or sustainability, although the fourth edition (1999) had sections on public bodies such as the then Countryside Commission which listed aims that included sustainability.

Sports studies saw significant publications on the environment in the 1990s and early 2000s. In 1994 Chernushenko published *Greening Our Games: Running Sports Events and Facilities That Won't Cost the Earth* and in 2001 daCosta published 'International trends in sport and the environment – a 2001 overview'. In 1999 the Council of Europe published 'Mens sana in corpore sano: a scientific review of the information available on the links between sport and the environment' (Oittinen and Tiezzi 1999). Sports textbooks began to feature significant sections on sport and the environment, notably B.F. Collins's contribution to *Sport and Society: A Student Introduction* (Houlihan 2003). His chapter discusses sustainability specifically and the word features in the book's index. It details a number of specific environmental impacts and provides case studies to illustrate the issues.

Early texts on event management made little reference to the environment. Bowdin has already been cited. *Successful Event Management* (Shone and Parry 2001) has a chapter on the implications of events and identifies social, economic, political and developmental ones. Environmental impacts gain a mention under the last heading. Sustainability does not feature as a chapter section/heading or index entry. From 2007 coverage began to change significantly. Getz's *Event Studies* (2007) has sections on environmental impacts and outcomes as well as coverage of sustainability, including a discussion of events and public policy. In 2009–10 two significant event books appeared. One was an academic collection of essays, *Event Management and Sustainability* (Raj and Musgrave 2009), the other a practical guide to managing events sustainably, *Sustainable Event Management* (Jones 2010).

Event Management and Sustainability is a welcome and scholarly contribution to the sustainability debate edited by two academics at Leeds Metro, a university offering courses in events and sustainability. However, the book treats the specific issue of environmental impacts lightly in a single chapter, of which five pages discuss principles and concepts before the presentation of a case study. Other chapters cover aspects such as supply chain management and techniques and policies, while urban regeneration is discussed in a separate chapter.

The overarching subject of business studies (within which many event management courses are run) has also spawned a large literature on sustainability, though relatively less on environmental impacts. Such general works on sustainability as *Making Sustainability Work* (Epstein 2008) look at topics such as impact evaluation systems, impact auditing and projects for improving corporate sustainability. Such works also link the concept of sustainability to other corporate concepts such as corporate social responsibility and the triple bottom line.

As well as books, conferences and academic papers have shaped environmental attitudes within the profession and education sector. These can be traced back to the 1980s and 1990s but have accelerated since 2000. Of particular significance was a conference entitled *Events beyond 2000: Setting the Agenda* that took place in Sydney in 2000 (Allen *et al.* 2000). Several papers featured environmental impacts. Of particular interest were two of the keynote papers, 'A future for event management: the analysis of major trends impacting the emerging profession' by Joe Jeff Goldblatt (Goldblatt 2000) and 'Developing a research agenda for the event management field' by Donald Getz (Getz 2000). The former identified 15 trends that would impact on the event profession over the next 25 years, five of which had environmental dimensions. Getz identified eight research perspectives, the first of which was environmental.

Since 2000 there have been many academic papers, ranging from the examination of environmental impacts and sustainability at particular events to conceptual reviews. The former include the FA Cup (Collins *et al.* 2007), which includes ecological footprint analysis, the Turin Winter Olympics (Frey *et al.* 2008) and the 2000 Americas Cup (Barker *et al.*). The latter include the sustainability of festivals (Getz and Anderson 2008) and the impact of mega-events (Hiller 1998). Recently there has been a plethora of papers on the sustainability and legacy of the 2012 Olympics, with no doubt more to follow.

Although academic journals have featured a range of articles on specific aspects of environmental impacts, there is still considerable scope for further detailed research in this area. It is pleasing to note that some of this research is already under way at undergraduate level. Recent undergraduate theses have covered the carbon footprint of university event programmes, the introduction of sustainability policies into Farnborough International Venue and Events (the student concerned helped shape these), public awareness of environmental issues at the Goodwood Festival of Speed and the carbon footprint of the Watercress Line. It is also of note that at least one event degree has been revalidated to align itself with the principles of responsible management education (PRME).

Developments in the industry

In recent years a growing number of guides and protocols have appeared on sustainable management. These are discussed more fully in Chapters 7 and 9. Some of these are sector-specific, such as the greening of the American Meetings Industry. Some focus on the environment, such as ISO 14001, while others take a more comprehensive approach to sustainability, such as BS 8901.

Musgrave and Raj (in Raj and Musgrave 2009) selected six examples and identified their key principles. The guides are:

- *Sustainable Events Guide* (Defra 2007);
- *Sexi: The Sustainable Exhibition Industry Project* (MEBC 2002);
- *The Hanover Principles: Design for Sustainability – Expo 2000* (McDonough 1992);

- *BS 8901: 2007 Specification for a Sustainable Event Management System with Guidance for Use Developed* (BSI 2007);
- *Staging Major Sports Events: The Guide* (UK Sport 2005); and
- *The Sustainable Music Festival: A Strategic Guide* (Brooks *et al.* 2007).

There are many others, such as the *2010 Copenhagen Sustainable Meetings Protocol* (Bigwood and Leuhrs 2010), the *Greenpeace Olympic Environmental Guidelines* (Greenpeace 2000), *The Green Meetings Guide* (UN 2009), the IOC's *Manual on Sport and the Environment* (IOC 2005), *The Green Meetings Report* (Convention Industry Council 2004), *Sustainable Events Guide* (Seventeen Events 2010) and *ISO 14001*. A number of these documents are discussed elsewhere.

BS 8901 has already been revised. Event managers can no longer complain of a lack of guidelines if they wish to use them. Neither is there a shortage of techniques or metrics. Griffin (Raj and Musgrave 2009: 43–55) identifies indicators and tools for management while in the same work Lambert *et al.* (ibid.: 119–31) discuss methods for assessing and monitoring the performances of a sustainable event. These issues are discussed further in Chapter 10. Advice also exists on environmental impact analysis, environmental cost accounting and ecological and carbon footprint calculation. Recently, Meegan Jones has provided a wealth of practical advice in her 2010 book, *Sustainable Event Management*. She devotes chapters to marketing and communications, energy and emissions, transport (possibly the most intractable problem for the industry), water, purchasing and resource use and waste.

Green events

One aspect of developments in the industry relates to 'green meetings'. This focus dates back some time, particularly in the hospitality industry. A significant report, *The Green Meetings Report*, was produced in 2004 by the Green Meetings Task Force, an initiative of the Convention Industry Council. The task force was charged with creating minimum best practices for event organisers and suppliers to use as guidelines for implementing policies of sustainability. It defined a green meeting as one that 'incorporates environmental considerations to minimize its negative impact on the environment' (Convention Industry Council 2004). It outlined detailed advice to both event suppliers and event organisers. Significantly it noted that as well as environmental benefits, there were also economic benefits to be had from adopting a green approach.

In 2009 the UN produced its *Green Meeting Guide*, designed to 'assist organisers and hosts of small- to medium-sized meetings of up to 200 participants in greening their meetings – from partners meetings to small conferences. It is applicable to all organisations, not just those within the UN system' (UN 2009). It has two sections, the first on what to know and the second on what to do. The latter is very practical and includes detailed recommendations that meeting organisers can adopt. The first checklist relates to venue selection:

- Headquarters of IGOs, offices of regional commissions etc. should be chosen for the venue, rather than ad hoc locations or commercial establishments, thus reducing the need of staff to travel.

- Venues certified with a recognised green building rating system or another recognised environmental management system should be preferred wherever possible.
- The venue should have an environmental policy and action plan, ideally covering: sustainable procurement, energy saving, catering services, transportation, and waste.
- The venue should have training courses for staff on environmental duties in place.
- The venue should have good access (ideally within walking distance) to the main public transport connections and town centre.
- The venue should be near to hotels where participants and speakers can stay or even provide accommodation facilities in the venue itself.
- If possible locally, all waste produced at the venue should be separated (e.g. paper, plastic, metal, organic) at source and sufficient, well-marked bins should be provided in both participant and staff areas.
- If catering is provided by the venue, the facilities should meet the recommendations outlined in the 'Catering' section.
- Cleaning services for the venue should meet the recommendations provided in the 'Accommodation' section.
- It should be possible to regulate the temperature within the building. (Ibid.)

TASK

Review a recent meeting/conference in your area. How well did it comply with the recommendations given above?

This guide is very practical and readers would benefit from reviewing the entire document which is available online free of charge.

A number of organisations, some of them academic, have sought to produce their own advice to participants in their meetings. An example of this is the Extremes Conference held in 2009. It advocates the following guidelines:

1. Participants and presenters are advised in advance that the meeting will strive to minimise environmental impacts and greenhouse gas emissions. The registration materials ask that participants respect and assist this process as they feel appropriate.
2. For all goods procured for the meeting, preference is given to the most environmentally-appropriate, locally-produced alternatives that are available at a reasonable price. We are willing to pay more for environmental responsibility.
3. Printed materials are kept to a minimum, and all printed paper (i.e. conference proceedings, registration papers, photocopying, etc.) aims to have certified recycled content, with a high proportion of post-consumer content. Chlorine-bleached paper is avoided.
4. Gifts for participants are minimised, but when provided are minimally packaged and aim to minimise the use of toxic materials.

5. Conference CDs are not offered, rather materials such as abstracts and proceedings are provided online.
6. Attendees are provided with options to offset their transportation-related emissions at the time of registration.
7. Steps are taken to minimise environmental impact of transportation to the conference and during the conference. This includes choosing a locale accessible by public transportation, walking and biking.
8. Attendees and organisers are encouraged to walk, bicycle, carpool or use public transit to attend meetings and events whenever possible. Venues are evaluated in part based on their environmental policies and practices.
9. Attendees who fly are encouraged to travel by direct flights.
10. Steps are taken to promote the sharing of hotel rooms by attendees. Hotels are chosen that have effective and comprehensive environmentally friendly policies and operations.
11. Sponsors and donors are actively sought who reflect positive environmental values and practices. (9ICSHMO 2009)

TASK

If you are a university student identify a recent conference held in your institution. Did it comply with the guidelines? Did it produce its own guidelines? If it did neither, try to ascertain from the organisers why this was so.

Interest in green meetings in higher education continues as attending conferences has been a traditional core activity of academics. Readers are referred to the Greening Events website for a detailed bibliography (http://greeningevents.ilrt.bris.ac.uk).

Sustainable event management protocols, principles and policies: some definitions

It has been noted earlier in this chapter that sustainability is a contested and elusive concept. While it is useful for those working in events to be aware of the complexity of the idea, it is useful for pragmatic purposes to have a working definition, at least in terms of what sustainable event management is. Many texts, such as *The Hannover Principles* (McDonough 1992), refer to the Brundtland Report as the basis of their understanding of sustainability. Some, however, attempt to go beyond this. For example, Bigwood and Luehrs define it as follows:

Sustainable Event Management (SEM) is the process of designing and organising an event following sustainable development principles in order to achieve strategic goals which serve the economic, environmental and social interests of organisers, delegates and host communities. Sustainable events bring positive results for the local and global society through diversity and inclusivity, promoting healthy, creative and effective meetings. (Bigwood and Luehrs 2010: 6)

They go on to note that:

> SEM is more than eliminating bottled water or offsetting the event-related carbon emissions. SEM is a strategic way to lead and operate events and meetings. It includes strategies, policies, processes, systems and actions that intertwine to support and manage events more efficiently, effectively and professionally. Unlike the concept of greening, sustainability is not something which can be just plugged into the event management function. Sustainability is a management competence which leads the integration of responsible business practices with a culture of values and principles that guide the organisation and its talent. (Ibid.: 6)

Although they are elusive about what sustainable principles are, they do introduce the idea of sustainability as being a 'management competence'. This is an important message to students of the subject, many of whom have not seen the issue as one central to their academic pursuit of event management.

Raj and Musgrave suggest that sustainable event management should:

- provide realistic and long-term economic event development and production, ensuring that socio-economic benefits are distributed fairly to all stakeholders;
- provide continuous employment opportunities, entrepreneurial opportunities and distribution of event income within host communities, thereby contributing to the reduction of socio-economic disparity;
- consider the use of environmental resources that assist in event development and production, complying with essential management processes and conservation techniques to help safeguard natural heritage and the biodiversity of the surrounding community; and
- develop and produce events in conjunction with host communities, protecting their sociological authenticity, built landmarks, traditions and cultural values by promoting intercultural understanding and tolerance. (Raj and Musgrave 2009: xv)

This is a very broad remit indeed that moves well beyond the environmental themes central to this book. While many would welcome the socio-cultural and ethical dimensions, others might wonder whether aspects of the proposals sound like extracts from a socialist manifesto.

The authors go on to suggest a conceptual framework for sustainable events management which they visualise in a management wheel. One aspect of their ideas is that sustainable management needs to be dynamic and is one 'that is a problem for each generation' (Raj and Musgrave 2009: 4). They cite Meadowcroft as follows: 'Each generation must take up the challenge anew, determining in what direction their development objectives lie, what constitutes the boundaries of the environmentally possible and the environmentally desirable, and what is their understanding of social injustice' (ibid.).

This could be described as the position of the reflective practitioner, a principle long utilised in teaching and the caring professions. Its incorporation into events management would seem appropriate.

Meegan Jones, in *Sustainable Events Management*, reverts to Brundtland for her definition of sustainability but introduces the pragmatic idea of a sustainability policy. She notes that there are many models for such a policy but that they should include:

- Commitment to sustainability, resourcing and staff.
- Consultation process and training of staff and education of key stakeholders.
- Statement of goals or objectives.
- Description of the Key Sustainability Indicators that performance will be measured against. (Jones 2010: 11)

She advocates an overview of energy use, transport, water consumption, resource consumption and purchasing and waste and effluent management along with details of compliance, auditing and monitoring.

There clearly exists a plethora of protocols, principles and policies for sustainable event management. These range from the quasi-theoretical to the extremely practical and from the relatively narrow to the catholic. All include environmental considerations but some are much wider than others and include principles that could be described as political. Acknowledgement that sustainable event management is a necessary management competence places sustainability at the heart of event training programmes and the idea of reflective practice aligns the industry's practitioners with other professions. The next chapter will look at some of the practicalities that flow from these protocols, principles and policies.

Case study: BS 8901 – sustainable event management system

Reference has already been made to BS 8901 as an industry response to the need to provide a framework for sustainable management. The BSI themselves describe the document as:

> the British Standard which has been developed specifically for the events industry with a purpose of helping the industry to operate in a more sustainable manner. The standard defines the requirements for a sustainability event management system to ensure an enduring and balanced approach to economic activity, environmental responsibility and social progress relating to events. It requires organisations to identify and understand the effects that their activities have on the environment, on society and on the economy both within the organisation and the wider economy; and put measure in place to minimise the negative effects. (BSI 2012b)

The BSI identifies the key requirements of the standard as:

- Sustainability Policy
- Issue identification and evaluation
- Stakeholder identification and engagement
- Objectives, targets and plans
- Performance against principles of sustainable development
- Operational controls
- Competence and training
- Supply chain management
- Communication
- Monitoring and measurement
- Corrective and preventive action
- Management system audits
- Management review. (Ibid.)

Use of such a standard is not a guarantee that any event will be as sustainable as it could be. Standards are about processes, not outcomes. If data, policies or plans are poor then so might be the event. The original publication was not perfect. Seventeen Events commented, 'BS8901 isn't the be all and end all when it comes to event sustainability. However, if you don't know where to begin, BS8901 could point you in the right direction. We believe it offers the best chance for industry wide consensus on a more sustainable approach' (Seventeen Events 2010). They went on to note that the 2009 review was intended to try to fix some of the points of confusion which had arisen around the standard. Revisions proposed included a more formal definition of the scope of compliance, an end to the three phase method of claiming compliance and a move to make some aspects of compliance such as the maturity matrix optional rather than compulsory.

Many organisations in the public and private sectors have incorporated the standard into their event management policies. Durham County Council, for example, in its *Use of Resources Improvement Plan 2010–13* (2010), outlined area for improvement number 9 as: 'Produce and implement a DCC Sustainable Events Management Policy for large scale promotional activities aligned to BS 8901'. Evidence that this had happened would be 'More sustainable events and better coordination and dissemination of best practice'. Given the size and range of events that county councils organise, successful implementation of such policies will see widespread utilisation of the ideas in BS 8901.

The 2012 Olympics in their guidance for event sustainability acknowledge the significance of BS 8901 when they state that 'These guidelines will help companies and organisations take the first steps towards establishing a BS 8901 compliant management system' (LOCOG 2010b). This is another powerful conduit through which the standard will be disseminated. Many private organisations have already implemented the standard. The BSI provides a number of case studies. Of sporting interest is Lord's Cricket Ground. The BSI case study notes a number of benefits, such as providing 'a valuable framework within which to set targets around waste recycling and energy usage. In turn, this activity brings the potential for cost savings, both in reducing landfill tax and energy bills' (BSI 2012a). These savings show that improving sustainability can have bottom-line effects such as cost reduction. However, the case study also identifies a number of difficulties such as 'getting supply chain partners to meet the requirements of the standard . . . [though the] supply chain requirements will be far more easily achieved three to five years down the line when the standard is better known' (ibid.).

Significantly, Lord's suggest that

> anyone contemplating putting the standard in place has to understand that it's a significant undertaking . . . affecting everything you do and everyone you work with. It's going to affect all your business relationships. There isn't an easy or shortcut way to implement the standard. It's for organizations with a genuine commitment to sustainability. (BSI 2012a)

This is undoubtedly true, as other case studies have shown, but it might act as a deterrent to smaller organisations or ones under current economic stress. However, the possibility of cost reduction may counter any reservations about implementing the system.

Conclusion

This chapter set out to:

- examine the development of ideas on sustainability and their political, cultural and social context;
- trace the evolution of the idea within event academe and the event industry;
- note the strand of green meetings;
- explore the scope of sustainable protocols, principles and policies; and
- evaluate aspects of the implementation of BS 8901 in the UK.

It has shown, first, that sustainability and its related terms have a complex history. A single definition has proven elusive and the ideas remain contested. Second, it has shown that there are many strands to the concept, most of which originate outside the subject of event management and outside the event industry. Third, it highlighted a specific aspect of sustainable event management concerned with green events, and showed this to be rich in practical advice and a particular concern of academics. Fourth, it looked a selection of protocols, principles and policies that have evolved in recent years. While these had much in common, including a frequent reliance on the Brundtland definition of sustainable development, they also differed in much, including their scope. Some took a very broad view of sustainability in practice, which included political and ethical issues. Significant among them was the identification of sustainable management as a 'management competence', and this could be described as critical to the future of the industry, as could the adoption of reflective practice. Finally, the origins and nature of BS 8901 were examined and aspects of its implementation evaluated.

Further reading

An extended treatment of this topic by this author can be found in chapter 24 of *The Routledge Handbook of Events* (2011).

9 Sustainable event management practices

Aims

The aims of this chapter are to:

- provide an overview of some of the practical guidance that exists to assist event managers in delivering sustainable events at a range of levels:
  - o lists, tips and flyers
  - o mini-guides
  - o books;
- provide case studies of guidance given for specific events; and
- suggest some of the difficulties that may be encountered in implementing sustainable management practices.

Introduction

As Chapters 7 and 8 have shown, the past few years have seen a substantial growth in environmental legislation accompanied by the development of a range of national and international standards and environmental reporting frameworks. Some of these are effectively guidance on issues to be addressed in delivering a sustainable event. Some of them are environmental management systems. Many, however, lack simple practical tips, particularly for small- and medium-sized enterprises (SMEs), sole traders and those in the voluntary sector who organise events at a modest scale. There is much advice that ranges from single-sheet sets of tips such as *Top 10 Tips for Green Events*, produced by In Any Event UK Ltd, through small booklets such as Defra's *Sustainable Events Guide*, to complete books such as Meegan Jones's excellent *Sustainable Event Management*. This chapter will indicate some of the advice available and where it can be obtained, and will cite examples of some of the content in the various materials. It will also discuss some of the difficulties in implementing sustainable management initiatives and illustrate this with a case study.

Lists and flyers

Over recent years many organisations have produced flyers of one or two pages listing a number of key points that event organisers might consider. While they have much

Table 9.1 Top ten tips for green events

	Item	Suggestions
1	Green venues	Consider environmental policies and supply chains
2	Save paper	Use electronic media
3	Re-use	Use used agendas for scrap paper, use recycled paper
4	Natural light	Use well-lit rooms, turn off lights/air conditioning after meeting
5	Food	Do not over order, source locally
6	Water	Use tap instead of bottled water
7	Name badges	Collect after event and re-use, use sustainable products
8	Event giveaways	Use recycled products
9	Location	Locate close to delegates, suggest public transport or car share
10	Signage	Use generic signage (non-event specific) that can be re-used

Source: Adapted from In Any Event UK (2007)

in common, they also have different emphases. In Any Event UK Ltd produces a list of ten tips (see Table 9.1).

Another flyer, from oursouthwest.com, is presented as a checklist (see Figure 9.1). It comes from a short guide, *Greener Events*, also available online. Organisers are invited to mark the boxes as they plan their event.

Another top ten list, from BlueGreen Events, based in the United States (which might be guessed from its reference to venues near airports), is shown in Figure 9.2.

The tips are consistent with many others but are notable for their inclusion of the 3 'Rs' – reduction, reuse and recycle, which now have widespread currency.

A final example of this type of advice comes from Cvent, who produce a short guide, *Green Meetings Made Easy*. On their website they produce a brief overview which includes Ten Key Ways to Go Green (Figure 9.3).

Mini-guides and brochures

As well as flyers and lists there are now many practical mini-guides and brochures on sustainable management of events. Most of these are available free online. A relatively early example of these was the Convention Industry Council's (CIC) *Green Meetings Report*, published in 2004. This followed the setting up of a task force 'charged with creating minimum best practices for event organizers and suppliers to use as guidelines for implementing policies of sustainability' (CIC 2004: 3). The guidelines defined a green meeting or event as one that 'incorporates environmental considerations to minimize its negative impact on the environment' (ibid.) and went on to outline the benefits of such meetings as both economic and environmental. In terms of the economic bottom line it noted that 'many of the minimum recommended guidelines in the Green Meetings Report can actually save money. For example, collecting name badge holders for reuse at an event of 1300 attendees can save approximately $975 for the event organizer' (ibid.). In relation to the environmental bottom line it pointed out that

GREENER EVENTS CHECKLIST

for discussions between event managers, venues and suppliers

Title (and date) of event: ....

This two page layout version of the checklist is to enable you to save the checklist document to your computer and retain it electronically as you plan your event.

Please note the checklist is updated periodically; you may wish to re-visit www.oursouthwest.com to ensure you have the latest version.

You can mark the appropriate boxes as you plan the delivery of your event.

Venue choice (and equipment)
❏ Choose a venue that has good access via public transport & for disabled people
❏ Ask potential venues for their in-house environmental policy & priorities
❏ Choose a venue interested in sustainability issues, and tell them that's why you chose them
❏ Venues offering in-house technical equipment & support (e.g. staging, audio-visual) can reduce equipment transportation
❏ Consider hiring rather than purchasing equipment; specify the most efficient available
❏ Consider video conferencing and/or recording the event for wider access via the internet

CO_2 Emissions (including travel)
(see "Reducing Waste" checklist also)
❏ Take measures to reduce CO_2 emissions from delegates travelling to the venue, i.e. provide information about local public transport (with pedestrian routes) and encourage its use. Where appropriate promote car sharing e.g. circulate attendees list in advance
❏ Minimise unnecessary lighting, heating / air-conditioning
❏ Offset the CO_2 emissions arising from your event

Catering & Locally Produced Food
❏ Plan food requirements carefully to avoid unnecessary waste (e.g. use event registration form to obtain information)
❏ Ensure that dietary requirements are catered for and offer vegetarian choices
❏ Plan meals using seasonal local produce wherever possible. Consider organic produce

Figure 9.1 Greener events checklist

Source: Oursouthwest (2005/2010)

❏ If serving fish, use fish from sustainable sources
❏ Wherever possible ensure fruit is provided as an alternative to sweet desserts
❏ Left over food: consider donating to local charity or sending for local composting
❏ Ensure tea/coffee is Fair Trade & provide tap water as an alternative (if you must use bottled water, make sure it is local!)
❏ Minimise use of individually packaged food/drink items (e.g. provide milk / cream in jugs rather than individual plastic cartons)
❏ Use reusable crockery, glassware & cutlery where possible (to reduce waste)

Reducing Waste (& costs)
Pre Event:
❏ Use websites & email lists to promote the event
❏ Use double-sided printing for promotional materials & hand-outs. Use recycled paper where possible without laminating it
❏ Use easily transportable & reusable display materials
❏ Seek naturally lighted meeting & exhibition areas
❏ Format any hand-outs so as to minimise the amount of paper used
❏ Where possible, write material in a re-usable format (general rather than event specific)
❏ Minimise the length of the registration form or use electronic registration where possible & publish the event itinerary on-line
❏ Ask the venue to recycle paper & cardboard waste etc – and to provide suitable recycling bins
❏ If required, make your own note pads from scrap paper

At Event:
❏ If you are providing delegate packs (if in a folder, make it re-usable), give these to delegates when they register on arrival – not beforehand – to avoid duplication
❏ Avoid mass distribution of hand-outs – allow attendees to download copies from the internet
❏ Ensure presenters are aware of electronic presentation facilities & that their presentation will be distributed electronically after the event
❏ Provide re-usable name badges (& remember to collect them at the end of the event!)
❏ Minimise use of accessories that are harmful to the environment (e.g. plastic leaflet wallets)
❏ Feature conference name & date on title slide rather than single use stage set graphics
❏ Minimise use of high wattage stage lighting

Figure 9.1 Continued

❑   Promote energy & water efficiency to participants – e.g. switch off lights when rooms are not in use

❑   Use dry mark eraser boards rather than paper in workshop presentations

❑   Request that any unused items be collected for use at another event

❑   Consider including a sustainability activity/session within the conference

Post Event:

❑   If not issued at the event, send out delegate feedback questionnaire by email

❑   Give any feedback you have to the venue

Figure 9.1 Continued

1. **Put it in writing.** Establish an environmental statement or policy for the meeting, and get buy in for it from the meeting host organization's management. Share the policy with suppliers, delegates and speakers. You'll be amazed at how far they'll go to help you make your event BlueGreen.

2. **Use paperless technology.** Use new media and electronic technology to cut down your paper use. Create a conference web site; offer electronic registration and confirmation; and advertise using the web and/or email.

3. **Meet close.** Reduce distances travelled by speakers and delegates. Choose a host city that's close to as many delegates as possible, and within the city choose a venue and hotel that are close to the airport and within walking distance of each other.

4. **Practice the 3Rs.** Ask your hotel and meeting venue to provide visible and accessible reduction, reuse and recycling services for paper, metal, plastic and glass.

5. **Bulk up.** Have your food and beverage service provider use bulk dispensers for sugar, salt, pepper, cream and other condiments.

6. **Lighten your stay.** Choose a hotel that offers a linen reuse program and bulk dispensers for shampoos and soaps in guest suites.

7. **Eat green.** Include vegetarian meals, and have meals planned using local, seasonal produce.

8. **Close the recycling loop.** Have all printed materials published on recycled paper, using vegetable-based inks, and on both sides of the page.

9. **Save energy.** Coordinate with the meeting venue to ensure that energy lights and air conditioning will be turned off when rooms are not in use.

10. **Spread the word!** Tell delegates, speakers and the media about your success. You'll be surprised – BlueGreen efforts are contagious.

Figure 9.2 Ten easy tips

Source: BlueGreen Meetings (2012)

Ten Key Ways to Go Green

1. Select hotels and suppliers with green policies and practices
2. Host all multi-session meetings at a central location to limit transportation needs
3. Minimize paper with web based invites, online event registration and electronic follow-up
4. Utilize double-sided printing for all collateral and meeting related materials
5. Give recycled materials precedence when making meeting supply purchases
6. Choose a venue with an in-house recycling program and encourage recycling
7. Decrease the usage of paper and plastic by using real china for all food and beverages
8. Select buffet style menus and donate leftovers to eliminate waste
9. Coordinate with venues to use bulk dispensers for all food and beverage
10. Encourage speakers to use electronic means of presentation

While this list may seem daunting, carefully selecting planning techniques automatically eliminates the headache. Technology providers such as Cvent offer event management tools that significantly decrease excessive waste of paper. Online site selection tools help planners find environmentally friendly venues, making the implementation and coordination of green meeting standards a breeze.

Figure 9.3 Ten key ways to go green

Source: Cvent (2012)

using recycled materials, recycling materials used, reusing items and reducing materials used can significantly lessen the environmental impact an event has. For example, if a five-day event serves 2200 people breaks, breakfasts, lunches and receptions using china instead of plastic disposables, it prevents 1,890 lbs. of plastic from going into a landfill. That's nearly one ton! Another example is by not pre-filling water glasses at banquet tables during three days of served lunches for 2200 attendees; 520 gallons of water can be saved. (Ibid.)

The guide, which runs for 14 pages, is divided into two sections which identify best practices for event suppliers and event organisers. The former identifies practical tips under the following headings:

- convention and visitors bureaux/destination management companies
- accommodation (lodging/cruise lines)
- event venues
- transportation providers

- food and beverage providers
- exhibition service providers
- general office procedures and communications.

The latter identifies advice using the following headings:

- destination selection
- accommodation selection
- event venue selection
- transportation selection
- food and beverage
- exhibition production
- communications and marketing
- general office procedures.

Many of the best practices identified are consistent with those already discussed in the previous section, but there are some novel ideas. The strongest best recommended practice for Convention and visitors bureaus/destination management companies is to 'have maps of walking trails and local parks available and be ready to suggest off-site events and tours that involve event attendees in the area's natural environment with minimal impact' (CIC 2004: 5). For organisers they suggest, in respect of transport, that they should 'provide a public transit pass and map in attendees' registration packets' (ibid.: 12) and in respect of communication and marketing they suggest that they 'reduce transportation emissions and support local economies by using local talent and products whenever possible' (ibid.: 14)

Although more contemporary and attractively presented guidelines are now available, many of these best practices remain valid, and – particularly as they are available free online – continue to be of considerable value to students, individual event organisers and those with limited time and budgets.

Three years later, and still in advance of the appearance of BS 8901, Defra published its *Sustainable Events Guide* (2007). It comprises seven pages of advice and is attractively laid out. It incorporates much of the best practice of the time on environmental management systems, environmental reporting and practical sustainable management tips and is consistent with much that was to follow (see Chapters 8 and 10 for discussion of this). It includes issues that go beyond the purely environmental, such as social wellbeing. It was written 'to help governmental organisations plan successful and sustainable events' (Defra 2007: 1). It starts by questioning the need for an event at all: 'Before organising your event, it is worth checking to see if there are other ways you can fulfil your objectives. You might be able to share ideas or engage with stakeholders and customers through another means e.g. video or teleconferencing' (ibid.). It is organised around seven themes (see Figure 9.4).

It points out that sustainable management might do more than save the environment – it might also be profitable: 'Use these options from the very beginning and you could save money: cost-saving, sustainable options such as serving tap water instead of bottled

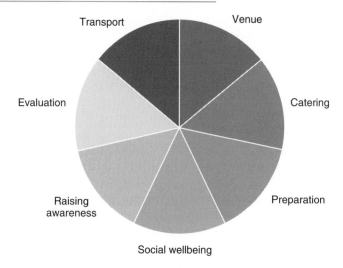

Figure 9.4 Themes for sustainable event management
Source: Defra 2007

water balances out more expensive choices like ordering sustainably-sourced fish; using electronic communication will save on paper, energy use and postage' (Defra 2007: 2). It also advocates monitoring (see Chapter 10 for a full discussion of this topic), noting that:

> Keeping a record of activities undertaken (e.g. energy/water used and waste produced) does not have to be an onerous exercise! It will enable effective evaluation and will allow delegates and other stakeholders to have confidence in your efforts. Measurements allow continuous improvement – by helping you to
>
> a)   minimise your negative sustainability impacts over time; and
> b)   become more ambitious with each event. (Ibid.)

It is very practical. Two extracts will illustrate this. In commenting on getting the best value out of the venue it suggests:

- Make sure all electrical equipment and power supplies are turned off when not in use, encourage delegates to use the stairs instead of the lifts.
- Use heating and air conditioning sparingly – heating above 21 degrees is not required and use natural ventilation where possible rather than air conditioning.
- Arrange stands/displays etc to maximise use of natural light.
- Provide clearly labelled recycling bins for different types of waste and advertise their presence. (Defra 2007: 4)

On the topic of providing literature for delegates it suggests:

- If providing delegate packs, hand them out on arrival to avoid duplication.
- Format hand-outs to minimise amount of paper required e.g. reduce the margins in page setup, print double-sided and print more than one page per sheet (this particularly applies to PowerPoint hand-outs).
- Provide links to downloads of literature rather than providing large hand-outs, or offer documents on CDs or memory sticks. Have a laptop and printer on site so that literature can be printed out on demand if delegates require hard copies. And ensure that all paper waste is collected and recycled. (Ibid.: 6)

It also highlights four top tips:

- Use low emission vehicles such as hybrid cars if possible.
- Have attendees sign up for meals in advance to reduce wastage and ask which sessions they plan to attend e.g. morning, afternoon or both.
- To enable signage to be reused – avoid putting the date on.
- Improving the wellbeing of your delegates, for example by minimising travel, providing plenty of fruit and water and maximising natural daylight, will help them to stay engaged and productive. (Ibid.)

Overall it is a concise, well-thought through piece of basic guidance. It is still of value to individuals who organise events, particularly those who are pressed for time and perhaps are not event professionals but have to run events as part of a broader job remit.

An interesting development in recent years has been the evolution of sustainable event guidelines for specific institutions such as universities. One such is Duke University, which produces a four page online mini-guide (Rhodes, undated). It produces advice under six headings: recycling waste, managing waste, recycling, food service, conserving energy and purchasing environmentally aware materials. The headings are unsurprising, as is most of the content, but as is the case with many such guides, there are individual and innovative ideas. These include the following tips: 'During event announcements, remind participants what and where to recycle . . . If centrepieces [sic] or decoration items are not reusable, consider donating them to a local charity' (Rhodes, undated: 2).

This example of an institution-specific set of guidelines is indicative of the extent to which environmentally friendly practices are now being used, a welcome contrast with 20 years ago.

TASK

Investigate the organisation you work for or study at. Does it have a set of sustainable event guidelines or does it subscribe to an external set?
    If not, why not?
    If not, work with others to write a set.

Event-specific guidelines

A recent development has been the establishment of guidelines for specific events or the endorsement of existing codes for them. These range from global conferences such as the World Summit on Sustainable Development, held in Johannesburg in 2002, to modest-sized academic meetings such as the 9th International Conference on Southern Hemisphere Meteorology and Oceanography, held in Melbourne in 2009. The presentation of these guidelines is variable and relates to the resources available for such events and their international significance. They may be glossy electronic brochures incorporating reportage of the event organisers' efforts to make the event sustainable alongside advice to delegates on how to make their contributions to sustainability. Alternatively they may be lists of practical tips. Two case studies will illustrate opposite ends of the spectrum.

Case study: the World Summit on Sustainable Development in Johannesburg, 2002

Given the theme of the World Summit on Sustainable Development (WSSD), it is not surprising that it wished to make the conference an emblematic example of its content. In its introduction to *Greening the WSSD – Leaving a Greening Legacy: Thousands Are Doing Their Bit. Are You?* the organisers state that 'Greening the WSSD is the first attempt to reduce the environmental impacts of a major UN Summit on the host city. In this case, the people of Johannesburg. By working with them, we aim to protect, conserve and improve the city's environment and natural resources' (UNDP *et al.* 2002: 2). It goes on to ask delegates to play their part: 'As participants, you have an important role to play. You too can make global issues work in Johannesburg. After all, good ideas have currency when they are put into practice. We encourage you to make a positive difference during your stay here' (ibid.). It points out that 'Your actions will make a difference. You have choices in areas such as water, transport and waste. We encourage you to choose "green" options wherever possible' (ibid.: 3)

The brochure is an eclectic publication combining reportage of the efforts already made by the organisers and local community to be sustainable with appeals to delegates to act in a similar way. A typical example of this is its approach to the summit's carbon footprint (see Figure 9.5).

The organisers were smart and on the lookout to raise money. They wished the event to be water neutral and suggested that:

> It is estimated you will consume 200 litres of water per day during the Summit – 90% of which will return to the sewage system. You can purchase a Water Neutral Certificate for R340 ($35). There are 5 000 certificates, the sale of which will raise R1,7 million to fund water and sanitation supply projects in poor communities in South Africa. You have the opportunity to make a difference. (UNDP *et al.* 2002: 11)

Again, taking a left-field approach to the wider context of the event, delegates are invited to

Johannesburg Climate Legacy

The Summit will produce an estimated 500 000 tonnes of carbon dioxide, the gas that contributes towards global warming. Most of it will be generated by you as participants, flying to Johannesburg and while in South Africa. We would like the Summit to be 'carbon neutral'. If you would like to offset the impact you make, you can invest in corporate or individual 'Climate Legacy Certificates'. A R100 or US$10 legacy certificate is worth about one ton of carbon.

Purchase your certificate at www.climatelegacy.org and become part of the Johannesburg Climate Legacy (JCL) project. JCL is led by a South African association of business, government, NGOs, business and academia working in partnership with the World Business Council for Sustainable Development, IIEC, Future Forests, KPMG, the Development Bank of Southern Africa, IUCN and others.

The project aims to raise US$5 million. The funds will be used to support South African projects that permanently reduce carbon emissions. The aim is to invest in enough projects to offset the carbon emissions produced by the Summit.

You can use the website to calculate how much carbon you generate during the Summit. A Summit Carbon Calculator will also show you how emissions from the Summit are being offset.

Your contribution will become part of an investment in energy-saving technology, helping replace 'dirty' fuel sources, and improve quality of life in poor communities in South Africa.

Figure 9.5 The Johannesburg Summit's climate legacy

Source – UNDP *et al.* 2002

Take the tour to Soweto. At the Ecohouse you'll meet Johannes Malahlela and his family, who will share with you the benefits of living in the house. Then you'll visit SOMOHO. At Mandla Mentoor's house you'll receive an overview of the project and you'll see people sculpting from re-cycled paper. Next, it's time to walk up to the Mountain of Hope and be taken on a brief tour. As a finale, you'll take part in an African drumming session. (Ibid.: 21)

TASK

Review the brochure in full online at www.johannesburgsummit.org/html/links/booklet%20greening%20wssd.pdf.

How effective, as an invitation to behave in a particular way, is the combination of reportage of the organisers' contribution to sustainability and exhortation to delegates?

Case study: 9th International Conference on Southern Hemisphere Meteorology and Oceanography held in Melbourne, 2009

A different approach came from the 9th International Conference on Southern Hemisphere Meteorology and Oceanography which was held at the Melbourne Convention Centre in 2009. It was a joint conference of the American Meteorological Society (AMS) and Australian Meteorological and Oceanographic Society (AMOS) organised around the broad theme of 'Extremes: Climate and Water in the Southern Hemisphere'. It was

> committed to being as carbon neutral as possible, and as such will adhere to recently adopted Green Meeting Guidelines from the AMS that demonstrates a commitment to environmental stewardship and in particular to reducing greenhouse gas emissions associated with running the meeting. Therefore, the 9th ICSHMO web site will have opportunities for people to purchase carbon offsets related to their travel to the conference. (Prevention Web 2009)

It produced green guidelines online for organisers and delegates alike based on AMS guidelines, an example of a specific conference promoting and endorsing guidelines produced for its own use (see Figure 9.6). Like the WSSD guidelines, they are a mixture of things that organisers can achieve and those that delegates can achieve. Although relatively brief, they have much in common with guidance discussed in earlier sections and show that modest events can make clear their own guidelines when promoting and delivering an event.

TASK

Design a set of brief guidelines for a sustainable conference to be held at your place of work or study.

Books

Many recently published books now incorporate sections on sustainable management and some of these include practical tips as well as discussions of a more theoretical kind. One book stands out, however, as it is dedicated to the discussion of practical issues: *Sustainable Event Management: A Practical Guide* by Meegan Jones, published in 2010. Its discussion of theory is minimal and it adopts, somewhat uncritically, Brundtland's definition of sustainability in its opening chapter (see Chapter 8). However, what follows is over 300 pages of practical guidance for running events sustainably that result from a career in the event industry, partly in Australia. The book is organised around six themes – marketing and communications, energy and emissions, transport, water, purchasing and resource use and waste. It is full of checklists and case studies and is an

Green Guidelines: Conference Organisation and Planning

As a scientific and professional organisation whose members are keenly aware of environmental issues, the AMS strives to be in the forefront of environmental stewardship. As atmospheric scientists, we are particularly concerned about rapidly increasing atmospheric greenhouse gas concentrations and associated climate change. The following guidelines summarise the AMS's commitment to conducting conferences in a manner that stresses responsible use of natural resources and minimisation of greenhouse gas emissions and other waste and pollutants. These guidelines are provided for coordinators, committees, contractors and all AMS members, and aim to educate and inspire continued mitigation of greenhouse gas emissions both within AMS and the larger society. These guidelines should be continually evaluated as technologies and mitigation options continue to develop.

1. Participants and presenters are advised in advance that the meeting will strive to minimise environmental impacts and greenhouse gas emissions. The registration materials ask that participants respect and assist this process as they feel appropriate.
2. For all goods procured for the meeting, preference is given to the most environmentally appropriate, locally produced alternatives that are available at a reasonable price. We are willing to pay more for environmental responsibility.
3. Printed materials are kept to a minimum, and all printed paper (i.e. conference proceedings, registration papers, photocopying etc.) aims to have certified recycled content, with a high proportion of post-consumer content. Chlorine-bleached paper is avoided.
4. Gifts for participants are minimised, but when provided are minimally packaged and aim to minimise the use of toxic materials.
5. Conference CDs are not offered, rather materials such as abstracts and proceedings are provided online.
6. Attendees are provided with options to offset their transportation-related emissions at the time of registration.
7. Steps are taken to minimise environmental impact of transportation to the conference and during the conference. This includes choosing a locale accessible by public transportation, walking and biking.
8. Attendees and organisers are encouraged to walk, bicycle, carpool or use public transit to attend meetings and events whenever possible. Venues are evaluated in part based on their environmental policies and practices.
9. Attendees who fly are encouraged to travel by direct flights.
10. Steps are taken to promote the sharing of hotel rooms by attendees. Hotels are chosen that have effective and comprehensive environmentally friendly policies and operations.
11 Sponsors and donors are actively sought who reflect positive environmental values and practices.

Figure 9.6 Green guidelines: conference organisation and planning
Source: 9ICSHMO 2009

invaluable source of practical advice to all event organisers. Given its comprehensive nature, this chapter will not pursue similar ground.

A note of caution

Reading this chapter, or Meegan Jones's book, will, it is hoped, enthuse event organisers to manage their future events in a sustainable manner. However, they must be prepared for a degree of disappointment. There may not always be suppliers available who conform to the highest standards of sustainable sourcing. The location of the event may preclude use of the most environmentally friendly venues and carbon efficient transport systems. Business and legal agreements may constrain the choice of suppliers. Financial resources imposed by management or external circumstances may limit the range of options. Time limitations may restrict the potential for adequate research. Recycling waste facilities may not be readily available. Above all, delegates may disappoint you, as the following brief case study illustrates.

Case study: Climate Change: Finding Solutions Conference held at the University of Winchester, 2008

In 2008 European Law Monitor – Europe Direct, the University of Winchester, and the European Commission Representation in London held a successful conference entitled 'Climate Change: Finding Solutions'. The conference was aimed at businesses that wish to develop low carbon products, or organisations that are looking to reduce their carbon footprint but are not sure how to set about this or are unaware of the financial incentives that exist to assist progress towards a low carbon economy. It was a free conference with an interesting range of speakers that included Professor Joy Carter (the university vice-chancellor), Dr Caroline Lucas (now Green Party MP for Brighton), representatives from green industries, the Carbon Trust, Defra and the South East England Development Agency. As might be expected given the nature of the event, the organisers were keen to manage the conference in as sustainable way as possible. Press releases were available electronically and places could be booked over the internet. Catering was provided by the university caterers, who subscribed to fair trade products and local sourcing. The venue was in a renovated building incorporating environmentally friendly facilities and the location, Winchester, was the county town with excellent public transport facilities. To encourage further the use of public transport, a minibus was provided free to pick up delegates from the railway station. It has to be said that the minibus initiative was not a great success – only 4 participants out of 80 made use of the facility and most delegates used cars to reach the conference.

As this case study shows, delegates do not always respond to green initiatives. This may be for a variety of reasons. In the Winchester case these included convenience, trying to combine the conference with other activities and time constraints. There is also still much scepticism about the impacts of fossil fuel use and it takes time and education to change behaviour. As other sections of this book have aimed to show, event organisers should not be in any doubt about the threats to the environment posed by unsustainable management of events. Neither should they be deterred by setbacks when sustainable initiatives fall short of expectation, As the old adage goes, if at first you don't succeed, try, try, try again. Finally, organisers should dwell on positives as well as negatives – the Winchester Conference was successful in many ways as a green event despite the disappointment relating to public transport.

Conclusion

This chapter set out to:

- provide an overview of some of the practical guidance that exists to assist event managers in delivering sustainable events at a range of levels:
    o   lists, tips and flyers
    o   mini-guides
    o   books;
- provide case studies of guidance given for specific events; and
- suggest some of the difficulties that may be encountered in implementing sustainable management practices

It has identified and detailed a number of lists outlining top tips for event organisers, such as those provided by BlueGreen Events and In Any Event UK. It has reviewed a number of mini-guides such as those produced by the CIC and Defra and outlined their approach as well as giving examples of their content. Attention has been drawn to book sources, notably that written by Meegan Jones. Case studies have been provided of how specific conferences have adopted their own sustainable guidelines or adopted those of others. These have shown a mixture of organisers' efforts and exhortations to potential delegates. There has been discussion of some of the difficulties that may be encountered in implementing sustainable practices, particularly with respect to use of transport. Finally, event organisers have been advised not to be deterred by any setbacks.

Further reading

The key text for further reading is *Sustainable Event Management: A Practical Guide* by Meegan Jones.

10 Monitoring the environmental performance of events

Aims

The aims of this chapter are to:

- briefly review the history of environmental performance monitoring;
- explore some of the indicators that can be used for monitoring;
- examine a range of monitoring approaches, including
  - ISO 14031
  - United Nations manuals
  - European Union directives
  - Defra's *Environmental Key Performance Indicators: Reporting Guidelines for UK Business*
  - Global Reporting Initiative (GRI)
  - *Event Organizers Sector Supplement*
  - DIT-ACHIEV model
  - other approaches; and
- review some of the environmental indicators used or advocated within the event industry.

Introduction

It can be argued that legislation relating to the environmental performance of events can only be effective if the performance can be accurately measured and sanctions applied if performance is unsatisfactory. An analogy is the law relating to theft – if theft cannot be detected, details of it given as evidence, and its perpetrators punished, the law will be ineffective. However, many in the event industry would probably be offended by such a comparison. Irresponsible environmental behaviour would not be considered comparable to criminal activity such as theft or assault. And yet, as other sections of this book have illustrated, the consequences of irresponsible environmental behaviour could be very serious indeed for the coherence of human society and possibly its very existence. The reasons we have a legal system relate to our need to organise our affairs in a way that minimises risk to society as a whole. If there were no laws against theft and assault life would become insecure and only the most brutal would prevail. Similarly it could be argued that depletion of resources, environmental pollution and global warming, will lead to a world of scarcity and extreme environmental events in which only the strong and privileged will enjoy a reasonable quality of life.

Many sceptics might argue that this is an apocalyptic view of the future that is unlikely to unfold. However, there are real environmental risks, even if the extent of them is debatable. In such a situation it seems appropriate to employ what is known as the precautionary principle. This involves taking action to prevent the worst type of scenarios unfolding. Just as overfishing requires legislation, quotas and legal action against those who break them, so might profligate environmental behaviour by the event industry. As has been noted elsewhere in this book, a considerable amount of environmental legislation already exists in many countries. In addition to this there are a number of industry standards, notably BS 8901 and ISO 20121, that have been discussed earlier in this book. The number of these standards is unlikely to decline. Given this, it is essential that the event industry is able to document its environmental performance and it is with this issue that the remainder of this chapter will be concerned. The focus of discussion will be on a relatively narrow range of environmental indicators. It is acknowledged that much of the discussion of sustainability indicators encompasses a range of social, economic and other factors that goes well beyond the purely environmental. However, the focus of this book is environmental and while the links with other factors are discussed, the environment remains the key factor.

History of environmental performance monitoring

In June 1972 the United Nations held a conference in Stockholm on the human environment. It produced 26 principles. Principle 2 stated that:

> The natural resources of the earth, including the air, water, land, flora and fauna and especially representative samples of natural ecosystems, must be safeguarded for the benefit of present and future generations through careful planning or management, as appropriate. (UNEP 1972)

Principle 25 stated that:

> States shall ensure that international organizations play a coordinated, efficient and dynamic role for the protection and improvement of the environment. (Ibid.)

Although, as noted elsewhere in this book, environmental concern dated back long before 1972, this conference was probably instrumental in the development of global approaches to environmental protection. It led in 1973 to the establishment of the United Nations Environment Programme (UNEP) and a series of international agreements and protocols. This culminated in the 1992 Rio Summit.

If agreements and protocols were to be justified and, when implemented, maintained, it was essential to have systems that could monitor and manage them. Crucial to these systems were indicators of the state of the environment and mechanisms for these to be reported. These began to be developed in the academic world and subsequently in the establishment of international standards. In the 1980s the ISO 9000 series began this process, which continued after the 1992 Rio Summit in the ISO 14000 series. In 1999 ISO 14031 on Environmental Performance Evaluation was published. Since then a range of documents has emerged that have built on ISO 14031. These have sought to identify particular environmental indicators and mechanisms for reporting these. They include the United Nations *Manual on the Preparation of Indicators for Eco-efficiency*, Defra's *Environmental Key Performance Indicators* (2006), the Global Reporting Initiative and, most recently, the *Event Organizers Sector Supplement* (2012). In addition to these, academic research has developed alternative approaches such as the DIT-ACHIEV Model, which originated as a model for evaluating environmental performance for tourism development but has been adapted by Griffin (2009) to stand as a more specific model for event management. Other authors, notably Meegan Jones, have built on personal experience, and the evolution of the standards mentioned above, to develop individual clusters of indicators around a range of themes such as waste and air pollution.

ISO 14031 Environmental Performance Evaluation

As noted above, the 1990s saw the development of the ISO 14000 series of environmental standards. ISO 14031 provided 'guidance on how an organization can evaluate its environmental performance. The standard also addresses the selection of suitable performance indicators, so that performance can be assessed against criteria set by management. This information can be used as a basis for internal and external reporting on environmental performance' (ISO 2000: 6). The standard sets out a methodology for environmental performance evaluation. As Putnam noted in his seminal paper on the subject, 'Environmental Performance Evaluation (EPE) is based on the adage, "what gets measured, gets managed"' (Putnam 2002: 1). Putnam goes on to describe EPE as 'a relatively new term used to describe a formal process of measuring, analysing, reporting, and communicating an organization's environmental performance against criteria set by its management. The process involves collecting information and measuring how effectively an organization manages its environmental aspects on an ongoing basis' (ibid.).

He outlines the objectives and benefits for such a scheme:

The objectives of implementing an EPE program include:
- Better understanding of an organization's impacts on the environment;
- Providing a basis for benchmarking management, operational and environmental performance;
- Identifying opportunities for improving efficiency of energy and resource usage;
- Determining whether environmental objectives and targets are being met;
- Demonstrating compliance with regulations;
- Determining proper allocation of resources;
- Increasing the awareness of employees; and
- Improving community and customer relations.

Once achieved these objectives are realized as benefits. One of the first steps in applying EPE involves identifying environmental aspects and impacts and establishing performance indicators to monitor. (Ibid.)

The system is effectively a plan, do, check, act model, an example of which can be seen in Figure 10.1. As the title implies, this is a development of the systems theory approach to scientific investigation that characterised subjects such as geography and environmental science during the 1950s and 1960s. In such approaches systems comprise components and processes with flows between the components. Self-regulating systems have feedback loops capable of altering the performance of the system. A good example would be a thermostat in a central heating system – when temperatures rise, the thermostat cuts out the heating; when temperatures fall below a set threshold, the heating is restarted. This maintains the system in a state of dynamic equilibrium, a state that allows change while keeping the system stable.

Adherence to the model allows an organisation to change through the improvement of its environmental performance without compromising its stability.

ISO 14031 outlines a number of indicators that may be used to support environmental management:

- environmental condition indicators (ECI)
- environmental performance indicators (EPI)

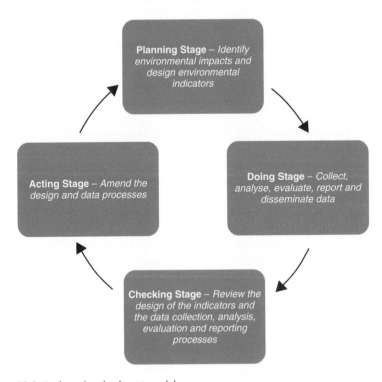

Figure 10.1 A plan, do, check, act model

- management performance indicators (MPI)
- operational performance indicators (OPI).

Some potential examples of OPIs for events are given in Figure 10.2.

As well as identifying the importance of environmental indicators, the standard also emphasises the importance of reporting the findings. Without such reporting the improvement process is liable to being ineffective. Notwithstanding the significance it attached to reporting to stakeholders, ISO 14031 has been criticised for its narrow focus on the environmental and economic at the expense of the social. Such a criticism relates to the more catholic views of sustainability discussed in Chapter 7. Given the negative views held by many businesses about the environment in the latter half of the 20th century, the emphasis on the environment seems appropriate and timely. The emphasis on reporting was also welcome and was taken up by the Defra, GRI and EOSS initiatives discussed below.

TASK

Review the indicators outlined in Figure 10.2. Which ones could be realistically put into practice for a local event such as a fireworks display?

Possible Environmental Condition Indicators (ECIs) for Events

- Carbon dioxide emissions for the event in tonnes
- Total area of soil compaction on the event site and approaches caused by trampling in M 2
- Urine concentrations in ground or surface water on the event site in millilitres per litre
- Weight of surface litter in kilograms
- Number of complaints to police and local authorities about noise levels at the event
- Sulphur dioxide and trioxide emissions in kilograms
- Nitric acid emissions in kilograms
- Death of fauna (insects and mammals) on the event site in kilograms
- Loss of vegetation on the event site in kilograms
- Levels of congestion expressed as total hours spent by stationary vehicles on approach roads
- Number of hospital admissions or doctor visits for respiratory complaints within 24 hours of the event
- Level of graffiti associated with the event in £/$ for cost of restoration.

Figure 10.2 Examples of potential performance indicators and metrics for events

United Nations: the UN Conference on Trade and Development and Environmental Accounting

During the 1990s the United Nations developed a different, but complementary, aspect of business's approach to the environment, that of environmental accounting. The Intergovernmental Working Group of Experts on International Standards of Accounting and Reporting (ISAR) discovered in 1989 that 'there were no national accounting standards specific to environmental information disclosure. Furthermore, some CEOs believed that environmental information was not necessary for a true and fair view of the enterprise's performance or that it was too difficult to obtain' (UNCTAD 2004: iv). In an attempt to counter this attitude the UN published *Accounting and Financial Reporting for Environmental Costs and Liabilities* (1999) and *Integrating Environmental and Financial Performance at the Enterprise Level* (2000). In 2004 it published *A Manual for the Preparers and Users of Eco-efficiency Indicators Version 1.1*. The main objective of the manual was 'to describe the method that enterprises can use to provide information on environmental performance vis-à-vis financial performance in a systematic and consistent manner over periods of time' (UNCTAD 2004: 2).

It linked the method to the concept of eco-efficiency and cited the World Business Council for Sustainable Development (WBCSD) in describing this. 'Eco-efficiency is reached by the delivery of competitively priced goods and services that satisfy human needs and bring quality of life, while progressively reducing ecological impacts and resource intensity.' The WBCSD includes a clear target level: an eco-efficient state is reached when economic activities are at a level 'at least in line with the earth's estimated carrying capacity' (UNCTAD 2004: 1) Achieving eco-efficiency requires the use of eco-indicators:

> An eco-efficiency indicator is the ratio between an environmental and a financial variable. It measures the environmental performance of an enterprise with respect to its financial performance. The problem with constructing eco-efficiency indicators is that there are no agreed rules or standards for recognition, measurement and disclosure of environmental information either within the same industry or across industries. Most importantly, there are no rules for consolidating environmental information for an enterprise or for a group of enterprises so that it can be used together and in line with the enterprise's financial items. (Ibid.: 1)

This is a striking paragraph in two ways. First, it emphasises the link between the environmental and financial. Second, it identifies a lack of standards and rules for such indicators. To address these issues the manual outlines its purpose as follows:

(a) To give guidance on how to define, recognize, measure and disclose environmental and financial information as specified within the traditional accounting and reporting frameworks;

(b) To improve and harmonize the methods used so that enterprises are able to report eco-efficiency indicators in a standardized format so that they are meaningful to decision makers and can be compared across enterprises;

(c) To complement and support existing reporting guidelines (e.g. the UN Sustainability Reporting Guidelines developed by the Global Reporting Initiative (GRI)). (Ibid: 2–3)

The GRI initiative is discussed later in this chapter. The manual goes on to identify guidelines for the measurement of five environmental variables:

(a) Water consumption per net value added;
(b) Global warming contribution per unit of net value added;
(c) Energy requirement per unit of net value added;
(d) Dependency on ozone-depleting substances per unit of net value added;
(e) Waste generated per unit of net value added.

It also notes the linked financial issues:

(a) Value added and net value added, revenue, purchased goods and services;
(b) Consolidation.

Detailed advice is offered on the measurement of the variables. An example is given in Figure 10.3 for calculating ozone-depleting substances.

TASK

For an event known to you, how easy would it be to ascertain the level of waste created?

Using the internet, investigate some of the festival sites to identify the amount of waste they generate. The Glastonbury Festival could be a starting point at www.glastonburyfestivals.co.uk.

Measurement of Waste

296. Waste should be weighed or metered.
297. Waste should be measured in kilograms and metric tons, litres or cubic metres.
298. If an amount of waste is estimated or calculated the range of uncertainty should be recorded.
299. Waste shall be reported according to weight (kg, t) and not volume (litres, m3).

Figure 10.3 UN guidelines on measurement of waste

Source: UNCTAD 2004

The guidelines conclude by linking the environmental measures to the financial measures. In particular, it looks at the treatment of value added and net value added and how environmental costs should be accommodated in these measures.

The UNCTAD manual was an important step in developing standards for environmental auditing and was particularly useful in putting environmental performance measurement into a financial context that challenges environmental sceptics.

TASK

Discuss with colleagues the merits of relating environmental performance to financial performance.

European Union directives

The European Union has also been active in developing requirements for businesses to report on their environmental performance. These include the Accounts Modernisation Directive. Individual governments were responsible for implementing these requirements.

> As a result of UK implementation of the EU Accounts Modernisation Directive (AMD), the Companies Act 2006 requires directors' reports to include a business review unless the business qualifies as a small company. Depending on its relevance to the company's business, the business review should contain certain information about environmental matters and their impacts on its prospects. Large quoted companies also have to report on environmental risks, policies and key performance indicators (KPIs). (ICAEW/Environment Agency 2006: viii)

In addition to Defra's guidance, discussed below, the ICAEW teamed up with the Environment Agency to produce *Environmental Issues and Annual Financial Reporting* in 2006. The guide states that:

> The integration of environmental issues with the financial reporting framework is not only logical from the point of view of stewardship, enabling users of financial statements to make economic decisions regarding environmental impacts on assets, liabilities, income and expenditure; it can also reveal business opportunities, as well as offering a more holistic approach to risk management. This could result in enhanced profitability, reputation and relationships with employees and customers. (Ibid.: 2)

The guidance identifies the implications of various European Union directives relating to the environment and discusses how these may be reported and audited. It summarises all the relevant European law on the environment (see Figure 10.4). It draws attention to the importance of KPIs and some of the difficulties that may be encountered in measuring the financial effects of environmental matters. It notes that there is often a considerable delay between the activity that causes an environmental issue, such as the contamination of a site due to industrial activity, and its identification by the entity or the regulators, and that accounting estimates do not necessarily have an established historical pattern and can exhibit wide ranges of reasonableness because of the number and nature of assumptions underlying the determination of these estimates.

Additionally the guide notes that environmental laws and regulations are evolving and interpretation can be difficult or ambiguous, so that consultation with an adviser may be necessary to assess their impact on the measurement of assets and liabilities. Finally, it points out that liabilities can arise other than as a result of legal or contractual obligations, for example, a voluntary commitment.

The guidance goes on to provide advice to companies and auditors on how to deal with these problems and how to produce reports that are compliant with the legislation. It can be seen, as might be expected, that the EU directives are generally consistent with both global and national standards. Some would argue that the European Union has been a powerful agent in promoting environmental issues within business, one that has sometimes pushed national governments beyond what they would wish to do. The United Kingdom has been generally compliant with the European directives, a compliance that has not always been welcomed in all parts of the business community.

Accounts Modernisation Directive 2003/51/EC

Air Quality Framework Directive 96/62/EC

Drinking Water Directive 98/83/EC

Eco-Management and Audit Scheme Council Regulation 761/01

End-of-Life Vehicles Directive 2000/53/EC

Environmental Assessment of Plans and Programmes Regulations (2005)

Environmental Impact Assessment Directive 85/337/EEC subsequently amended by 97/11/EC

Environmental Liability Directive 2004/35/EC

Habitats Directive 92/43/EEC

Integrated Pollution Prevention and Control Directive 96/61/EC

Landfill Directive 1999/31/EC

Large Combustion Plant Directive 2001/80/EC

Registration, Evaluation, Authorisation and Restriction of Chemicals Regulation EC/2006/1907

Restriction of Hazardous Substances Directive 2002/95/EC

Strategic Environmental Assessment Directive 2001/42/EC

Transparency Directive 2004/109/EC

Waste Electrical and Electronic Equipment Directive 2002/95/EC

Water Framework Directive 2000/60/E

Figure 10.4 EU laws and standards relevant to environmental issues

Source: ICEAW/Environment Agency 2006

TASK

Which of the laws listed above do you think may apply to an event venue?

Defra: *Environmental KPIs: Reporting Guidelines for UK Business*

In 2006 the Department of Environment and Rural Affairs (Defra) in the United Kingdom published its *Environmental Key Performance Indicators: Reporting Guidelines for UK Business*. The purpose of these guidelines was to:

- Give clear guidance to companies on how to report on their environmental performance using environmental Key Performance Indicators (KPIs)
- Define which KPIs are most relevant to which sectors, and
- Set out the business rationale for managing environmental performance using KPIs. (Defra 2006)

In a sensitive comment aimed at avoiding conflict with the business sector the guidelines note that 'These Guidelines place no new mandatory requirements on business and they have been designed, as far as possible, to be compatible with other reporting guidelines and frameworks' (ibid.: 7).

They go on to state that:

> The Guidelines aim to help businesses address their most significant environmental impacts, and report on these impacts in a way that meets the needs of a range of stakeholders. They set out 22 environmental KPIs that are significant to UK businesses and describe which KPIs are most significant to which business sectors. The majority of sectors (c.80 per cent) have five or fewer relevant KPIs and no sector needs to report on more than ten. For most companies greenhouse gas emission is the most significant KPI and the Government expects business to tackle its climate change impacts. (Defra 2006: 7)

This paragraph identifies two particular points: the introduction of the term Key Performance Indicator, and the emphasis on climate change. Defra explains the importance of KPIs:

> Environmental Key Performance Indicators (KPIs) provide businesses with a tool for measurement. They are quantifiable metrics that reflect the environmental performance of a business in the context of achieving its wider goals and objectives. KPIs help businesses to implement strategies by linking various levels of an organisation (business units, departments and individuals) with clearly defined targets and benchmarks. (Ibid.: 12)

Defra goes on to emphasise the importance of managing business in an environmentally responsible way:

> The impact of environmental matters on business performance is increasing and will continue to do so. For example, poor management of energy, natural resources or waste can affect current performance; failure to plan for a future in which environmental factors are likely to be significant may risk the long-term value and future of a business. (Ibid.)

This is a dictum that has often been ignored by business students in the past, including those specialising in event management. To make the message more palatable the guidelines also emphasise the commercial advantages. These are said to include cost savings and productivity gains, improved sales, preferred supplier status, increased attractiveness to the investment community, product and service innovation, employee recruitment and licences to operate. Some of these, however, have an element of threat.

Defra's KPIs are grouped into a number of categories, as shown in Figure 10.5.

TASK

Review an event that you have helped organise. Look at the list of KPIs – which ones would have been applicable to your event? How might you have measured them?

Emissions to air
1. Greenhouse Gases
2. Acid Rain, Eutrophication and Smog Precursors
3. Dust and Particles
4. Ozone Depleting Substances
5. Volatile Organic Compounds
6. Metal emissions to air

Emissions to water
7. Nutrients and Organic Pollutants
8. Metal emissions to water

Emissions to land
9. Pesticides and Fertilisers
10. Metal emissions to land

11. Acids and Organic Pollutants
12. Waste (Landfill, Incinerated and Recycled)
13. Radioactive Waste

Resource use
14. Water Use and Abstraction
15. Natural Gas
16. Oil
17. Metals
18. Coal
19. Minerals
20. Aggregates
21. Forestry
22. Agriculture

Figure 10.5 Defra's key performance indicators

Source: Defra 2006

These guidelines were significant in setting out the government's philosophy in relation to business and the environment. They were also congruent with the wish of the UK government to make the 2012 Olympic Games in London environmentally responsible and the most sustainable ever. More narrowly, they were a further step in the direction of more comprehensive environmental reporting, which, in the case of the event industry, culminated in the publication of the Global Reporting Initiative's *Event Organizers Sector Supplement* in 2012, discussed below.

Global Reporting Initiative (GRI)

GRI was founded in Boston in 1997. Its roots lie within the US non-profit organisations the Coalition for Environmentally Responsible Economies (CERES) and the Tellus Institute. Its mission was to 'to make sustainability reporting standard practice by providing guidance and support to organizations' (GRI 2012a). Its vision is 'a sustainable global economy where organizations manage their economic, environmental, social and governance performance and impacts responsibly and report transparently' (ibid.).

It produced the first version of its guidelines in 2000. The following year, on the advice of the Steering Committee, CERES separated GRI into an independent institution. A second generation of guidelines, known as G2, was unveiled in 2002 at the World Summit on Sustainable Development in Johannesburg. The G3 guidelines were published in 2006. The latest edition, G3.1, was published in March 2011.

The GRI Reporting Framework is designed to provide a reporting mechanism for the evaluation of an organisation's economic, environmental and social performance: 'It is designed for use by organisations of any size, sector, or location. It takes into account the practical considerations faced by a diverse range of organizations – from small enterprises to those with extensive and geographically dispersed operations' (GRI 2011). GRI sees sustainability reporting as 'the practice of measuring, disclosing, and being accountable to internal and external stakeholders for organizational performance towards the goal of sustainable development' (ibid.).

The guidelines 'consist of Principles for defining report content and ensuring the quality of reported information. It also includes Standard Disclosures made up of Performance Indicators and other disclosure items, as well as guidance on specific technical topics in reporting' (GRI 2011: 3)

Of particular interest to this chapter is the section on sustainability performance indicators. It identifies three main categories – economic, environmental and social. Social indicators are sub-divided into labour, human rights, society, and product responsibility. These indicators are divided into core and additional. An example of a core indicator is EN16 – Total direct and indirect greenhouse gas emissions by weight – and an example of an additional indicator is EN10 – Percentage and total volume of water recycled and reused. The other 28 environmental indicators, and two additional ones identified for the event industry, are discussed below in the section on the EOSS.

The guidelines use the Brundtland Report definition of sustainability and conceptually they thus have some of the weaknesses that attach to that definition (see Chapter 7). However, they have been recognised internationally and GRI has become an organisation affiliated to UNEP. A strength of the guidelines is their pragmatic nature, although there are limitations to the pragmatism when it comes to compiling the environmental data. There is no specific advice on how to measure carbon dioxide emissions, for example. It is fortunate for the event industry that the GRI chose it as a target for a supplement. This is discussed below.

Event Organizers Sector Supplement (EOSS)

In early 2012 a set of performance indicators was published that related very directly to the event industry. It is entitled the *Event Organizers Sector Supplement* and is based on the GRI's G3.1 *Sustainability Reporting Guidelines*. It is similarly focused on reporting sustainability, including environmental performance – what should be reported and how it should be presented within each reporting cycle. It is another initiative that has links to London 2012. As the GRI website reports:

> GRI started the development of the Event Organizers Sector Supplement in collaboration with its project funders: the Austrian and Swiss governments who jointly hosted the 2008 European Soccer Championships, The London Organising Committee of the Olympic and Paralympic Games (LOCOG), who will host the London 2012 Olympic Games, and the International Olympic Committee (IOC).

> The Event Organizers Sector Supplement was developed by multi-stakeholder, geographically diverse Working Groups, formed by volunteers from event organizers companies and organizations, investors, labor, non-governmental organizations and research organizations. Members take part in the GRI Working Groups as individuals and do not necessarily represent the view of their organization. (GRI 2012c)

In response to the question as to why the industry needs its own supplement the GRI comments:

> The EOSS provides sustainability performance indicators and disclosures that are important or unique to the event organizers sector. Stakeholder expectations for transparency and requirements for sustainability disclosure are increasing. The Supplement provides event organizers with an opportunity to communicate their sustainability journey, at the same time as generating economic, environmental and social benefits. (GRI 2012b)

The supplement takes a very broad view of sustainability (see Chapter 8) and is not focused on the environment alone. In advocating its use the supplement comments:

> Event organizers that report their management approach and the results of their practices can benefit in a number of ways, including:
> o   Brand enhancement and associated economic benefits
> o   Financial savings resulting from increased monitoring and evaluation of resource use

o   Increased understanding of potential economic, environmental and social impacts

o   Ability to benchmark and compare data

o   Risk avoidance. (GRI 2012b)

This is very much a triple bottom-line approach. Indicators cover economic, environmental and social issues as well as product responsibility, sourcing and legacy. Development of the supplement involved the creation of 13 new indicators. This chapter has a specific focus and fortunately the supplement does cover the environment in some detail. It identifies 32 environmental performance indicators including two new indicators relating to transport. Given the significance of transport in the running of events this is not surprising. As noted elsewhere in this book, transport to an event is an intrinsic part of most events and remains one of the industry's most intractable environmental problems. The indicators are grouped into nine aspects – materials, energy, water, biodiversity, emissions, effluents and waste, products and services, compliance, transport and overall. These are listed in Figure 10.6.

As the supplement notes:

> The Aspects in the Environment Indicator set are structured to reflect the inputs, outputs, and modes of impact an organization has on the environment. Energy, water, and materials represent three standard types of inputs used by most organizations. These inputs result in outputs of environmental significance, which are captured under the Aspects of Emissions, Effluents, and Waste. Biodiversity is also related to the concepts of inputs to the extent that it can be viewed as a natural resource. However, biodiversity is also directly impacted by outputs such as pollutants. The Aspects of Transport and Products and Services represent areas in which an organization can further impact the environment, but often through other parties such as customers or suppliers of logistics services. Compliance and Overall Aspects are specific measures the organization takes to manage environmental performance. (GRI 2012b: 3)

After listing the indicators, the supplement examines each one in further detail. It discusses its relevance, how the information may be compiled, relevant definitions, sources of documentation and references. Throughout it provides specific advice for event organisers. For example, in respect of EN1 (materials used by weight or volume), it comments: 'Event organizers usually do not manufacture products, but instead purchase finished products and services from their supply chains, which are diverse. Refer to the Sourcing Category to disclose the management approach for sourcing materials' (ibid.: 5).

In terms of EN3 (direct energy consumption by primary energy source) it notes:

> In the context of events, direct energy is generated and consumed on-site and not supplied by an external grid. It may include permanent or temporary power generation using purchased energy sources within venues or facilities (e.g., a temporary generator), and fuel combustion in vehicles owned or controlled by the

Environmental Performance Indicators

Aspect: Materials
EN1   Materials used by weight or volume.
EN2   Percentage of materials used that are recycled input materials.

Aspect: Energy
EN3   Direct energy consumption by primary energy source.
EN4   Indirect energy consumption by primary source.
EN5   Energy saved due to conservation and efficiency improvements.
EN6   Initiatives to provide energy-efficient or renewable energy based events, products and services, and reductions in energy requirements as a result of these initiatives.
EN7   Initiatives to reduce indirect energy consumption and reductions achieved.

Aspect: Water
EN8   Total water withdrawal by source, conservation and improvement initiatives and results.
EN9   Water sources significantly affected by withdrawal of water.
EN10   Percentage and total volume of water recycled and reused.

Aspect: Biodiversity
EN11   Location and size of land owned, leased, managed in, or adjacent to, protected areas and areas of high biodiversity value outside protected areas.
EN12   Description of significant impacts of activities, products, and services on biodiversity in protected areas and areas of high biodiversity value outside protected areas.
EN13   Habitats protected or restored.
EN14   Strategies, current actions, and future plans for managing impacts on biodiversity.
EN15   Number of IUCN Red List species and national conservation list species with habitats in areas affected by operations, by level of extinction risk.

Aspect: Emissions, Effluents, and Waste
EN16   Total direct and indirect greenhouse gas emissions by weight.
EN17   Other relevant indirect greenhouse gas emissions by weight.
EN18   Initiatives to reduce greenhouse gas emissions and reductions achieved.
EN19   Emissions of ozone-depleting substances by weight.

Figure 10.6 The EOSS environment performance indicators

Source: GRI 2012b

EN20   NO, SO, and other significant air emissions by type and weight.

EN21   Total water discharge by quality and destination, and improvement initiatives and results.

EN22   Total weight of waste by type and disposal method, and initiatives to manage waste and their results.

EN23   Total number and volume of significant spills.

EN24   Weight of transported, imported, exported, or treated waste deemed hazardous under the terms of the Basel Convention Annex I, II, III, and VIII, and percentage of transported waste shipped internationally.

EN25   Identity, size, protected status, and biodiversity value of water bodies and related habitats significantly affected by the reporting organization's discharges of water and runoff.

Aspect: Products and Services

EN26   Initiatives to mitigate environmental impacts of events, products and services, and extent of impact mitigation.

EN27   Percentage of products sold or provided, and their packaging materials, that are reclaimed by category.

Aspect: Compliance

EN28   Monetary value of significant fines and total number of non-monetary sanctions for noncompliance with environmental laws and regulations.

Aspect: Transport

EN29   Significant environmental and socio-economic impacts of transporting products and other goods and materials used for the organization's operations, and transporting members of the workforce.

EO2   Modes of transport taken by attendees and participants as a percentage of total transportation, and initiatives to encourage the use of sustainable transport options.

EO3   Significant environmental and socioeconomic impacts of transporting attendees and participants to and from the event and initiatives taken to address the impacts.

Aspect: Overall

EN30   Total environmental protection expenditures and investments by type.

Figure 10.6 Continued

event organizer. Event organizers are invited not only to report about primary source, but also about their mix of energy sources, potentially including small-scale renewable energy production (solar, wind, etc.). (GRI 2012b: 7).

While this statement is not strictly true (some events do use electricity supply from an external grid), this focus on advice to event organisers is particularly helpful as it helps clarify responsibility for a group whose knowledge may be limited, even if they are environmentally committed.

While this list is not exhaustive and, in places, the details relating to indicators are lacking (e.g. in the area of biodiversity), this supplement does provide a substantial and significant set of guidelines for measuring the environmental impact of events. It is most welcome in an industry that has not always prioritised the environment in its planning or operations, and in some ways, if extensively implemented, could put the industry in the van of environmentally responsible management. Given London 2012's involvement with this initiative, post-event evaluation may provide some indicator of the supplement's early success and future prospects.

TASK

1. Review the list of environmental indicators given above and, if possible, access the whole document via the internet (www.globalreporting.org/reporting/sector-guidance/event-organizers). Identify any omissions. Identify any indicators that you think are unnecessary or superfluous. Justify your decision.

2. Working on your own, or in a group, reflect on an event you have organised or planned. Produce an environmental report of the event using the list of indicators provided in the EOSS. If you cannot obtain precise data for some indicators, suggest how you might obtain it in future.

3. Hold a group debate to discuss the following motion:

    'Environmental reporting wastes event organisers' time and the event profitability without enhancing the state of the environment.'

The DIT-ACHIEV Model

In the field of tourism, researchers have focused for some time on the development of environmental indicators. In 2004 the World Tourism Organisation suggested ways in which this could be brought about. This was taken up by the Dublin Institute of Technology (DIT) in its ACHIEV project, 'a research project developing a tourism destination management tool designed to guide and encourage a destination towards true sustainability' (Fitzgerald 2010).

'The main aim of this research is to develop and test methodologies/processes for stakeholder engagement and empowerment in local tourism development' (DIT 2011). The model reflects six components of their approach to sustainable development, namely

Administration, Community, Heritage, Infrastructure, Enterprise and Visitor (hence ACHIEV).

While the project and its associated model were focused on local tourism development, they are relevant to this chapter for two reasons. First, the model did develop indicators, and second, in 2009 Griffin adapted the model as a basis for developing indicators for events in his chapter in *Event Management and Sustainability* (Raj and Musgrave 2009). Griffin suggested that the model could be used to:

- establish a baseline for the state of an area in an objective and robust manner;
- develop a methodology for the identification of when carrying capacity is negatively impacted by an event; and
- assist in the development of an overall policy plan for the management of sustainable events. (Griffin 2009: 49)

In advocating the use of indicators, Griffin argued that they can be used to identify:

- stress in an area for example traffic congestion, water shortages, visitor dissatisfaction;
- the impacts of events for example seasonality, habitat damage, local community employment;
- management effort for example funding of pollution and litter clean-ups; and
- the effects of management actions for example changed water quality, number of repeat visitors to subsequent events. (Ibid.: 49)

He also suggests that 'indicators can also provide an early warning when policy change or new action may be needed as well as providing a basis for the long-term planning and review of events' (ibid.). This is consistent with the ISO 14031 and UNCTAD approaches outlined above. He goes on to provide some samples of indicators and assessable parameters. Some of these are environmental, such as air quality and road congestion and pressure; some are social, such as disability access and the importance and state of local culture; and others are economic, such as visitor spend. Like most current manifestations of the concept of sustainability, the model extends well beyond the purely environmental. In conclusion, Griffin calls for 'champions who are willing to adopt the model and test its applicability both spatially and temporally' (ibid.: 55).

However, while the tourism perspective is an interesting and relevant one, the advent of the *Event Organizers Sector Supplement* and its approach, discussed above, is likely to become the focus of event organisers' efforts to measure their environmental performance.

Other approaches

There have been other approaches to developing indicators of environmental performance. One of these is worthy of mention as it represents the outcome of the experience of Meegan Jones, an event organiser who has worked at a number of festivals such as Reading, Leeds and Glastonbury in the United Kingdom and the Peats Ridge Festival in Australia. In 2010 she published *Sustainable Event Management*. In the first chapter, entitled 'Sustainability and events', she identifies four sets of key sustainability

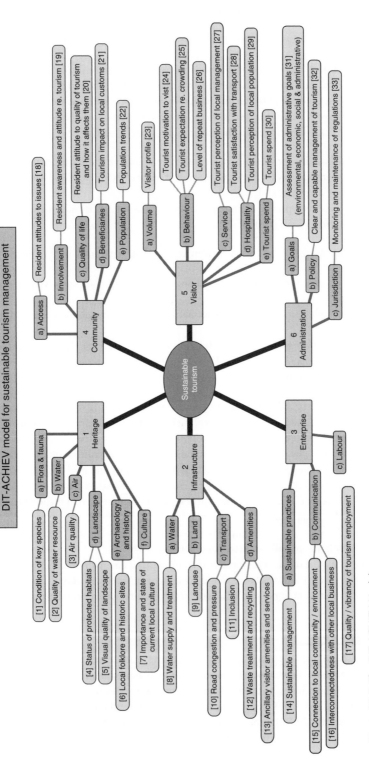

DIT-ACHIEV model for sustainable tourism management

4 Community
- a) Access
  - Resident attitudes to issues [18]
- b) Involvement
  - Resident awareness and attitude re. tourism [19]
  - Resident attitude to quality of tourism and how it affects them [20]
- c) Quality of life
  - Tourism impact on local customs [21]
- d) Beneficiaries
- e) Population
  - Population trends [22]

5 Visitor
- a) Volume
  - Visitor profile [23]
- b) Behaviour
  - Tourist motivation to vist [24]
  - Tourist expectation re. crowding [25]
  - Level of repeat business [26]
- c) Service
  - Tourist perception of local management [27]
  - Tourist satisfaction with transport [28]
- d) Hospitality
  - Tourist perception of local population [29]
- e) Tourist spend
  - Tourist spend [30]

6 Administration
- a) Goals
  - Assessment of administrative goals [31] (environmental, economic, social & administrative)
- b) Policy
  - Clear and capable management of tourism [32]
- c) Jurisdiction
  - Monitoring and maintenance of regulations [33]

Sustainable tourism

1 Heritage
- a) Flora & fauna
  - [1] Condition of key species
- b) Water
  - [2] Quality of water resource
- c) Air
  - [3] Air quality
- d) Landscape
  - [4] Status of protected habitats
  - [5] Visual quality of landscape
- e) Archaeology and history
  - [6] Local folklore and historic sites
- f) Culture
  - [7] Importance and state of current local culture

2 Infrastructure
- a) Water
  - [8] Water supply and treatment
- b) Land
  - [9] Landuse
- c) Transport
  - [10] Road congestion and pressure
  - [11] Inclusion
- d) Amenities
  - [12] Waste treatment and recycling
  - [13] Ancillary visitor amenities and services

3 Enterprise
- a) Sustainable practices
  - [14] Sustainable management
- b) Communication
  - [15] Connection to local community / environment
  - [16] Interconnectedness with other local business
- c) Labour
  - [17] Quality / vibrancy of tourism employment

Figure 10.7 The DIT-ACHIEV Model

Source: DIT 2011

indicators that 'will indicate your event's sustainability performance and, where relevant, a corresponding greenhouse gas emissions factor' (Jones 2010: 22). The first two tables relate to transport. One looks at terrestrial transport – cars, coaches, buses, trains and taxis – and the other at air travel, ferry travel, metro travel and, somewhat curiously, motorbike travel (why is this not in the first table?). The second two tables look at energy, waste and water. She additionally suggests that event organisers might want to record the impacts of freight transport to the event site and hotel accommodation related to the event. Each table suggests specific indicators, most of which originate from the United Kingdom's Department for the Environment and Rural Affairs (Defra). For transport by car, for example, she suggests that event organisers measure the number of cars, occupancy rate, average distance travelled and tons of carbon dioxide emitted. For each category of indicator she cites an emissions factor. These make startling reading, as Table 10.1 demonstrates.

TASK

For the next event which you organise, conduct a mini survey of attendees. Ask them how they travelled and how far they travelled. Use the figures given below to calculate how many kilograms of carbon dioxide were generated by the event. Tips

- To avoid disruption carry out only a sample survey. Ten per cent of attendees would be a useful figure.
- Use an appropriate sampling method such as systematic or stratified sampling.

This is only one of many methods of calculating the carbon footprint resulting from transport to events. You may wish to try other methods and compare the results.

Table 10.1 Carbon dioxide emissions by mode of transport

Mode of transport	Emissions factor in kg CO_2/km
Car	0.2151
Coach	0.6744
Bus	0.6106
Train	0.0602
Taxi	0.2229
Domestic flight	0.1753
Short haul international flight	0.0983
Long haul international flight	0.1106
Metro	0.0650
Ferry	0.1152
Motorbike	0.1067

Source: Jones 2010

Jones's identification of KPIs is consistent with many of the other approaches discussed in this chapter. However, it is distinctive not only because Jones is a practitioner but also because of the way the information is presented in her book – it is accessible and attractively laid out and likely to be more appealing to many who find the austere formats of some of the reports discussed above somewhat forbidding.

Conclusion

The aims of this chapter were to:

- briefly review the history of environmental performance monitoring;
- explore some of the indicators that can be used for monitoring;
- examine a range of monitoring approaches, including
  o ISO 14031
  o United Nations Manuals
  o European Union Directives
  o Defra – Environmental Key Performance Indicators : Reporting Guidelines for UK Business
  o Global Reporting Initiative
  o Event Organisers Sector Supplement
  o DIT-ACHIEV model
  o other approaches; and
- review some of the environmental indictors used or advocated within the event industry.

It has shown that the history of environmental performance management is a long and complex one, containing at least two strands. On the one hand there was a drive towards the measurement of the environmental impacts of business, and on the other was a concern to make companies account financially for their environmental impacts. The growing concern over sustainability, in its many guises, saw these strands merge through a series of initiatives that included global regional and national approaches. These initiatives have seen the development of KPIs, environmental auditing and a range of reporting mechanisms.

Many of the early initiatives were not focused on the event industry as such. In recent times, however, perhaps abetted by the preparations for London 2012, there has been a greater focus on events, culminating in the publication in 2012 of the *Event Organizers Sector Supplement*. It could be argued that the event industry has gone from being a laggard in monitoring its environmental impacts to one that is now in the van of such developments.

Further reading

There is no single reference that covers all the material in this chapter. However, the *Event Organizers Sector Supplement* published in 2012 gives a clear account of a range of performance indicators that can be used by event organisers with advice on how to use them.

11 Future issues

Aims

The aims of this chapter are to:

- review briefly the progress of environmental awareness in the event industry and event academe over the last 20 years;
- reflect on the content of previous chapters; and
- evaluate some of the issues that may affect developments in good environmental practice over the next 20 years.

Introduction

The last 20 years have seen much change in the relationship of the event industry and event academe with the environment. The event industry has seen a host of environmental initiatives and developments, ranging from the use of environmental management systems and environmental performance monitoring, through guidelines on green events such as that produced by Defra, to the development of BS 8901 and the *Event Organizers Sector Supplement* and the publication of Meegan Jones's book on sustainable environmental management.

These initiatives are reflected notably in the performance of the Olympic movement, which has moved from an era of environmental protests such as those that characterised the Albertville Games to the enshrining of sustainability into the London 2012 Olympics and its association with the new ISO 20120 standard. The academic world has seen a growing volume of research ranging from papers on the carbon footprint of sports events to evaluating overall event environmental performance. The publication of Raj and Musgrave's *Event Management and Sustainability* in 2009 in some ways symbolised this progress. While this record of improving environmental awareness is important, there remain a number of issues that will have an impact on the way in which environmental issues are addressed in the future. These include environmental scepticism, global recession, the education system, the intrinsic nature of events, the political system and the incentive framework for sustainable management.

Environmental scepticism

Many environmental scientists are concerned that environmental scepticism gains publicity disproportionate to the number of scientists who espouse such views. Often this publicity is funded – somewhat discreetly – by organisations, such as energy companies, which have an interest in maintaining the status quo. The publicity can have widespread influence. A particular problem arises with public broadcasters, who have a responsibility to provide balanced coverage of news items. Thus, if one view is put forward, any contrary view must also be presented, even if it is a minority view. An example of this is the debate over global warming where the majority of climate scientists and the Inter-Governmental Panel on Climate Change, which is the UN body charged with investigating the issue, believe that anthropological contributions are almost certainly adding to atmospheric warming. However, other views, such as those put forward by Nigel Lawson, who states that 'the second big lie is that global warming is actually taking place' (Lawson 2009: 108), still gain much media coverage. Even he acknowledges that surveys show that 66 per cent of climate scientists agree or strongly agree with the contention that climate change is mostly the result of anthropogenic causes while stating that this is 'nothing approaching a consensus' (ibid.). This is pedantry – consensus can mean unanimity (how often is this achieved?) but also can mean a trend of opinion: two-thirds represents a very clear trend of opinion, one which far exceeds what most governments get elected on in the United Kingdom. Readers wishing to pursue the theme of environmental scepticism are referred to the works of Blomborg (Blomborg 1998 and 2009) and Lawson (Lawson 2009) among others.

Global recession

At the time of writing much of the western world continues to be locked into a global recession. This has a number of impacts on attitudes to environmental issues. First, the political climate becomes focused on growth to the detriment of other concerns. Second, there is a shortage of investment capital, and environmentally friendly innovation can be more expensive than the alternatives. While sustainable management of resources can often yield long-term savings, these do not always accrue in the short term. In a financial system that appears to reward early returns on investment, long-term approaches can be difficult to implement. This is exemplified by government policy – the Conservative–Liberal Democrat coalition government in Britain, elected in 2010, quickly appeared to soften its approach to coal-fired power stations and their environmental impacts (Stratton 2010) and this may set an example for others to follow (see below for further discussion of political issues). Third, perceptions and attitudes change when budgets are tight. As Lawson states, 'the recessionary blizzard that struck the world economy . . . has led most politicians to attach more importance to saving the world from economic disaster now than saving the planet from becoming warmer in a century or so's time' (Lawson 2009: 116). This gives more credence to the views of sceptics that have already been discussed. There is also a temptation to cut corners and revert to old ways. Momentum on progress in environmental management that has built up over many years can be quickly dissipated; it may take a long time to recover.

Education

The educational framework will affect environmental progress in the event industry in at least two ways. First, it will influence the environmental attitudes and values of all young people in general through the continuing teaching of such issues in the curriculum. Knowledge and understanding of the mechanisms that drive the planetary systems should lead to more responsible behaviour in respect of resource use and disposal. Second, the introduction of modules concerned with the environment and sustainability into event management courses should produce graduates capable of becoming environmentally responsible event practitioners. Some courses, such as that at the University of Winchester in the mid-2000s, embedded environmental modules into each of the three years of the undergraduate event management course, though this was later, to some extent, diluted by the use of some generic sustainability modules rather than ones specifically written for event students. The University of Winchester course, which was validated in 2008, specifically aligned itself with the principles of responsible management education (PRME). These are:

Principle 1 – **Purpose**: We will develop the capabilities of students to be future generators of sustainable value for business and society at large and to work for an inclusive and sustainable global economy.

Principle 2 – **Values**: We will incorporate into our academic activities and curricula the values of global social responsibility as portrayed in international initiatives such as the United Nations Global Compact.

Principle 3 – **Method**: We will create educational frameworks, materials, processes and environments that enable effective learning experiences for responsible leadership.

Principle 4 – **Research**: We will engage in conceptual and empirical research that advances our understanding about the role, dynamics, and impact of corporations in the creation of sustainable social, environmental and economic value.

Principle 5 – **Partnership**: We will interact with managers of business corporations to extend our knowledge of their challenges in meeting social and environmental responsibilities and to explore jointly effective approaches to meeting these challenges.

Principle 6 – **Dialogue**: We will facilitate and support dialog and debate among educators, students, business, government, consumers, media, civil society organisations and other interested groups and stakeholders on critical issues related to global social responsibility and sustainability. (PRME 2012)

Most undergraduate event management courses now incorporate at least one sustainability module or cover the subject across a range of modules. Leeds Metro now offers an MA in Responsible Events, which is effectively about sustainable event management, and other higher education establishments such as University College, Falmouth, are running new event courses at postgraduate level (in this case on music events) focused on sustainable management. However, the reluctance of some event management undergraduates to study, let alone believe in, environmental issues and sustainability has been the experience of this author – it has been cited elsewhere in this book and has implications for the immediate future. Some event lecturers also remain environmental sceptics and influence their students accordingly. Nonetheless, it is possible to be optimistic about the increasing amount of embedding of the issues in degree curricula even if this is sometimes, as indicated above, generic rather than being centred on industry-specific issues and practices. There remains, however, plenty of scope for further curriculum development supported by an expansion of research into events and the environment.

The intrinsic nature of events

Traditionally, events have been designed to bring people together. It is the travel involved in modern events that contributes substantially to their negative environmental impacts. The sheer scale of the problem is a deterrent to many. Recently, one major event company introduced a progressive sustainability policy. Energy used in the events and travel to them was excluded, however, as the apparent intractability of the problem could have undermined the implementation of more restricted policies. Transport will have to tackled, however. Virtual experience of events is one way forward. Many guidelines, such as Defra's, already advocate the use of electronic replacements for events. Some progress has been made on e-conferencing, particularly in the professions. However, its popularity remains limited. Speaking into webcams and watching large screens makes some uncomfortable, though a younger generation brought up with computer technology and social websites may find the experience less threatening. Given that body language is a large component of communication, any limitation on this – even with imagery – means the potential for misinterpreting people's intentions and meanings is greater.

For many, getting out of the office to a meeting is one of the perks of the job. Academe, for example, has always prioritised the importance of holding and attending conferences as a means of promoting and disseminating research. Such conferences have not only facilitated professional networking but provided opportunities for travel at the employer's expense. Many are the professors who have added a week's leave to a foreign conference or perhaps taken a partner with them (admittedly at their own expense) to enrich the experience. The same is true of many meetings held in the private sector and a massive conferencing industry has developed to service this apparent need to travel.

A massive change in the way business is structured and consequently behaves is necessary if the carbon footprint of commerce is to be permanently reduced in the absence of carbon-free travel. Taking away perks, with implications for terms and conditions of work, is never easy. Historical evidence shows that this can achieved as recession usually results in a downturn in air travel in particular. However, when prosperity returns, traditional practices often reassert themselves.

The problem with non-conference events is even greater. Two of the prime characteristics of events are the opportunity to socialise and to share the intangible nature of the event experience itself. Watching a cup final on television, even on a big screen, does not have the excitement of being in a large crowd cheering on its teams. This is equally true of festivals where the atmosphere of live performance is unique and thus a principal motivator for being involved in such an event. Again, even with the stereo at full volume (with a possible outcome of antagonising neighbours), broadcasts of such events cannot capture the experience of being there. Yet these events can generate very significant environmental consequences, as earlier chapters in the book have shown. The virtual world so familiar to the young does not offer the same opportunities for substitution as it does for conferencing. For these events the experience is intrinsic to its purpose, unlike a meeting which can be said to be instrumental in promoting research or disseminating good practice. Coming together for festivals appears to have been part of human nature since prehistoric times – consider Stonehenge as an early religious venue – and is an important aspect of our ludic culture, and perhaps our spiritual development. Although despotic governments may rein in such activities, except for their own ends, it is difficult to foresee such limitations in democratic, capitalist societies.

The environmental imperative for such events lies therefore in sustainable transport management – practices such as greater use of public transport, more careful venue selection, car sharing and other such initiatives. While such practice can be equally applied to conferences, these are not all necessary to achieve their instrumental ends and society perhaps needs to ask itself which events can be substituted and which cannot. This is not an easy task in so-called free societies but in an age of environmental degradation it is, perhaps, a necessary one. Future technology may resolve some of these issues but in the meantime this is an important area for further research and innovation.

The political process

Green issues often feature in political party manifestos but the track record of parties in power is variable. In the US, in particular, Republican presidencies have been perceived as less progressive environmentally than Democratic ones, as the Bush presidencies would indicate. However, the Democrats also equivocate, as the record on Kyoto and Copenhagen demonstrates. The coalition government in the United Kingdom has often emphasised its green credentials yet it has also vacillated over a number of issues such as wind power. It has reduced tariffs for those who install solar energy and feed surpluses to the national grid, and apparently relaxed its attitude to coal-fired power stations. It is in the process of changing the planning framework, which some argue will allow more development on greenfield sites.

Planning permission for events is an interesting issue in itself. While such permission is needed for venue construction in most countries, it is often not needed to hold particular events, particularly those of modest size. Mega-events such as the Olympics and festivals such as Glastonbury may be scrutinised closely for their environmental impact, but local events are often not. They may require permissions but they do not usually (see Chapter 4 for exceptions) have to account for their environmental impacts.

Such events as school fetes and village bring-and-buy sales may be small scale but their aggregate environmental impact is considerable. It may seem fanciful but it could be argued that in future all organised events involving travel to a venue (whether commercial, public sector or voluntary) should require environmental approval before they can proceed. Using some of the checklists and pro formas discussed in earlier chapters can make such a task less onerous than it may first appear but in many countries, including the UK, such a process is likely to be seen as bureaucratic and a further piece of red tape for business. For these reasons, such an approach appears unlikely to be taken up at present, except at the larger scale.

Sustainable management incentives

Human behaviour is known to respond to incentives, particularly economic ones. Given this, thought might be given to creating a reward system for sustainable event management. This could apply to rewards for internal initiatives in organisations as well as external rewards through the taxation and grant awarding systems. Successful sustainable management could become a criterion for appraisal and performance-related pay – indicators such as fuel and water use, attendees travelling by public transport and recycling rates could provide the data for such reward schemes.

Externally, green initiatives for industry and individuals have often been short-term and isolated rather than holistic. They do exist, however, such as those for energy-efficient investment for UK entrepreneurs. In the 2010/11 tax year for example there were '100% first year allowances for investments in certain energy saving technologies and new, unused cars that have CO_2 emissions of 110g/km or less' (HMRC 2010: 3). It is unclear how well-known these are, particularly for sole traders, which many event entrepreneurs are. They also relate to capital rather than revenue items. A more integrated and comprehensive approach might improve sustainable performance, and could be linked to the environmental reporting mechanisms discussed in Chapter 10. Reductions in key indicators such as energy or water use could be rewarded with tax breaks. Brief environmental reports could become part of tax returns just as income and expenditure need to be reported. HMRC could safeguard itself against fraud with the possibility of spot checks, just as they can other information. Although this would be bureaucratic, businesses would be willing to provide the information if tax burdens are relieved. Of course, given the current recession and cutbacks in public expenditure, such radical innovation is unlikely, even if it could be shown to have long-term financial benefits.

Conclusion

The aims of this chapter were to:

- review briefly the progress of environmental awareness in the event industry and event academe over the last 20 years;
- reflect on the content of previous chapters; and
- evaluate some of the issues that may affect developments in good environmental practice over the next 20 years.

It has commented positively on the positive progress in environmental management within the event industry and the educational infrastructure that lies behind it. It has considered many of the observations made elsewhere in the book in the context of a number of current issues that may affect the development of environmental attitudes and practices within the industry in the future. It has evaluated, in particular, the roles of environmental scepticism (particularly in the media), the economic recession, education, the intrinsic nature of events (particularly the problem of transport), political structures and processes, and the possibility of providing more incentives to support sustainable management. Many of these pose threats, such as the recession and environmental scepticism. Others provide opportunities, such as developments in education and changes in political processes and frameworks for incentives. Some, notably the intrinsic nature of events, provide challenges for event practitioners and the wider technological society to overcome in the pursuit of a more sustainable and environmentally responsible future.

As this chapter indicates, there has been progress over the past 20 years in the complex relationship between the event industry and the environment but there remains much to be achieved at all levels of the industry. Environmental problems, including the legacy created by past practices, will not go away. Even if there is debate over climate change, there is less discussion of the degradation of our oceans, air pollution such as ozone depletion and acid rain, and despoliation of soil, vegetation and landscape. Resource depletion is likely to become more problematic as the global population continues to grow. Already it is impossible to supply the resources needed to bring all the world's population up to the material standards of the United States. There is cause for optimism in the developments of the past 20 years but complacency and other threats could easily compromise this. It is hoped that this volume will help students of, and participants in, a youthful and dynamic industry to appreciate the wider context of the complex relationship between events and the environment and remain, or become, ambassadors for responsible environmental behaviour in the future. Such is the underlying aim of the book.

Further reading

There is now a growing literature about events and how they relate to the environment. However, much of this is dispersed, as the references cited in previous chapters indicate. Two substantive volumes exist which address substantial sections of the issues raised in this book, particularly those covered in the latter part on sustainability: Raj and Musgrave's *Event Management and Sustainability* and Meegan Jones's *Sustainable Event Management*.

Bibliography

9ICSHMO (2009) Green Guidelines: Conference Organisation and Planning, www.bom.gov.au/events/9icshmo/green_guidelines.shtml, accessed 9 August 2012.

Allen, J., Harris, R., Jago, L.K. and Veal, A.J. (eds) (2000) *Events Beyond 2000: Setting the Agenda*, Proceedings of Conference on Event Evaluation, Research and Education Sydney 2000, Sydney: Australian Centre for Event Management.

Aronson, L. (2000) *The Development of Sustainable Tourism*, London: Continuum.

Baim, D. (2009) Olympic-driven urban development, in G. Poynter and I. MacRury, pp. 73–86. *Olympic Cities: 2012 and the Remaking of London*, Farnham: Ashgate.

Barker, M., Page, S.J. and Meyer, D. (2002) Evaluating the impact of the 2000 America's Cup on Auckland, New Zealand, *Event Management*, 7: 79–92.

Barrow, C.J. (2006) *Environmental Management for Sustainable Development*, Abingdon: Routledge.

BBC News (2003a) Fans go wild for Robbie, http://news.bbc.co.uk/1/hi/entertainment/3116113.stm, accessed 7 August 2012.

BBC News (2003b) Robbie gigs 'a success', http://news.bbc.co.uk/1/hi/england/beds/bucks/herts/3123269.stm, accessed 7 August 2012.

BBC News (2009) IPL confirms South Africa switch, http://news.bbc.co.uk/sport1/hi/cricket/7958664.stm, accessed 6 October 2011.

BBC News (2012) Beijing to release more air pollution data, www.bbc.co.uk/news/world-asia-china-16438315, accessed 7 January 2012.

Belshaw, C. (2001) *Environmental Philosophy: Reason, Nature and Human Concern*, Chesham: Acumen.

Bigwood, G. and Leuhrs, M. (2010) *The Copenhagen Sustainable Meetings Protocol*, Copenhagen: CSMC.

Blomborg, B. (1998) *The Sceptical Environmentalist*, Cambridge: Cambridge University Press.

Blomborg, B. (2009) *Global Crises, Global Solutions*, Cambridge: Cambridge University Press.

BlueGreen Meetings (2012) *10 Easy Tips*, www.bluegreenmeetings.org/HostsAndPlanners/10EasyTips.htm, accessed 6 August 2012.

Blunden, J. (1977) *Section 1: Man and the Environment; Units 4–6, Parts 1 and 2*, Milton Keynes: Open University Press.

Boers, H. and Bosch, M. (1994) *The Earth as a Holiday Resort: An Introduction to Tourism and the Environment*, Utrecht: SME.

Bowdin, G., Allen, J., O'Toole, W., Harris, R. and McDonnell, I. (2001) *Events Management* (3rd edn pub. 2010), Oxford: Butterworth-Heinemann.

Brooks, S., Magnin, A. and O'Halloran, D. (2007) *The Sustainable Music Festival: A Strategic Guide*, www.gmicglobal.org/resource/collection/47C838A0-D177-4D6A-84FA-0EC254420949/The_Sustainable_Music_Festival_Guide.pdf, accessed 6 August 2012.

Brunet, F. (2009) The economy of the Barcelona Olympic games, in G. Poynter and I. MacRury, *Olympic Cities: 2012 and the Remaking of London*, Farnham: Ashgate, pp. 97–120.

BSI (2007) *BS 8901:2007 Specification for a Sustainable Event Management System with Guidance for Use*, London: BSI, www.bsigroup.com/upload/Standards%20&%20 Publications/Environment/case_studies/organise.pdf, accessed 30 January 2012.

BSI (2012a) Lord's Cricket Ground: Sustainability Events Management Case Study, www.bsigroup.com/upload/Standards%20&%20Publications/Environment/case_st udies/lords.pdf, accessed 9 August 2012.

BSI (2012b) Positive Impact Case Study: Understanding BS 8901 Educational Workshop, www.organisethis.co.uk/assets/uploads/page_content/image/13837 B65-90F1-16EF-E2AA14FB7CC75257.pdf, accessed 30 January 2012.

BSI (2012c) BS 8901 Sustainability ManagementSystems for Events, /www.bsigroup. co.uk/en/Assessment-and-Certification-services/Management-systems/Standards-and-Schemes/BS-8901, accessed 8 August 2012.

Carson, R. (1962) *Silent Spring*, Harmondsworth: Penguin.

Carter, N. (2007) *The Politics of the Environment: Ideas, Activism, Policy*, 2nd edition, Cambridge: Cambridge University Press.

Case, R. (1997) Managing the Wessex coast: Christchurch Bay, *Geography Review*, 10(3): 20–25.

Case, R. (2007) *A Tale of Two Stadia: Greenfield v Brownfield Sites for Sports Stadia*, Geo Factsheet No. 149, Shrewsbury.

Case, R. (2011) Event impacts and environmental sustainability, in Page and Connell 2011, pp. 362–84.

Cater, E. and Lowman, G. (eds) (1994) *Ecotourism: A Sustainable Option*, Chichester: Wiley.

Centre on Housing Rights and Evictions (2007) *Fair Play for Housing Rights: Mega-events, Olympic Games and Housing Rights*, Geneva: COHRE, http://iocc.ca/documents/ FairPlayForHousingRights-COHRE.pdf, accessed 6 August 2012.

Chaffey, J. (1996) *Managing Wilderness Regions,* London: Hodder and Stoughton.

Chernushenko, D. (1994) *Greening Our Games: Running Sports Events and Facilities that Won't Cost the Earth*, Ottawa: Centurion.

CIC (2004) *Green Meetings Report*, Alexandria: Convention Industry Council, www. conventionindustry.org/Files/CIC_Green_Meetings_Report.pdf, accessed 6 August 2012.

CIOSS (2005) Eutrophication: too much fertiliser, http://cioss.coas.oregonstate. edu/CIOSS/Documents/Outreach/Aug05/Eutrophication.pdf, accessed 6 August 2012.

Cole, D.N. (1993) Minimizing conflict between recreation and nature conservation, in D.S. Smith and P.C. Hellmund (eds) *Ecology of Greenways: Design and Function of Linear Conservation Areas*, Minneapolis: University of Minnesota Press, pp. 105–22.

Collins, A., Flynn, A., Munday, M. and Roberts, A. (2007) Assessing the environmental consequences of major sporting events: the 2003/04 FA Cup Final, *Urban Studies*, 44(3): 457–76.

Craig, I. (2004) Pop show warning call to curb road chaos, http://menmedia. co.uk/manchestereveningnews/news/s/138/138270_pop_show_warning_call_to_ curb_road_chaos.html, accessed 6 August 2012.

Croall, J. (1995) *Preserve or Destroy: Tourism and the Environment*, London: Calouste Gulbenkian Foundation.

Cumming, P. and Pelham, F. (2011), *Making Events More Sustainable: A Guide to BS8901*, London: BSI.

Cvent (2012) Green Meetings Made Easy, www.cvent.com/en/resources/green-meetings-made-easy.shtml, accessed 6 August 2012.

Cybriwsky, R. (1998) *Tokyo*, New York: Wiley.

daCosta, L.P. (2001) International trends in sport and environment – a 2001 overview, in daCosta, L.P. (ed.) *Book of Abstracts: Sixth Annual Congress of the European College of Sports Science*, Cologne: ECSS.

Dartmoor NPA (2012) Erosion on public rights of way and on public open space within Dartmoor National Park, www.dartmoor-npa.gov.uk/learningabout/lab-printableresources/lab-factsheetshome/lab-erosion, accessed 7 August 2012.

Defra (2006) *Environmental Key Performance Indicators: Reporting Guidelines for UK Business*, London: HMSO.

Defra (2007) *Sustainable Events Guide*, http://archive.defra.gov.uk/sustainable/ government/advice/documents/SustainableEventsGuide.pdf, accessed 8 March 2012.

Defra (2012) *UK Climate Projections*, http://ukclimateprojections.defra.gov.uk/, accessed 24 August 2012.

Dernbach, J. and Feldman, I. (2003) After Johannesburg: sustainable development begins at home, *Environmental Quality Management*, 12(3), 87–90.

Digby, B. (2008) *Fieldwork: Background to the 2012 Site,* London: RGS–IBG.

DIT (2011) ACHIEVing Sustainable Tourism Management: Putting the DIT-ACHIEV Model into Practice, http://dit.ie/dit-achiev/dit-achievmodel, accessed 7 February 2012.

Doyle, C. (2010) *Weather Forecasts for the 2010 Winter Olympic Games: Pre-Games Challenges and User Requirements in an el Niño Season,* 14th Conference on Mountain Meteorology, https://ams.confex.com/ams/14MountMet/techprogram/paper_170 046.htm, accessed 6 August 2012.

Durham County Council (2010) *Resources Group Service Improvement Plan 2010–2013*, Durham: Durham County Council.

Dzioubinski, O. and Chipman, R. (1999) *Trends in Consumption and Production: Selected Minerals*, DESA Discussion Paper No. 5, New York: United Nations.

ECB (2012) 2012 Major Match Tickets Refund Scheme, www.ecb.co.uk/tickets/2012-major-match-tickets-refund-scheme,2662,BP.html, accessed 7 August 2012.

ECO-3 (2012) Protecting Our Soil, Water & Air, www.eco-3.com/SeattleWaRFP.htm, accessed 7 August 2012.

Environment Agency (2012a) Directives, www.environment-agency.gov.uk/business/regulation/31865.aspx, accessed 20 January 2012.

Environment Agency (2012b) English environmental legislation, www.environment-agency.gov.uk/netregs/legislation/current/63594.aspx, accessed 19 January 2012.

Environment Agency (2012c) Mobile hospitality, leisure and tourism businesses, www.environment-agency.gov.uk/netregs/businesses/62693.aspx, accessed 19 January 2012.

Environment Agency (2012d) Vehicle emissions from hospitality, leisure and tourism, www.environment-agency.gov.uk/netregs/businesses/62655.aspx, accessed 19 January 2012.

Epstein, M.J. (2008) *Making Sustainability Work*, Sheffield: Greenleaf Publishing.

Festival Gardens Liverpool (2012) The site: history, www.festivalgardens.com/the-site/history, accessed 4 January 2012.

Fitzgerald, J. (2010) *ACHIEVing Sustainable Tourism Management: Putting the DIT-ACHIEV Model into Practice*, http://etfi.live.addsite.nl/site/download/0Gl0YT7cvxan?type=open, accessed 7 February 2012.

Foreign and Commonwealth Office (1999) *Antarctica* (Schools Pack), London: FCO.

Frey, M., Iraldo, F. and Melis, M. (2008) *The Impact of Wide-Scale Sport Events on Local Development: An Assessment of the XXth Torino Olympics through the Sustainability Report*, Working Paper No. 10, Milan: Istituto di Economia e Politica dell'Energia e dell'Ambiente.

Getz, D. (2000) Developing a research agenda for the event management field, in J. Allen, R. Harris, L.K. Jago and A.J. Veal (eds) *Proceedings of Conference on Event Evaluation, Research and Education*, Sydney: Australia Centre for Event Management, School of Leisure, Sport and Tourism, University of Technology, Sydney, pp. 9–20.

Getz, D. (2007) *Event Studies*, Oxford: Butterworth-Heinemann.

Getz, D. and Anderson, T.D. (2008) Sustainable festivals: on becoming an institution, *Event Management*, 12: 1–17.

Goldblatt, J.J. (2000) A future for event management: the analysis of major trends impacting the profession, in J. Allen, R. Harris, L.K. Jago and A.J. Veal (eds) *Proceedings of Conference on Event Evaluation, Research and Education*, Sydney: Australia Centre for Event Management, School of Leisure, Sport and Tourism, University of Technology, Sydney, pp. 1–8.

Goldenberg, S. (2010) Winter Olympics: they're bringing in snow by the truckload, www.guardian.co.uk/sport/audio/2010/feb/11/winter-olympics-vancouver-no-snow, accessed 6 August 2012.

Goldsmith, E. and Allen, R. (1972) *Blueprint for Survival*, Harmondsworth: Penguin.

Greenpeace (2008) *Beijing Summary*, Greenpeace.

Greenpeace Australia (2000) *Greenpeace Olympic Environmental Guidelines: A Guide to Sustainable Events*, Sydney: Greenpeace Australia.

GRI (2011) *Sustainability Reporting Guidelines*, Amsterdam: GRI.

GRI (2012a) About GRI, www.globalreporting.org/information/about-gri/Pages/default.aspx, accessed 9 August 2012.

GRI (2012b) *Event Organisers Sector Supplement*, Amsterdam: GRI, www.global reporting.org/resourcelibrary/EOSS-G3.1-SummaryGuide-QRS.pdf, accessed 9 August 2012.

GRI (2012c) Who developed this guidance and how?, www.globalreporting.org/reporting/sector-guidance/event-organizers/Pages/development-of-the-event-organizers-supplement.aspx, accessed 9 August 2012.

Griffin, K.A. (2009) Indicators and tools for sustainable event management, in R. Raj and J. Musgrave (eds) *Event Management and Sustainability*, Wellingford: CABI, pp. 43–55.

Haggett, P. (1965) *Locational Analysis in Human Geography*, London: Edward Arnold.

Hay, P. (2002) *A Companion to Environmental Thought*, Edinburgh: Edinburgh University Press.

Hiller, H.H. (1998) Assessing the impact of mega-events: a linkage model, *Current Issues in Tourism*, 1(1): 47–57.

HMRC (2010) *Capital Allowances and Balancing Charges*, London: HMSO.

Holden, A. (2000) *Environment and Tourism*, London: Routledge.

Honey, M. (1999) *Ecotourism and Sustainable Development: Who Owns Paradise?*, Washington DC: Island Press.

Houlihan, B. (2003) *Sport and Society: A Student Introduction*, London: Sage.

IAATO (2012) Guidance for visitors to the Antarctic, http://iaato.org/c/document_library/get_file?uuid=022e237f, accessed 8 August 2012.

ICAEW/Environment Agency (2006) *Environmental Issues and Annual Financial Reporting,* London: ICAEW/Environment Agency.

IIED (2002), Mining, minerals and sustainable development ten years on, London: IIED, www.iied.org/mining-minerals-sustainable-development-10-years-mmsd-10 [see Chapter 4: The need for and availability of minerals]

In Any Event UK (2007) Sustainable events, www.inanyevent-uk.com/pages/sustainable-events/sustainable-events.php, accessed 6 August 2012.

Internet Geography (2012) World climate zones, www.geography.learnontheinternet.co.uk/topics/climatezones.html, accessed 12 April 2012.

IOC (2005) *Manual on Sport and the Environment*, Geneva: IOC.

IPCC (2005) *Second Assessment Report – Climate Change*, Geneva: IPCC, available online at www.ipcc.ch/publications_and_data/publications_and_data_reports.shtml, accessed 7 August 2012.

IPCC (2007a) *Fourth Assessment Report – Climate Change*, Geneva: IPCC, available online at www.ipcc.ch/publications_and_data/publications_and_data_reports.shtml, accessed 7 August 2012.

IPCC (2007b) *Climate Change 2007: Synthesis Report. Contribution of Working Groups I, II and III to the Fourth Assessment Report of the Intergovernmental Panel on Climate Change* [Core Writing Team: Pachauri, R.K and Reisinger, A.], Geneva: IPCC, www.ipcc.ch/pdf/assessment-report/ar4/syr/ar4_syr.pdf, accessed 7 August 2012.

ISO (2000) *Environmental Management: The ISO 14000 Family of International Standards,* Geneva: ISO.

Jadhav, R. (2004) LEEDing Green in India, *Architecture Week* (22 September 2004), E1.1, www.architectureweek.com/2004/0922/environment_1-1.html, accessed 16 April 2012.

James, O. (2007) *Affluenza*, London: Vermillion.

Johnston, R.J., Gregory, D., Pratt, G. and Watts, M. (1994) *The Dictionary of Human Geography*, 3rd edition, Oxford: Wiley-Blackwell.

Jones, M. (2010) *Sustainable Event Management*, London: Earthscan.

Jones, R., Pilgrim, A., Thompson, G. and Macgregor, C. (2008) *Assessing the Environmental Impact of Special Events: Examination of Nine Special Events in Western Australia with Particular Reference to the Approval Process and Identification of Potential Environmental Impacts,* Western Australia: Cooperative Research Centre for Sustainable Tourism, available online at www.sustainabletourismonline.com/83/events-and-festivals/assessing-the-environmental-impacts-of-special-events-examination-of-nine-special-events-in-western-australia, accessed 7 August 2012.

Kearins, K. and Pavlovich, K. (2002) The role of stakeholders on Sydney's Green Games, *Corporate Social Responsibility and Environmental Management*, 9: 157–69.

Knebworth House (2012) Directions to Knebworth House, www.knebworthhouse.com/directions/directions.html, accessed 7 August 2012.

Lambert, L., Fava, I. and Noci, G. (2009) Assessing and monitoring the performance of a sustainable event, in R. Raj and J. Musgrave (eds) *Event Management and Sustainability*, Wellingford: CABI, pp. 119–31.

Lawson, N. (2009) *An Appeal to Reason: A Cool Look at Global Warming (with a New Afterword)*, London: Duckworth.

LearnMarketing.net (2012) SMART objectives, www.learnmarketing.net/smart.htm, accessed 30 January 2012.

Levi, P. (1980) *Atlas of the Greek World*, Oxford: Phaidon.

LOCOG (2007) *Towards a One Planet 2012 – London 2012 Sustainability Plan*, London: LOCOG [later version at www.london2012.com/documents/locog-publications/london-2012-sustainability-plan.pdf, accessed 6 August 2012].

LOCOG (2009) *Greenwich Park Venue Update*, London: LOCOG.

LOCOG (2010a) *London 2012 Carbon Footprint Study – Methodology and Reference Footprint*, London: LOCOG, www.london2012.com/documents/locog-publications/carbon-footprint-study.pdf, accessed 6 August 2012.

LOCOG (2010b) *London 2012 Sustainability Guidelines: Corporate and Public Events*, 2nd edition, London: LOCOG.

Lovelock, J. (2006) *Revenge of Gaia*, Harmondsworth: Allen Lane.

Ma, S.-C., Egan, D., Rotherham, I. and Ma, S.-M. (2010) A framework for monitoring during the planning stage for a sports mega-event, *Journal of Sustainable Tourism* 19(1), www.ukeconet.co.uk/images/stories/sports%20mega%20events%20jnl%20of%20sustainable%20tourism.pdf, accessed 27 August 2010.

Malone, A. (2008) Abandoned, derelict, covered in graffiti and rubbish: What is left of Athens' £9 billion Olympic 'glory', *Daily Mail* (18 July 2008), www.dailymail.co.uk/news/article-1036373/Abandoned-derelict-covered-graffiti-rubbish-What-left-Athens-9billion-Olympic-glory.html, accessed 12 January 2012.

Maslow, M. (1968) *Towards a Psychology of Being* (2nd edition), New York: van Nostrand.

Matheson, C.M. (2010) Legacy planning, regeneration and events: the Glasgow 2014 Commonwealth Games, *Local Economy*, 25(1): 10–23.

McDonough, W. (1992) *The Hannover Principles: Design for Sustainability*, Charlottesville, VA: William McDonough and Partners.

Meadows, D.H., Meadows, D.L., Randers, J. and Behrens III, W.W. (1972) *The Limits to Growth: A Report for the Club of Rome's Project for the Predicament of Mankind*, New York: Universe.

MEBC (2002) *Sexi: The Sustainable Exhibition Industry Project*, Birmingham: MEBC.

Met Office (2012) Hadley Centre Central England Temperature (HadCET) dataset, www.metoffice.gov.uk/hadobs/hadcet/, accessed 17 April 2012.

Middleton, N. (1995) The *Global Casino*, London: Hodder and Stoughton.

Middleton, N. and O'Keefe, P. (2003) *Rio plus Ten*, London: Pluto Press.

Mowforth, M. and Munt, I. (1998) *Tourism and Sustainability: New Tourism in the Third World*, London: Routledge.

NOGOE (2010) National heritage and the Olympics: a clash of values, *NOGOE Newsletter* (January 2010), www.nogoe2012.com/downloads/2010-january-newsletter-nogoe.pdf, accessed 8 August 2010.

OECD (2010) *Local Development Benefits from Staging Global Events: Achieving the Local Development Legacy from 2012*, Paris: OECD, www.oecd.org/regional/leedprogramme localeconomicandemploymentdevelopment/46207013.pdf, accessed 7 August 2012.

Oittinen, A. and Tiezi, E. (1999) A scientific review of information available on the link between the environment and sport, in Council of Europe (ed.) *Proceedings of the CDDS Bureau Meeting*, Strasbourg: Council of Europe, pp. 1–33.

Otto, I. and Heath, E.T. (2009) The potential contribution of the 2010 Soccer World Cup to climate change: an exploratory study among tourism industry stakeholders in the Tshwane Metropole of South Africa, *Journal of Sport and Tourism*, 14(2): 169–91.

Oursouthwest (2005/2010) Greener Events, www.oursouthwest.com/SusBus/gevents. html, accessed 6 August 2012.

Pacione, M. (2011) The role of events in urban regeneration, in S.J. Page and J. Connell *The Routledge Handbook of Events*, London: Routledge, pp. 385–400.

Page, S.J. and Connell, J. (2006) *Tourism: A Modern Synthesis*, 2nd edition, London: Thomson.

Page, S.J. and Connell, J. (2011) *The Routledge Handbook of Events*, Abingdon: Routledge.

Page, S.J. and Dowling, J. (2002) *Ecotourism*, Harlow: Prentice Hall.

Panagiotopolou, R. (2009) The 28th Olympic Games in Athens 2004, in G. Poynter and I. MacRury (eds) *Olympic Cities: 2012 and the Remaking of London*, Farnham: Ashgate, pp. 145–62.

Parks Canada (2011) *Special Events in the National Historic Sites of Canada in Cape Breton: Replacement Class Screening Report*, Quebec: Parks Canada, www.ceaa.gc.ca/050/documents/16392/16392E.pdf, accessed 8 August 2012.

Pearsall, J. and Hanks, P. (2001) *New Oxford Dictionary of English*, Oxford: Oxford University Press.

People 1st (2010) *Labour Market Review of the Events Industry*, Uxbridge: People 1st, www.businesstourismpartnership.com/pubs/Labour%20Market%20Review%20of%20the%20events%20Industry%20January%202010.pdf, accessed 6 August 2012.

Porter, L. (2009) Planning displacement: the real legacy of major sporting events, *Planning Theory & Practice*, 10(3), 395–418.

Poynter, G. and MacRury, I. (2009) *Olympic Cities: 2012 and the Remaking of London*, Farnham: Ashgate.

Prevention Web (2009) 9th international conference on Southern Hemisphere meteorology and oceanography, www.preventionweb.net/english/professional/trainings-events/events/v.php?id=3628, accessed 9 August 2012.

PRME (2012) The Principles for Responsible Management Education, www.unprme.org/the-6-principles/index.php, accessed 27 February 2012.

Putnam, D. (2002) *ISO 14031: Environmental Performance Evaluation*, draft submitted to Confederation of Indian Industry for publication in their Journal, http://inbec.com.br/josimardealmeida/wp-content/uploads/2012/01/AVALIA%C3%87%C3%83O-AMBIENTAL.ARTIGO-CIENT%C3%8DFICO.Performace-Ambiental1.pdf, accessed 6 August 2012.

Quinn, N.W. and Morgan, R.P.C. (1980) Simulation of soil erosion induced by human trampling, *Journal of Environmental Management*, 10, 155–65.

Raj, R. and Musgrave, J. (eds) (2009) *Event Management and Sustainability*, Wallingford: CABI.

Rechkemmer, A. (2005) *The Rio Earth Summit as a Locus for Postmodernity*, Working Paper FG 8, 2005/1, Berlin: SWP.

Rhodes, J. (undated) Green Event Planning Guide for Duke University, http://cme.mc.duke.edu/wysiwyg/downloads/Duke_Green_Event_Planning_Guide.pdf, accessed 6 August 2012.

Robison, J. (2002) Copper, in *Energy and Environmental Profile of the US Mining Industry*, Washington DC: US Department of Energy, www1.eere.energy.gov/manufacturing/industries_technologies/mining/pdfs/copper.pdf, accessed 27 August 2012.

Safe Concerts (2004) Official – North Herts admit Code of Practice Failures, www.safeconcerts.com/newsitem.asp?nurn=111, accessed 7 August 2012.

Saunders, R. (2012) *How to Implement BS 8901: A Practical Guide*, Positive Impact Events, www.eibtm.com/files/how_to_implement_bs_8901.pdf, accessed 30 January 2012.

Seventeen Events (2010) *Sustainable Events Guide*, London: Seventeen Events, www.seventeenevents.co.uk/wp-content/uploads/downloads/2010/08/Sustainable-Events-Guide-final-1.pdf, accessed 11 April 2012.

SGS (2012) Turf isn't the only thing that should be green, www.sgs.com/~/media/Global/Documents/Brochures/5658-SGS-BS8901-Brochure-EN-A4-11-Low-Res.pdf, accessed 8 August 2012.

Shone, A. and Parry, B. (2001) *Successful Event Management: A Practical Guide*, London: Continuum.

Smith, D.S. and Hellmund, P.C. (eds) (1993) *Ecology of Greenways: Design and Function of Linear Conservation Areas*, Minneapolis: University of Minnesota Press, pp. 105–22.

Solway, A. (2009) *Sustainable Tourism*, London: Hachette Children's Books.

Spink, J. (1994) *Leisure and the Environment*, Oxford: Butterworth-Heinemann.

Spivey, N. (2004) *The Ancient Olympics: A History*, Oxford: Oxford University Press.

Stratton, A. (2010) Coal-fired power stations win reprieve, *The Guardian* (15 August 2010), www.guardian.co.uk/environment/2010/aug/15/coal-fired-power-stations-coalition, accessed 24 August 2012.

Sustainable Event Alliance (2011) Event GHG Inventory, http://sustainable-event-alliance.org/?page_id=9131, accessed 9 December 2011.

Sustainable Event Solutions (2012) Background, http://www.sustainableeventsolutions.com/BS8901WhatIsIt.aspx, accessed 19 January 2012.

Terrell, S. (2004) *The Geography of Sport and Leisure*, Sevenoaks: Hodder and Stoughton.

Theobold, W.F. (1994) *Global Tourism*, Oxford: Butterworth-Heinemann.

Thomson, A, Leopkey, B., Schlenker, K. and Schulenkorf, N. (2010) *Sport Event Legacies: Implications for Meaningful Legacy Outcomes*, www.eventsandfestivalsresearch.com/files/proceedings/THOMSON,%20LEOPKEY,%20SMALL%20&%20SCHULENKORF.pdf, accessed 16 January 2012.

Torkildsen, G. (1983) *Leisure and Recreation Management*, 1st edition, London: Spon.

Torkildsen, G. (1999) *Leisure and Recreation Management*, 4th edition, London: Spon.

Toyne, P. (2009) London 2012 – winning the Olympic 'green' medal, in G. Poynter and I. MacRury, *Olympic Cities: 2012 and the Remaking of London*, Farnham: Ashgate, pp. 231–42.

Tziralis, G., Tolis, A., Tatsiopoulos, I. and Aravossis, K. (2006) Economic aspects and sustainability impact of the Athens 2004 Olympic Games, in Aravossis, K. et al (eds), *Environmental Economics and Investment Assessment*, WIT Transactions on Ecology and the Environment Vol 98, Southampton: WIT Press, pp. 21–33.

University of East London (2007) *A Lasting Legacy for London? Assessing the Legacy of the Olympic Games and Paralympic Games*, London: Greater London Authority, www.uel.ac.uk/londoneast/research/documents/lasting-legacy.pdf, accessed 7 August 2012.

UK Sport (2005) *Staging Major Sports Events: The Guide*, London, UK Sport, www.uksport.gov.uk/publications/major-sports-events-the-guide-april-2005, accessed 6 August 2012.

UN (2009) *Green Meeting Guide 2009 – Rolling Out the Green Carpet for Your Participants*, New York: UN, www.unep.org/pdf/GreenMeetingGuide.pdf, accessed 8 August 2012.

UN (2012a) Earth Summit 2012, www.earthsummit2012.org, accessed 12 April 2012.

UN (2012b) UN Conference on Environment and Development, www.un.org/geninfo/bp/enviro.html, accessed 12 April 2012.

UNCED (1992) *Agenda 21*, New York: UN, www.un.org/esa/dsd/agenda21/res_agenda21_01.shtml, accessed 12 April 2012.

UNCTAD (2004) *A Manual for the Preparers and Users of Eco-efficiency Indicators Version 1.1*, New York: United Nations.

UNDP et al (2002) *Greening the WSSD – Leaving a Greening Legacy: Thousands Are Doing Their Bit. Are You?*, www.johannesburgsummit.org/html/links/booklet%20greening%20wssd.pdf, accessed 6 August 2012.

UNEP (1972) Declaration of the United Nations Conference on the Human Environment, www.unep.org/Documents.Multilingual/Default.asp?documentid=97&articleid=1503, accessed 3 February 2012.

UNEP (2009) Beijing Olympics get big green tick, www.unep.org/documents.multilingual/default.asp?documentid=562&articleid=6086&l=en, accessed 7 January 2012.

UNEP (2012) About the programme, www.unep.org/law/About_prog/introduction.asp, accessed 20 January 2012.

UN Framework Convention on Climate Change (2012) Climate Change Information Sheet 6, http://unfccc.int/essential_background/background_publications_html pdf/climate_change_information_kit/items/282txt.php, accessed 24 August 2012.

Usborne, S. (2008) After the party: what happens when the Olympics leave town, *The Independent* (19 August 2008), www.independent.co.uk/sport/olympics/after-the-party-what-happens-when-the-olympics-leave-town-901629.html, accessed 12 January 2012.

US Green Building Council (2011) What LEED is, www.usgbc.org/DisplayPage.aspx?CMSPageID=1988, accessed 12 April 2012.

WCED (World Commission on Environment and Development) (1987) *Our Common Future*, Oxford: Oxford University Press.

WCU/UNEP/WWFN (World Conservation Union/United Nations Environment Programme/World Wide Fund for Nature) (1991) *Caring for the Earth*, Gland: WCU/UNEP/WWFN.

Weathernetwork (2011) Statistics: Vancouver International, BC, Canada, www.theweathernetwork.com/index.php?product=statistics&pagecontent=C02096, accessed 10 October 2011.

Weaver, T. and Dale, D. (1978) Trampling effects of hikers, motorcycles and horses, *Journal of Applied Ecology*, 15, 451–7.

Webster, T.B.L. (1969) *Everyday Life in Classical Athens*, London: Batsford.

Wood, K. and House, S. (1991) *The Good Tourist*, London: Mandarin.

Index